NOT SEEING GOD

Atheism in the 21st Century

Edited by
JONATHAN MS PEARCE

Foreword by Ed Buckner

Afterword by Dale McGowan

Not Seeing God: Atheism in the 21st Century

Copyright © 2017 Onus Books

Published by *Onus Books*

Printed by Lightning Source International

All rights reserved. No part of this publication may be reproduced, stored in a retrieval system, or transmitted in any form by any means, electronic, mechanical, photocopy, recording, or otherwise, without the prior permission of the publisher, except as provided for by UK and US copyright law.

Cover design: Onus Books and Tristan Vick

Trade paperback ISBN: 978-0-9935102-2-9

OB 13/23

Praise for this volume:

In *Not Seeing God*, philosopher and author Jonathan MS Pearce has collected the top writers on Patheos Nonreligious and set them to work deconstructing god and reconstructing our view of what it means to be godless, both today and in the future. From showing how god as a construct is a side effect of our natural psychology to how the stories in the Bible are folklore rather than truth, from musings on being non-religious across areas of the globe as diverse as Africa, the Middle East, and Latin America, to thoughts on how life holds purpose without the supernatural, this collection has something for everyone to enjoy and ponder. This book should be considered required reading for the well-informed non-theist.
 –Dr. Caleb Lack, author of *Critical Thinking, Science, and Pseudoscience: Why You Can't Trust Your Brain* and *Psychology Gone Astray: A Selection of Racist & Sexist Literature from Early Psychological Research*, blogger at *Great Plains Skeptic*

Anyone who has even a passing interest in religion or atheism has much—interesting things, important things, fun things—to learn from the writers included in this book…. [A] fascinating, interesting, useful book.
 –Ed Buckner, author (with Michael E. Buckner) *of In Freedom We Trust: An Atheist Guide to Religious Liberty*, Former President of American Atheists

An original collection of essays ranging from positive arguments for atheism to godlessness in different parts of the world, from the raising of children to meaning and purpose without God. The real surprise here is the number of new ideas presented.
 –Franz Kiekeben, philosopher and author of *The Truth about God* and of *Atheism: Q&A*

In *Not Seeing God*, Jonathan MS Pearce has done a wonderful job of providing a very wide range of thoughtful and personal perspectives that give the reader every reason to doubt belief in God. This volume provides a unique contribution to the canon of contemporary god-skeptical literature and is recommended to every curious reader interested in such discussions.
 –James A. Lindsay, author of *Dot, Dot, Dot: Infinity Plus God Equals Folly* and *Everybody Is Wrong About God*

A varied and interesting collection of work from a great variety of contributors, all weaving together a compelling theme of places and cultures where no god is found.
    –Ed Suominen, co-author of *Evolving out of Eden*; editor, Tellectual Press.

Not Seeing God is the perfect sequel and antidote to Catholic philosopher Michael Novak's *No One Sees God* in which he confessed: "The atheist does not see God—but neither does the believer.... Believers in God well know, in the night, that what the atheist holds may be true."
    –David Warden, Chairman of Dorset Humanists (the UK's largest humanist group) and Honorary Member of Humanists UK

Not Seeing God is a concentrated blend of the classical and contemporary arguments against religious dogma from some of today's most popular philosophical thinkers comprising rapid fire rationality sprinkled with clarity, wisdom and cutting wit. A thoroughly entertaining read that will undoubtedly rattle the cages of dogmatic certainty.
    –Paul Thompson, *The Skepticule Podcast*

Not Seeing God is an excellent collection of some of the best skeptical writers working today. As one would expect from the writers at *Patheos Nonreligious*, each piece is well crafted, often humorous, occasionally moving, and always deeply insightful. The quality and diversity of writers and their approaches to not seeing god(s) makes this text a handy reference tool for the next time you find yourself embroiled in a formal debate on the existence of God, or a conversation with a cantankerous relative at a family reunion, or even (OmniGod forbid) a Facebook argument. From defeating Pascal's Wager (see "Using Common Sense to Not See God" by Bob Seidensticker), to navigating the waters of raising your kids in a religion soaked world (see "Not Seeing God when Raising your Kids" by Stephanie Savage) this book has so much to offer that I suspect it'll spend a lot more time sitting on my desk than it will on a shelf.
    –David Fletcher, author of *Myth Education: A Guide to Gods, Goddesses, and Other Supernatural Beings*

Acknowledgements

This book would not have been possible without the contributors themselves, to whom a massive thanks is owed. Please check out all of their respective blogs at *Patheos Nonreligious*. A big thanks also goes to Geoff Benson, for looking over the manuscript, as well as… As ever, Helen, my partner, deserves enormous credit for her patience.

About the Editor

Jonathan MS Pearce is a philosopher, author, blogger, public speaker and teacher who lives in Fareham, Hampshire, UK with his partner and twin boys. He has spent many years philosophizing about all things religious and…well, all things, actually. He has a penchant for discussing free will, or its illusion, and how this affects society. Pearce has written a number of books (including fiction: check out his zombie apocalypse series dealing with aspects of philosophy), edited others, and contributed to more still, and public speaks to various groups around the UK concerning the topics he covers. He is surprised there is any time left in the day to breathe. You can find him on the *Patheos* network, blogging at *A Tippling Philosopher* (patheos.com/blogs/tippling).

Other books by Jonathan MS Pearce include:

> *Free Will? An investigation into whether we have free will or whether I was always going to write this book*
> *The Little Book of Unholy Questions*
> *The Nativity: A Critical Examination*
> *Did God Create the Universe from Nothing? Countering William Lane Craig's Kalam Cosmological Argument*
> *Beyond An Absence of Faith: Stories about the Loss of Faith and the Discovery of Self* (ed.)
> *The Problem with "God"* (ebook)
> *13 Reasons to Doubt* (ed.)

And as Johnny Pearce:
> *Survival of the Fittest: Metamorphosis*
> *Twins: A Survival Guide for Dads*

*To freethought bloggers everywhere:
we are spreading the light
of critical thinking
to the darkest parts of the globe.*

*One day, we hope
there will be no
nefarious shadows.*

CONTENTS

FOREWORD - SOMETHING TO LEARN BY ED BUCKNER 1

INTRODUCTION BY JONATHAN MS PEARCE 7

PART ONE: DECONSTRUCTING GOD 11

   NOT SEEING OMNIGOD™ THROUGH PHILOSOPHY AND LOGIC 13
      Jonathan MS Pearce, A Tippling Philosopher ....
   NOT SEEING GOD THROUGH PSYCHOLOGY AND NEUROSCIENCE 23
      Matthew Facciani, According to Matthew ....
   USING COMMON SENSE TO NOT SEE GOD 35
      Bob Seidensticker, Cross Examined ....
   NOT SEEING GOD, BUT SEEING FOLKLORE, IN THE BIBLE 49
      Jeana Jorgensen, PhD, Foxy Folklorist ....
   NOT FINDING GOD IN ETHICS 61
      Dan Fincke, Camels With Hammers ....
   SEEING GOD IN THE BIBLE AS RIDICULOUS 79
      Andrew Hall, Laughing in Disbelief ....
   RATIONALLY NOT SEEING GOD: BEING BORN AGAIN. AGAIN. 89
      Jonathan Burrello, Blinky & Sal ....

PART TWO: REFLECTING ON GODLESSNESS IN MODERN SOCIETY 103

   NOT SEEING GOD IN THE MIND 105
      Nail Carter, Godless in Dixie ....
   IT STARTED WITH YOGA: UNRAVELLING THE THREADS TOWARDS NOT SEEING GOD 113
      Suzanne Titkemeyer, No Longer Qivering ....
   SCIENCE AND MEDICINE: NOT SEEING GOD IN YOUR PRAYERS, THANK YOU VERY MUCH 119
      Kevin Davis, SecularVoices ....
   NOT SEEING GOD THROUGH CELEBRATIONS IN LIFE 125
      Galen Broaddus, Across Rivers Wide ....
   NOT SEEING GOD AT THE MOVIES 131
      Andrew Spitznas, Atheist Cinephile ....
   HUMANISM AND WITCHCRAFT: NOT SEEING GOD IN AFRICA 145

Warren Alan Tidwell, Kudzu in the Pines ....
THE IMPORTANCE OF VISIBILITY WHEN NOT SEEING GOD IN LATIN AMERICA..........155
Luciano Gonzalez, Sin God ....
POLITICS AND RELIGION: NOT SEEING GOD IN THE ISLAMIC REPUBLIC 165
Kaveh Mousavi, On the Margin of Error ....
NOT SEEING ATHEISTS IN CONGRESS 175
Hemant Mehta, The Friendly Atheist ....
NOT SEEING GOD IN THE MILITARY 181
Kathleen Johnson, NoGodBlog ....
SEEING GOD IN EDUCATION AS CHILD ABUSE 189
Michael Stone, Progressive Secular Humanist ....
NOT WANTING TO SEE GOD IN EDUCATION, BUT DAMN, HE'S STILL THERE 199
Jonny Scaramanga, Leaving Fundamentalism ....

PART THREE: LOOKING TOWARD A FUTURE IN A GODLESS WORLD 211

HOW TO PREPARE FOR NOT SEEING GOD 215
Martin Hughes, barrierbreaker ....
NOT SEEING GOD IN LIFE'S MEANING AND PURPOSE 221
Gleb Tsipursky, Intentional Insights ....
NOT SEEING GOD WHEN RAISING YOUR KIDS 233
Stephanie Savage, Miracle Girl ....
NOT SEEING GOD IN RELIGION 243
Alan Duval, A Tippling Philosopher ....
WHAT COMES AFTER NOT SEEING GOD 257
Hank Fox, A Citizen of Earth ....

AFTERWORD - STARING BACK AT THE ALL-SEEING GOD BY DALE MCGOWAN **279**

AUTHOR BIOGRAPHIES **281**

Foreword

Something to Learn

By Ed Buckner

I served a satisfying three years as executive director of the Council for Secular Humanism, working with and for leading atheists like Paul Kurtz and Tom Flynn. Then, a few years later, I served for over two years as the president of American Atheists, with bright, inspiring colleagues like Kathleen Johnson and David Silverman. (Silverman, by the way, is likely to be best pleased by Hank Fox's opening lines, since Fox aptly credits an event arguably most important in Silverman's professional atheist career.)

I'm a smart, well-read, well-educated guy (modest, too) and relished talking with many hundreds of my fellow secular humanists and atheists before, during, and since those periods. I thought I would be justified by now in thinking that I honestly did not have much to learn about atheism and religion any more. It gives me great pleasure to tell you I was wrong. Anyone who has even a passing interest in religion or atheism has much—interesting things, important things, fun things—to learn from the writers included in this book.

If you, even you the longtime student of (and activist for or against) atheism over there in the corner, think you don't have something to learn by reading these essays, think again. Learn, with zesty delight, how yoga and atheism relate (thanks to Suzanne Titkemeyer), how American military troops and leaders are twisted by religion, how real conversions from Christianity to atheism come about (hint: it's not just rebelling against "proper" authority), how the claimed omniscience for God renders him impotent, and so much more. Laughs are also abundantly available.

There are two groups of people who owe it to themselves to read this book: 1. Thoughtful atheists who want to understand more about their irreligious conclusions from a wide variety of practical, moral, and philosophical perspectives; and 2. Thoughtful theists who really want to understand more about their religious conclusions and to learn why thoughtful atheists wisely don't accept those religious conclusions (or, often enough, don't even consider the religious conclusions reasonable).

Those two categories surely include millions of potential readers but not everyone. Atheists blasé enough to hold an important conclusion or lack of belief without Socrates's famous imperative to make life worthwhile by examining such things can ignore all this. Theists who ignore this book can meander through life, wasting time, focus, money, and energy shoring up religious leaders and institutions when there are far better ways to live. The latter can even be smug, as long as no one has ever introduced them to the gospel (the real "good news" conveyed in these pages).

Atheists can even learn how we might be blindly (religiously?) following Richard Dawkins and not know it, or that we really shouldn't consider theists "stupid" or see religion as a "mental illness." If these things puzzle or irritate you, blame Matthew Facciani, not me. Facciani is also the one who can sort you out on why a detective agency and agency detection aren't the same animal.

The atheist writers included in this book are all over the map in many ways—professional philosophers and military crime scene analysts, young and old (oh, OK, from my stance at least, they're all damned young), men and women, cheerful sorts and more grave ones, etc. But they do all have stuff in common—

- An ability to write and explain things clearly
- Care in directing readers to real news, credible sources, sound logic, and actual evidence (Gleb Tsipursky's advocacy for a "Pro-Truth Pledge" fits well with all the essays here, not just his own)
- An uncanny ability to look at matters in fresh, original ways
- The power to use satire, wit, humor [insert a further "u" here as needed], and lively writing without undercutting serious analyses (this last certainly applies to Andrew Hall, Stephanie Savage, and Jonathan Burrello but also consistently to the other writers featured here—not a dull plodder in the bunch)
- An ability to peer fearlessly into the future and map out clearly what's to come (or at least to provide a reasonable, plausible facsimile thereof), whether by Citizen Hank Fox, Dale McGowan, or others less explicitly focused on what's to come.

The all-over-the map nature of these writers also applies to them pretty literally. Jonathan Pearce, the editor (and chief contributor), is a Brit, while most of the others are in one sense or another widely spread out Yanks, but there is nevertheless geographic diversity. Suzanne Titkemeyer represents Costa Rica (oh, OK—she never even mentions Costa Rica in her essay, but she lives there now, so that counts, right?). More serious diversity comes from Ghana (thanks to an Old South Alabaman-American, Warren Tidwell), from Jonny Scaramanga (who, like Pearce, toils primarily in the fertile fields of the United Kingdom, and from Luciano Gonzales, and from Kaveh Mousavi. Like all Puerto Ricans, Gonzalez qualifies as a Yank, but he also represents an unusual perspective for an American atheist. He does not restrict himself to Puerto Rico but analyzes atheism and religion throughout Latin America (or Hispanic America, if you prefer). Gonzalez is also a bilingual punster.

Mousavi is another clear-headed, clear-thinking-and-writing contributor and he adds to the geographic diversity (he's an Iranian living in Iran) but more crucially he enlarges the perspectives regarding religion (most of the other contributors primarily address Christianity). Mousavi is not the only contributor to touch on Islam, of course, but his is the most direct, forceful, effective take on the marriage—a bad one, for those of us who're atheists but also for anyone committed to religious liberty—between Islam and politics or government. He's not optimistic about the chances for an amicable divorce, either.

As you'd expect, there is plenty of attention paid in these pages to connections among children, parents, science, and atheism vs. religion. And toys and God. And if you've never quite understood that whole "it's not a religion—it's a personal relationship with Jesus" trope, Neil Carter will sort you out in ways that perhaps only he and "Buzz Lightyear" can grasp.

Stephanie Savage has a nice metaphor about the parallels between second-hand smoke and religion, while Michael Stone, citing Richard Dawkins and others (Dawkins has promoted similar ideas at least since *The God Delusion* [2006]), makes a convincing case that teaching "scientific" creationism to children is a form of child abuse as well as an abuse of science. Alan Duval makes a much broader, more philosophical, case about the importance of protecting our future and our children from religious nonsense. Hank Fox offers a clarion call to protect our future—our children and our culture—from religion-based dishonesty and depredations.

Readers, atheists and theists alike, should beware of presumptions. As with many other atheist writings, there's plenty here to refute theistic claims (philosophical, social, psychological, and moral), but Jonathan Pearce, Bob Seidensticker, and several others lay out cogent arguments *for* atheism as well as shredding theistic claims. And Savage can fill you in on the plain fact that mythology is a communicable disease. Martin Hughes discusses, eloquently, the fact that atheists who leave a religion can—unintentionally—hurt family and friends. Galen Broaddus makes the strong case that atheists need and should have access to rituals and ceremony, and that these can be powerful without any god-talk whatsoever.

Many contributors—especially Dan Fincke, but also Burrello, Duval, and others—bring fresh insights to the ancient questions supposedly raised by the connections of morality and religiosity.

Probably my personal favorite subject that intersects with atheism—secularism—gets strong analysis by Kevin Davis as a blogger on secularism on Patheos, for which I here give him gratitude and respect—though his essay in this book is focused more on prayer, support for his premature baby, and a moving story about presumptions and a nurse. Secularism is defended or at least touched on by many of these writers, probably most strikingly by Mousavi (who doesn't use the term but provides cogent examples for its need), Mehta (who ties it directly to American politics and voting), and Tsipursky (who explains the necessary connections among morality, ethics, government, and rationality).

After decades of conversations with atheists and theists (mostly but not all Christians), I can attest that this book is much needed by atheists—many of whom will read it—and by religious believers, few of whom will. Misconceptions, misunderstandings, and even outright lies about atheism—about silly things and deadly serious things—pervade the globe (unevenly, to be sure). Far too many atheists might reasonably be called "unexamining atheists" (mostly from isolation rather than from willful ignorance). These atheists often seem to be people who cannot bring themselves to swallow the preposterous claims of believers but who nevertheless remain defensive or even afraid. Ignorance stands in those atheists' way and only the kind of understanding that writers like the contributors here can supply can lead them to kind of lives they want and deserve. Many of these "unexamining atheists" think, I've discovered, that they are alone or in a tiny, weird minority. These atheists need to grasp the richness—the incredible diversity of opinions, experiences, and approaches—shown by this book, and to give up false notions of atheism as monolithic, immoral, or illogical. Peace of mind and deep satisfaction await.

The absurd, false ideas about atheism held by billions of human beings could be largely rebutted and eliminated if all the believers would read these essays with an open mind. That won't happen, but there may be hopes of nudging some significant fraction of them toward the light. And the atheists who read this book will be incomparably better prepared to enlighten those believers in their own lives (at least the ones who will read or hear). Humankind's future literally depends on more rationality, more humanistic ways, and more applied intelligence. This book offers real help with all three.

Writers like Jeana Jorgensen, Warren Tidwell (one of my heroes, if you must know—a near-perfect example of a man who thinks that humanism means more than anything else that our fellow humans deserve our help), Kathleen Johnson (another hero and another person I'm proud to call friend), Hemant Mehta (a friend, I think and hope), Neil Carter, and Andrew Spitznas all come at all this in ways, personal or academic, quite different from my own. They show how atheism and misconceptions about atheism and religion are worth examining with tools from anthropology, sociology, art (especially film), politics (electoral and intra-organizational), cultural and philanthropic activism, military organizations, and psychology.

Time to start reading a fascinating, interesting, useful book. Oddly enough, you'd do well to start with the afterword (just to get an idea where all the writers are headed), by probably the best writer (and speaker—never miss a chance to hear a talk from him) in the movement in America, Dale McGowan. Wherever you start, you're in for a series of treats, so enjoy.

Ed Buckner, author (with Michael E. Buckner) *of In Freedom We Trust: An Atheist Guide to Religious Liberty*, Former President of American Atheists

Patheos Nonreligious

Introduction

By Jonathan MS Pearce

The Patheos network is an interesting place for conversation between people of faith, of all persuasions, and those without. And the Patheos Nonreligious channel is the home to an eclectic mix of writers who cover a vast array of areas concerning life for atheists and the nonreligious alike. In today's societies, talks and debates over religion often take place front and center. In many countries, the platform has opened up to allow citizens to question, to permit freethought to blossom and bear fruit. Equally, though, there are many corners of the world where such discussion is sign of heresy, and will lead to risk. Very great risk. It is a time of flux, and in these times, places like Patheos Nonreligious can offer refuge, strength, inspiration, resources and springboards for positive action. It is in this vein, from this fertile philosophical and sociological earth that the seed of this book germinated. Here it is, in full flower.

How best do we showcase all of these great writers and their typical content? The book is split into three sections. The first, "Deconstructing God," does what it says on the tin. The resident philosophers and scientists look to tackle the idea of God and see whether it stands up to scrutiny. It doesn't, you may either be pleased or shocked to find out. My own chapter ("Not Seeing OmniGod™ through Philosophy and Logic") looks at a range of philosophical arguments against the existence of the classical representation of God (being all-knowing, all-powerful and all-loving). Matthew Facciani (in his chapter "Not Seeing God through Psychology and Neuroscience") looks at God from a neuroscientific and psychological point of view, explaining some of the reasons why many people *do* believe in God. In "Using Common Sense to Not See God", Bob Seidensticker uses seven of his favorite arguments to dismember the Godhead. I get the feeling that God is already in trouble, and his project is terminal. But alas, let's drive the stake further in.

In "Not Seeing God, but Seeing Folklore in the Bible," Jeana Jorgensen puts her knowledge of folklore to good use in showing the folkloric aspects of the Bible, which takes the good book down a peg or two. Next off in this section is the deep-thinking Dan Fincke, with some original thought on morality (which is something of a rarity after thousands of years of moral philosophy). He discusses morality as a functional aspect of our human nature. Thus atheists are justified in claiming objective morality.

Penultimately, with the smoldering, albeit ethereal, corpse of God lying dejected on the intellectual battlefield, what can we do but laugh? Or at least smugly smirk. There is no better smug smirker in the business than Patheos Nonreligious' own Andrew Hall in his withering retelling of the biblical story of Cain and Abel: "Seeing God in the Bible as Ridiculous."

To act as a deconversion sandwich over the threshold of the first and second sections, we turn to that release of belief, that shedding of clothes that no longer fit. In this section, Jonathan Burrello, with the help of his exquisite cartoonery (that's now a word), takes us through his rational approach to giving up his Christian beliefs. "Rationally Not Seeing God: Being Born Again. Again." shows that people do give up their beliefs for philosophical reasons, not just psychological ones.

The second section of the book moves away from the conceptual and toward the practical. "Reflecting on Godlessness in Modern Society" contains a great variety of subject matter concerning differing views on atheism from within a modern societal context. We start with Neil Carter, whose experiences of God were very much relational. In "Not Seeing God in the Mind," Carter shows the difficulty in coming to terms with considering that the entity with whom you are having such an important relationship does not actually exist. Managing that in the Deep South comes with its own challenges.

Next is Suzanne Tiktemeyer's "It Started with Yoga: Unravelling the Threads towards Not Seeing God," which looks at the process of losing one's religion, from a fundamentalist context, and how the threads to that comfort blanket can start unravelling in the light of the most mundane of things. In this case, yoga. Damn that devilish enterprise! Prayer is a really important part of the believer's life. However, it is somewhat less important to the non-believer. What happens when believers, in number, pray for the non-believer? Keven Davis recalls his experiences of such in "Science and Medicine: Not Seeing God in Your Prayers, Thank You Very Much" when a difficult pregnancy and birth made for a challenging time in dealing with believing well-wishers and the fallout from politely denying their requests for Godly intervention.

Following on is "Not Seeing God through Celebrations in Life," from Galen Broaddus, expressing his delight in doing what he loves: being a humanist celebrant. Such ceremonial celebrations of important moments in life are not the sole, exclusive property of religious organizations. Andrew Spitznas takes us on a romp through the world of cinema in his chapter "Not Seeing God at the Movies." My own movie wish list expanded a title or two in reading his piece, as I am sure yours will, too!

We move on to geographically-centered approaches to atheism next, starting with Warren Alan Tidwell's experiences with humanist charity work in Africa in "Humanism and Witchcraft: Not Seeing God in Africa." It's great to see humanism put into a real-world, practical context. Next, Luciano Gonzalez spreads the word about being outspoken and spreading the atheistic word in his part of the world, in his chapter "The Importance of Visibility when Not Seeing God in Latin America." From Latin America, we jump seamlessly to Iran with one big freethinking leap. Kaveh Mousavi steadies our feet on landing with his chapter "Politics and Religion: Not Seeing God in the Islamic Republic," showing that there is still so far to go for so many people around the world before they can openly proclaim their beliefs (or lack thereof). And, quite often, this is entwined with politics.

Politics is where Hemant Mehta lingers. And lingering is what Christianity does, in the corridors and offices of U.S. power. Why, Mehta asks, do atheists not feature as a voting bloc or in office, and as candidates for office? "Not Seeing Atheists in Congress" is a whistle-stop tour along those governmental roads. Politics and the military are closely linked and so it is no surprise that Kathleen Johnson's valuable insights into secularism and nonbelief in the army follow on. Her chapter, "Not Seeing God in the Military" tackles issues surrounding the pervasive religionism found in parts of society many of us have little access to.

From politics and unbelief, we move to education. Michael Stone chips in on education, expressing how creeping creationism in the U.S. school system (as advocated by organizations like *Answers in Genesis*—sorry, dirty words for some) represents a form of child abuse for our children and harm for our future. "Not Wanting to See God in Science Education because It Is Child Abuse" does what it says on the tin. Jonny Scaramanga then gives his personal insight into Christian education in the UK, and schools that belong to the Accelerated Christian Education fold. "Not Wanting to See God in Education" is a window into his efforts in campaigning to expose the huge problems associated with such schools.

The third and final section of the book is "Looking toward a Future in the Godless World" where we look forward into the unknown. In some respects, the future looks good for secularism and the nonreligious. It is growing. However, it is growing in the context of established, mature and post-industrialized countries. Places like the US and the UK now have growing atheist populations who feel emboldened to publicly proclaim their lack of faith. On the other hand, the growth populations in the world are not based in these sorts of nations. Islamic countries, if trends are to be trusted, are the hotbed for childbirth and population growth, for a whole host of reasons. Thus, for secularism and the nonreligious, prognosis is mixed.

Martin Hughes gets the ball rolling here with offering vital preparation hints for tackling deconversion. His experience of "embracing reality" is something many of us who have walked that road will be able to recognize. "How to Prepare for Not Seeing god" is a case of not wanting atheism to overpromise and underdeliver.

Gleb Tsipursky continues by looking at how atheists can interpret or claim meaning and purpose in comparison to our religious cousins. "Not Seeing God in Life's Meaning and Purpose" sets the record straight when religious commentators claim we must struggle for direction in these areas. Stephanie Savage takes the baton and runs with it in her look at secular parenting, especially considering her own culturally Jewish upbringing. If we want a growing secularization of society, then parenting plays a major role. In "Not Seeing God when Raising your Kids", Savage shares some important lessons for those godless parents embarking on their big parental journeys.

Alan Duval brings his expertise in psychology to the fore in "Not Seeing God in Religion" where he looks at what religion entails for believers and questions whether, looking to the future, the supernatural element of these psychological ideals might fall away to leave religion without a god.

Last, but certainly not least by any stretch, is Hank Fox's contribution. He doesn't hold back in his tour de force chapter that rounds off the book. He has a vision. His vision is *Beta Culture* and he's not backward in coming forward about it. "What Comes after Not Seeing God" is a manual for the future, a blueprint for how we build it. So let's get building.

There is enough in this smorgasbord of delight to keep the reader on their toes. Intellectual satisfaction as they consume the ideas herein. What I hope, though, is that if you are not a frequenter to the Patheos Nonreligious channel, there is enough here to pique your interest. Come drop by; we'd love a chat. We're usually a friendly bunch! If you're already a Patheos Nonreligious reader, then perhaps you have a favorite blog where you hang out, getting your kicks, digging the vibe. Well, here is your chance to have a little taster, a soupçon, of something equally as delectable.

Either way, though you may want to long savor the taste, you can always come back for seconds: http://www.patheos.com/Nonreligious.

Part One

DECONSTRUCTING GOD

People have been building God up for thousands of years. They've been doing a very good job of carrying out her PR work for him. The scale of divine miscommunication, given God's omniskills, is pretty catastrophic. No-one can quite agree on what it looks like, this God-thing. Moreover, we have also witnessed thousands of years of tussling and outright fighting as to what form this god or gods has or have, and what form the religions that follow on should have.

Luckily, we now live in a time of greater freethought. Not everywhere, as you will know, and as alluded to within this book. But the fact that this book can be published at all is testament to the current state of affairs.

While God has recently been rather absent from direct world-meddling (although there have been a number of hurricanes and tsunamis as a result of humanity's proclivities for sexually perverse activities, apparently), there is no shortage of people around the world shouting about how existent God is, and how offended he and they must be if we don't believe this to be the case.

God has very thin skin, it seems.

Many freethinkers have taken their own intellectual baseball bats to the edifice that is God. Here is but a small selection of arguments from the Patheos Nonreligious writers in this same vein. God is taken to task over existence, omniskills, and morality, as well as there being questions raised over the rather convenient idea that "God" provides a psychological function for us mere humans.

No doubt these arguments will be roundly ignored (or cognitively dissonantly harmonized) by believers *precisely because* God provides those all-important functions. But still, it's good to get these philosophical and psychological broadsides off our chests.

This is why philosophy is important. Of course, I would say that, as a philosopher. But it serves a purpose here as being the tool with which we approach finding an "ultimate" truth. And, like the scientific method, philosophical theories are ripe for challenge and refining in light of robust and warranted criticism. This is the reason why we blog, in many cases—we want to offer our thoughts and theories about God and atheism in order that they can be criticized, analyzed and generally taken to task. Without this process, our opinions and conclusions are potentially inoculated against contrary positions. They could be castles in the air.

And yet, here are our foundations. It's up to you to see how strong they are. If you find any weaknesses, please report back to our structural engineers so that they can resubmit some new plans.

Not Seeing OmniGod™ through Philosophy and Logic

Jonathan MS Pearce, A Tippling Philosopher

I have long had an interest in the notion of God in classical theism and how his attributes intersect. Or don't. I say "his", but I mean "hers" or "its". There's another headache right there.

By "classical theism", I mean the idea that God is omnipotent, omniscient and omnibenevolent. God is OmniGod™. I often give talks to various groups, one presentation of which is a set of arguments against the existence of God that I call "God on Trial", where I present five arguments against OmniGod's existence. One point that is sometimes raised is that this is a straw man conception of what God is. "My idea of God is very different to this version you are presenting; therefore you are wrong. I, too, admit that this idea of God is problematic!" Well, there are as many versions of God as there are believers, and theists of various stripes can always shift the goalposts. However, we have to start somewhere. I cannot present a case against God and take into account the several billion variations thereof. Instead, I pick the most prevalent understanding of God that has maintained through history, brought about by philosophical ruminations over time.

These ideas of omni- are popular and, some argue, necessary threads that weave their way through ideas of what God is. So I will settle for picking my philosophical fight against this understanding of this perfect God: all-powerful, all-knowing, and all-loving. If you want to propose another version of God, we can have that fight another time. Which will be sometime after you have wrangled free of your label of "heretic." Good luck with that.

Let's start properly conceptual, and narrow it down from there. Start big, I always say.

Why Create at all?

Imagine God, causally "before" creating anything, existing in total perfection, for that is what God must be. There is, or was, nothing greater than God in human (or any other) conception. Interestingly, there can have been no deliberation about creating. There was no time, after all. God's decisions were instantaneous. Necessary, even. God "chose" to create this world. Why? What reason could God have? In order to intend to do something, there must be some kind of desire (if we forget, for a while, that was no time in this process! Oh, it's all so problematic!). A desire signifies a lacking. If you want something, you lack what it is that that something gives you. If you have a lacking, then, it can be argued, you are imperfect. A perfect being will have no needs, no desires. If God has perfect foreknowledge, then God would know all future counterfactuals (if this happened, then that would happen). God would know the future. Heck, God could *feel* or *imagine* or *experience* the future, without *even* having to create it. Essentially, God could be sitting back in his virtual armchair *really* and *actually* imagining and sensing the universe without *really* and *actually* creating it.

Alas, I am here, *really* and *actually* experiencing stubbing my toe, and wondering whether that experience was real or not. So *I* exist, whatever *I* am.

But God apparently *did* create, so God *wanted* something out of this process, something he must not have had, rendering his perfection rather problematic.

He created imperfectly

Shelving the problem that he would have had no desire or need to create anything, existing, as he did, in perfection, let's consider actual creation. Anything created must necessarily have been a degradation of his perfect state of affairs. Unless, of course, he created absolute perfection there and then. Let's face it, although I'm pretty awesome, I'm not quite perfect, and it took me a few billion years of trial and error to get here, too.

A perfect painter is unlikely to produce a really shoddy painting and still maintain the moniker of a perfect painter. It's all about the deeds.

A perfect creator, a perfect chooser, as God must be (if we listen to great Christian philosophers who thought up syllogisms like the Ontological Argument to supposedly prove this, and his existence), would surely choose to create perfectly?

We are here. Good old humans, on the good old world, with its good old tsunamis and malaria, in this good old universe, with its supposed heat death, and life-sucking black holes. This here universe is a perfect creation. Somehow, at some point. Is it now? Jury's out. Could it be on a journey to perfection? Who knows…? I am just not sure that all the pain and suffering we see is necessary for the eventual perfection.

Okay, let's analogize (analogy: the philosopher's favorite toy). Imagine you are an extraordinarily good scientist in your lab. You have concocted a design for a new sentient creature. You know that this creature, if you were to create it, would, with one hundred percent certainty, go out and rape and pillage in the local town. These sentient beings, you *know*, would run amok, freely causing pain and suffering. They would also paint some lovely pictures, and be nice to people at times, too. Knowing all of this, you create anyway. And the creatures go out from your lab into the wider community and cause some mayhem, perfectly predicted. The police come knocking. They find you ultimately morally culpable for the crimes committed. You are deemed, rightly, to be some meddling, ne'er-do-well scientist.

If I was CEO (and chief designer) at a car company, and I designed a car that I knew would be faulty and would cause death when it malfunctioned, which it would, and decided to create that car anyway, releasing it to market, I would be morally and legally culpable for so doing.

These analogies show that God should not be let off the hook for the moral misdemeanors of these imperfect beings called humans. There is no way round this if God has that perfect foreknowledge, that omniscience, and was the ultimate creator of all there is and ever will be. He has chosen to create imperfect beings that he has designed, and whom he knows will cause untold havoc. And he is apparently perfect, and morally off the hook?

Adam and Eve

Let's put this design fault into biblical context. God creates Adam and Eve in this supposedly perfect scenario. They have been chosen to represent humanity in a big test: the test of not eating a fruit from the Tree of Knowledge. In other words, before eating from a fruit that gives them the knowledge of what is right and wrong, they have to know that it is wrong to disobey God and eat some forbidden fruit.

Damn this logic game.

Okay, let's let that issue slip and carry on with the story.

So, Adam and Eve represent humanity in this test. God presumably knows in advance the result of this test, but he picks Adam and Eve to do it anyway, and to knowingly fail. In other words, God is admitting a glaring design fault. If Adam and Eve are representative of humanity, then any given human taking that test would have failed, and we are all inherently faulty. This throws perfect design and creation down the pan.

If, however, Adam and Eve are *not* representative of humanity, then God has chosen non-representative people to take a test and fail, on account of which all other people, given the Fall, are punished. It's bad enough to know we are being punished for the choice of Adam and Eve because we are all equally as shoddy as they are, but it's quite another to think we are being punished for the wrongdoing of this brace when we could have *passed* the test ourselves!

Quite a two-horned dilemma.

God loves abortion

Another creative shortcoming concerns fetuses. Most religious people appear to be fervent pro-lifers. That is to say, they are not fans of abortion. No one is really a fan of abortion in and of itself, but it is useful a procedure for any number of reasons, and the fetus is often merely a group of cells or something that has no personhood and feels no pain. God has designed and created human beings, in some manner, and appears to love abortion, even though his denizens don't. Anywhere up to three quarters of fertilized eggs are naturally, spontaneously, aborted. They either fail to implant or are rejected by the body, or undergo other such problems.

This amounts to perhaps billions of individual blastocysts or embryos over time. God doesn't appear to lift a virtual finger to stop this. What's good for the goose…

God's not fair

We have, like it or not, this collection of human beings that God has designed and created. Or if you are a theistic evolutionist, God created the system that created the humans. Either way, with his omniscience, he knew that which would come to pass.

God created a whole range of people. Men, women and others (if you don't adhere to a gender binary) is one range. The neurotypical and people on the autistic spectrum might be another range.

I assume that, since heaven and hell appear to be the consequence of this here existence, the main point for earthly humans on earth is to enter into a loving relationship, freely, with God. Yes, you can ask what happened to people who existed before the Bible, or in the Amazon who have never heard the Gospel, who don't know the Bible. Theologians like William Lane Craig have argued that God has front-loaded all those souls whom he knew would freely reject him into those peoples. Dark. Fatalistic. Another answer might be that humans have morality written on their hearts and that we don't need the Bible, nor such a relationship with the Christian/Muslim/InsertNameHere God, in order to succeed in the Test of Life and get into heaven. Well, that's a whole problem for theists, meaning we are not needing God for morality, not needing the Bible for guidance, and it is a good argument for secular humanism!

Back to the point. God has created ranges of people, and science has shown that these different types of people have different probabilities in believing in God. Women, for whatever reason (it doesn't matter whether it is genetic, biological or environmental), are more likely to believe in God than men. Scientists less likely than others. And, interestingly, certain autistics far less likely than the neurotypical to believe in a personal deity.

One hypothesis about this last group, based on work by Norenzayan, Gervais and Trzesniewski[1], is that certain autistic people are less able to empathize, to see life from someone else's point of view. They are less able to put themselves in someone else's shoes. Where religious believers are consistently wondering how God, as a personal agent, is viewing their life, their moral actions, these autistic people are unable to do so. That kind of intersubjectivity is much more difficult for them. And so they end up not believing in God, being almost unable to believe in a personal entity out there who is watching their every move.

What this means is that God is unfair. He's stacking the cards, loading the dice, such that certain subgroups of people are more or less likely to freely come to love him. If that is at least part of the endgame, then God is not fair, and not omnibenevolent.

---

[1] Norenzayan A, Gervais WM, Trzesniewski KH (2012). "Mentalizing Deficits Constrain Belief in a Personal God". PLoS ONE 7(5): e36880. https://doi.org/10.1371/journal.pone.0036880

Heaven ain't justification

Please don't use heaven to justify the last point, or to justify how it is okay that a six-month-old baby dies of cancer. "It's alright," you or your theistic friend might say, "they will live for an eternity in heaven!"

This is compensation, and compensation is not moral justification, and certainly so if you are a religious believer. Theists invariably hate a moral value system called consequentialism (William Lane Craig called it a "terrible ethic") because it has no need for God. You derive your moral value from the consequences pertaining to a given action. If I walked up to you and punched you clean in the face and broke your jaw for no reason, then that would not be nice. It is not morally good on almost anyone's moral value system. But let's particularly think about theists who believe morality is divinely commanded, usually, in some manner: this certainly wouldn't be good. If I am made to pay you $10,000, or even if I give it to you voluntarily, it does not make the punch suddenly morally good. You may even enjoy getting that money and think it was worth it, but it is compensation; it is not *moral justification*. Don't let theists fool you with this sleight of hand.

God is a consequentialist anyway

It doesn't get any easier for God, though. The Problem of Evil is the argument that asks why there is so much suffering in the world given his omni-characteristics. He should surely know what to do about all the suffering, would be able to do it, and would be caring enough to want to do it. But, alas, there is still so much suffering. Therefore, the theist says, it is not gratuitous. It does not exist for no reason; we can reason why it is there. We have free will; it is a natural by-product. We have souls; suffering helps to build them into greater entities. Et cetera, et cetera. However, these *theodicies*, as they are called, are all built upon notions of consequentialism. Suffering happens so that we can obtain a greater good, whether it be free will, better souls, or whatnot.

Take Noah's flood, or the death of Jesus. These things happened to obtain greater goods. All of humanity and virtually every ecosystem and animal died. Why? For a greater good, of course! Not sure it worked, but there you go.

The whole moral system involved in proposing theodicies as defenses against the Problem of Evil is consequentialist in nature. God, in allowing these seeming evils, because they can't be gratuitous, must be a consequentialist.

Why don't we photosynthesize?

Let's get back to God's creating us. It turns out that mere existence is predicated upon a whole raft of pain and suffering. Carnivorousness is a system whereby, in order to just exist, many organisms require the pain and death of other organisms. This happens, literally, on an industrial scale, from farming to the Serengeti. I once watched an online video of a water buffalo being eaten alive by a pride of lions just so I could understand this point.

It was terrible.

But that's life, or death as may be. And it has happened for a very long time. All that pain and suffering—every unit—has been built into the design of so many organisms.

It doesn't have to be that way. God could have it any other way, surely, with his omni-skills? Carnivorousness can't be necessary, can it? We could, for example, all photosynthesize. All organisms could derive all of the energy from the sun, thus not necessitating the death of other animals. God could either cook the physical constant to allow for this, or simply allow for perpetual miracles to take place in every organism.

You can take this a step or two further. We don't actually need energy. Conceptually, God could have created organisms, or a whole system, that didn't revolve around our understanding of energy.

No, further still, God did not need to create a physical world at all. God could just have created heaven, and populated heaven directly.

Heaven and Hell

If the endgame is indeed heaven, then why not just create heaven and put our ethereal beings within? Let's return to his divine foreknowledge, if God knew in advance whom the elect were, whom the people who would freely come to love him would be, then why not just create them? If he knew exactly whom on earth would freely come to love him, why bother creating all those majority of others? All those others who are condemned to an eternity in hell? That seems unnecessarily harsh: punishing people infinitely for a finite failure that God knew would happen anyway.

No, just create heaven. Forget earth, the universe, and everything else; just create paradise and fill it with the people you were always going to fill it with.

Job done.
Suffering eradicated. (This creating job is a cinch.)

Satan as God's management executive

God is supposed to be omnipotent. You know, all powerful, almighty. The great-making characteristics of such a god are the paragon of abilities. He could achieve anything at the metaphorical click of his fingers.

So what the hell is Satan still doing hanging around? Well, of course, he doesn't exist either. But supposing you believe that both God and Satan are real entities. Well, then, you'd be making no sense at all. God could make Satan disappear, non-existent, just like that. Any ontological argument for God, or claim that he is perfect, such as under Perfect Being Theology, argues for God's supreme omni-abilities. To be the greatest being in conception, there can be no rival being as God could dispense with them on a whim. Satan cannot be God's equal.

This means that if the Devil exists, he does so at the behest of God. Either God actively wants him to exist, or his disappearance would cause more grief than good, like some embodiment of the Problem of Evil and consequentialism, as previously mentioned.

Thus it appears that Satan, if he exists, is doing a job for God; providing a service, if you will. God, then, must accept corporate responsibility for him. In other words, anything that is laid at the feet of Satan, in terms of blame and moral responsibility, should actually be laid at the invisible feet of God. God allows (either by design, direct causation or act of omission) everything that Satan does.

God's omniscience means he has no free will

Of course, simply knowing everything is not so simple. If God knew his own actions in advance, and was constrained by his own omni-characteristics, then he would not have free will and could not do otherwise than he had already predicted. If God had perfect foreknowledge, and knew in advance exactly what he was going to do, he could never change his mind, or deviate, otherwise he would invalidate his perfect foreknowledge.

Secondly, if he is perfectly loving, then everything that he did would have to be in terms of that kind of perfection. His course of action would always *have* to be the most loving option. He would have no freedom to do otherwise. He would have no freedom or ability to act against his own nature, a nature that he had no role in creating, it was just necessarily so.

If free will is all that and a bag of chips, as many theists claim, then the fact that God does not have it is a bit of a problem.

All he knows is that he doesn't know everything...

In many instances, you cannot know that you don't know something. If there is a situation where you cannot know something, then, if it is claimed that you are omniscient, this would invalidate that claim.

For example, there could conceivably be something that God does not know. Conceivably, perhaps another dimension run by another God exists that does not coincide at all with this dimension. If one eternal God can exist, why not another in an entirely different dimension and unbeknownst to the first God? Now, it is unimportant as to whether this is actually the case or not. What is important is that God could not *know* that he did not know this by the very nature of not knowing it! I think.

Where does this leave God? Well, God is in a situation whereby he cannot know that he knows everything. He might *think* he knows everything. Epistemologically speaking, though, he cannot *know* it. Of course, this whole point depends on the definition of "know" and "knowledge." But if we take a Cartesian sense of indubitably to be the case, then I think we can make something of a problem for God.

Remaining with Descartes and his Evil Daemon thought experiment (updated to *The Matrix* for modern times), there's always a chance that God is an experiment in an elaborate lab, programmed to think he is omnipotent and omniscient (yes, God could be plugged into the Matrix and he'd never know it!). There's a chance he is one of a trillion gods in a trillion different universes, that he has himself been created by another, more powerful god, but that the other god made it so God god was not aware of this.

It only takes one thing you cannot know to invalidate omniscience. God cannot know that he knows everything. It might not be the case, of course, that there is a whole procession of gods leading back from God, but God cannot know that this is indubitably not the case.

Phew, being God isn't as easy as it's cracked up to be.

And the list goes on

And so it goes for the classical notion of God. Problems beget problems, and they beget further problems. I look at many of these and more in a couple of my previous books: *The Little Book of Unholy Questions* and *The Problem with "God": Skeptical Theism under the Spotlight*.

I think what we *can* safely say is that this version of God is wholly unlikely, and problematic. Impossible, even, given the above. Something has to go. One of the omnis has to be dropped. Or all of them.

Or God.

Not Seeing God through Psychology and Neuroscience

Matthew Facciani, According to Matthew

How does religiosity impact our brains?

The neuroscience of religiosity is a recent and exciting subfield of research. Unfortunately, the popular media does not always do a great job of accurately explaining this area so I aim to counter this in my chapter, covering the science of religious belief, and focusing on some important findings from sociology, psychology, and neuroscience. Science cannot confirm whether or not God exists, but it can explain some of the popularity of religion, as well as the impact it has on our mind. This chapter is certainly not meant to be exhaustive, but, in it, I will share some important research that gives a brief introduction to the science of religious belief. My central point is that religion hijacks existing psychological processes and perpetuates itself. But first…

Who am I?

Before I jump into the science, I would like to go into a little bit of my background and explain how I got interested in this subject. After studying psychology and sociology as an undergraduate, I started a PhD in cognitive neuroscience at The University of South Carolina, specifically "quantitative neuroscience," which essentially focused on the methods behind neuroimaging research. However, after publishing a couple of papers, I realized I was more interested in directly studying human behavior than mapping the neurons from which it arguably derives. I quickly learned that I wasn't as interested in my area as I had originally hoped, instead reading studies and books about the science of religious belief, initially as more of a hobby. Because I had the science background, I gave a talk summarizing my findings to my local Secular Student Alliance group and people seemed to enjoy it (including myself!). So I continued to research this area and ended up giving similar talks to groups around the country as well as at a few national atheist/skeptic conferences. Eventually, I switched my academic focus to study the neuroscience of religion in order to reflect my hobby.

Realizing I was more interested in studying human behavior from a more "macro" perspective, I "changed majors" in graduate school and will be finishing my PhD in sociology (with a focus on social psychology). I have worked on a few academic papers that have investigated religion and atheism, but my main research focus now is looking at the social factors behind why people reject scientific evidence. So my academic background is a bit unorthodox as I have expertise in sociology, psychology, and even neuroscience. In this chapter, I'd like to use such an eclectic background to review some of the literature on the science of belief from a variety of fields and discuss how they collectively explain why religion is so universal.

What psychological processes does religiosity utilize?

There are several well-studied aspects of human behavior that we consistently see across many cultures. One of them is our deference to authority. In Stanley Milgram's famous experiment, he found that most people will induce a lethal shock in another person if an authority figure tells them to (Blass, 1999). Milgram's experiment had a participant believe that they had to instruct another person in a different room how to complete a task. Whenever the person in the other room made a mistake, they had to increase the electric shock voltage at the behest of a scientist in a white lab coat who was working with them. Importantly, there was not actually another person in the other room. It was a recording and the participant falsely believed they were shocking someone. Milgram found that the majority of people would induce a lethal shock just because someone with a white lab coat was telling them what to do! This, in part explains, how apparently good or normal people could have done terrible things during World War II.

Now how does this relate to religion? Well, if people are inclined to defer to authority, then churches can certainly take advantage of and benefit from that process. Priests can undoubtedly have a lot of influence over their congregations, tapping into these existing psychological processes. Indeed, God may be the ultimate authority figure, which may make people even more likely to carry out violence or bigotry in his name.

People also conform much more often than we would like to admit. Solomon Asch's classic conformity study showed that people will respond incorrectly along with other people in the room during a simple task, even if the answer to the task is fairly obvious (Asch, 1955). Asch asked his participants to determine which line was at a different length from a group of lines. The vast majority of people had no problem with this task in isolation, but once several people in front of them said the wrong answer, they were more likely to say the wrong answer as well. This is consistent with research that shows people are more likely to hold creationist beliefs when embedded in a social network of other creationists (Hill, 2014).

Importantly, any system can utilize these existing social psychological processes. For example, I've seen plenty of atheists blindly defer to Richard Dawkins or another "leader" in the atheist movement on any number of issues. Our human proclivity to conform and defer to authority figures impacts all of us.

Another psychological process that religion can certainly benefit from is our propensity to create agency and meaning in chaos. In 1944, Heider and Simmel created a task that demonstrated that people will attach meaning to completely random shapes on a screen. It may be interesting for you to go and watch this video on YouTube (just search for Heider & Simmel task) and see how quickly you get angry at the big triangle seeming to bully the other shapes, despite there being zero text or any information beyond moving shapes.

Many similar studies have captured this phenomenon of interpreting agency over the years. Andy Thompson argues in his book *Why we believe in Gods* that we possess a hyperactive agency detection device in our brains. This may have been adaptive for our ancestors: we would be more likely to survive if we thought the rustling in the bushes was a predator rather than thinking it was just the wind. Experimental evidence shows that people will search for meaning even more when they are feeling stressed as they seek a sense of control (Whitson & Galinksy, 2008). This is consistent with how religion can be comforting as we will see in several other studies.

This agency detection process seems to be a universal human process, but it may be even more pronounced in religious believers. Highly religious people tend to have a greater need for cognitive closure (Saroglou, 2002). In other words, they feel more uncomfortable when they cannot create meaning easily.

To test this more directly, a study by Reikki and colleagues (2014) found that supernatural believers (those who believe in God as well as ghosts) are more likely to create agency in random moving patterns than nonbelievers. Believers and nonbelievers watched a video much like the Heider and Simmel task and the believers rated the intentionality of the different moving shapes much higher than nonbelievers.

A follow up study had believers and nonbelievers do the same task, but this time they had their brain activity measured. Believers had higher activity brain areas associated with inferring meaning of social behavior (medial prefrontal cortex) during animation with random movement! This study provides some neuroscientific evidence that back up the psychological findings.

Speaking of the neuroscience of religion, you may have heard about some articles reporting on a "God area" of the brain, but this is overly simplistic. Neuroscience research hasn't found some special area that is only involved with religion. In fact, religious belief activates well-established brain areas involved with emotion, episodic memory, and imagery (Kapogiannis et al, 2009). So now that we've established some cognitive components religion utilizes on our whistle-stop tour, we can see if religious beliefs actually impact our psychology.

Can religion benefit people psychologically?

By creating agency and meaning in chaos, religion can help reduce uncertainty. It's easy to imagine how religion could have started as an explanation for uncertain events in our environment and continues to do so today. We all go through difficult times that may leave us asking "Why me"? Because humans are motivated to avoid cognitive dissonance (Festinger, 1962), creating meaning from thinking about "God's Plan" can reduce a great deal of uncertainty and anxiety. Given this, it's unsurprising that religion has been shown to reduce both uncertainty and anxiety.

Sociologists have argued that religion's rules and rigid boundaries for seeing the world allows the person to avoid processing contradictory information. For example, if a traumatic event happens, one can think that it is part of "God's plan" or that "God works in mysterious ways." (Hogg et al, 2010; 2014). However, being involved with any sort of extreme group with rigid rules (secular or religious) may reduce uncertainty because such groups have an inflexible view of the world. Importantly, an ideology must have strong and rigid beliefs that provide a meaning system and framework for understanding the environment in order to reduce uncertainty (Hogg, 2014). Given that religion can be more accessible and flexible than other ideologies, it can do a better job at reducing uncertainty in more situations, but we can also see similar effects with strongly held political beliefs (Kay and Eibach, 2013).

The above sociological evidence is consistent with psychological findings as well. Research has shown that strongly religious people often have reduced anxiety, which has been theorized because of their strong meaning-making for chaotic events (Park, 2005) and social support (Salsman et al, 2005). However, it's important to note that highly religious people can have increased anxiety as well, if they are following a doctrine that makes them feel guilty about their behavior (Pargament, 2002). For example, those who believe God is punishing when they get an illness tend to have more anxiety.

Essentially, having strong conviction in one's beliefs creates a framework for understanding their environment (Pargament, 2002). Kay and Eibach (2013) saw this effect with strong political beliefs and Farias and colleagues (2013) found that secular people's belief in science increases in the face of stress and existential anxiety. However, it does seem that generally having strong religious conviction can act as a particularly strong buffer against uncertainty. These psychological findings are supported by neuroscientific evidence that looks at error detection through the anterior cingulate cortex (Inzlicht et al, 2009).

The anterior cingulate cortex (ACC) is a part of the brain associated with error detection and the experience of anxiety. Brain activity in the ACC has been shown to be associated with error detection, with greater activity following an error in cognitive tasks (Yeung et al, 2004). An example of such a task would be the classic Stroop task (Stroop, 1935). The Stroop task has participants name the text color of a word that is printed in a color not represented by the word they have to read (e.g., reading the word "blue" printed in red ink instead of blue ink). Error detection would occur whenever the participant accidently says the wrong color while trying to name the text color.

Essentially, errors on these cognitive tasks activate a basic "uh oh" response in the brain. Individuals who are more anxious tend to also have higher ACC activity during the "uh oh" response when detecting they made an error (Hajcak, 2003). Thus, if religiosity does reduce anxiety we should see less ACC activity during an error detection task associated with anxiety.

Inzlicht and his colleagues (2009) conducted a study where they measured the neural processes of anxiety in both religious believers and non-believers. They had both groups complete a cognitive task which is known to activate processes involved with error detection (and the corresponding "uh oh" response). An electroencephalograph (EEG) measured brain activity while the believers and non-believers completed the cognitive task. The researchers found that religious believers had less activity in the ACC during errors on the task. This effect was found despite controlling for personality factors and cognitive ability! These findings suggest that high levels of religiosity might buffer the anxiety caused by uncertainty.

This finding has since been replicated in other studies using similar experimental paradigms (Inzlicht, Tullet, & Good 2011). In one such study, participants who strongly believed in God were broken up into two experimental groups. In one group, participants wrote what their religion meant and explained in their lives before completing the cognitive task, while the other group did not. Like the 2009 study, Inzlicht and colleagues (2010) had participants complete an error detection task associated with anxiety while they had their brain activity measured. The group that reflected on God before the experiment had less ACC activity during errors than the group that did not reflect on God. However, this effect was only seen in religious believers because it likely affirmed their religiosity.

In a study that focused on specific aspects of a religion, Good and colleagues (2014) demonstrated that Mormons experienced less anxiety (reduced ACC activity) when thinking about alcohol after they were primed to think about God's forgiveness. Again, affirming one's convictions to a particular ideology appears to be the crux of reducing anxiety. Though religion is particularly good at creating this effect, we can see affirming other values has self-protective effects as well (Sherman & Cohen, 2006).

These neuroscientific studies suggest that what we believe does appear to have a top-down effect on how our brain processes information. After we parse and operationalize these beliefs, neuroscience can allow us to study their effects on the brain. Psychological research has previously supported the role that religious belief can play in helping to reduce anxiety (Park, 2005) and now we can observe this effect on a neural level (Inzlicht, Tullet, & Good 2011). High religiosity seems to provide a strong anxiety of uncertainty buffer by providing a framework for understanding one's environment. Parsing the specific components of religiosity that create this uncertainty buffer can be addressed with future research.

Can psychological research explain why there are atheists?

So we have seen that psychological science has shown that religiosity taps into existing cognitive processes and can act as a buffer for anxiety and uncertainty. This seems like a very adaptive function, so the question arises of why atheists even exist at all!

Well, there is a cocktail of psychological, environmental, and genetic components that lead to any belief system or behavior. No one main factor has been identified that causes someone to be religious or not. However, some psychological research has shown a few cognitive differences between believers and nonbelievers. It does seem that nonbelievers are more comfortable engaging in analytic thinking over intuitive thinking in certain tasks.

A common way to categorize this "intuitive" type of thinking is referred to as Type 1 processing. Basically, Type 1 thinking is intuitive, fast, and automatic. This kind of thinking leads to more rapid responses. Such intuitive types of thinking are difficult to override via slower Type 2 processing. The analytic Type 2 styles are slower and more deliberative (Kahneman, 2011).

In his book *Why Religion is Natural and Science is Not*, McCauley (2013) argues that religion uses Type 1 thinking which is cognitively natural for us. Conversely, scientific thinking uses Type 2 which is often counterintuitive and requires a great deal of practice.

Importantly, popular science is similar to popular religion! The website *I Fucking Love Science* is known for its overly simplistic representation of science that aims to make people feel good. I would argue this is cognitively similar to popular religion found in a typical church where people don't have to think too much and feel good about themselves. Conversely, a theologian may engage in much more analytic thinking when they are making their arguments.

There is research to back up these ideas as well, as atheism is strongly associated with more analytic thinking (Gervais & Norenzayan, 2012). Atheists tend to score higher on tasks that tap into analytic thinking than those who are strongly religious. Again, this doesn't mean that religious people as a group cannot think analytically, it means atheists tend to want to engage in analytic thinking more often than the most devoutly religious.

Lindeman and colleagues (2012) argue that skeptics inhibit some of the cognitively natural aspects of religious belief. Their study found that supernatural believers (combining a sample of those who believe supernatural things like God, ghosts, and spirits) are more likely to see "signs" than nonbelievers. The study had people think about certain scenarios and then showed them random pictures. For example, they would think about having an important job interview and then show them a picture of a nice suit. The supernatural believers would be more likely to say the suit was a "sign" that they did well in the interview.

In a neuroimaging experiment using the previous method, the authors found that believers see more signs than skeptics, again. However, the part of the brain associated with cognitive inhibition (right inferior frontal gyrus) had greater activity in skeptics! Thus, the authors argue that skeptics are inhibiting themselves from seeing signs. So it's not that skeptics cannot see the connections between the pictures and the scenarios, they may use their Type 2 thinking and override them!

Finally, research has shown that atheism tends to rise in areas that have more equality. So it could be that when there is less of a need for people to adhere to an anxiety reducing belief system, people tend to be less religious (Gray & Wegner, 2010). So while atheists do have some cognitive differences compared to religious people, there are also many social factors involved (which could be explained at length in several books!).

Now that I've discussed some of the neural and psychological differences of religiosity, it's important to note that our brains can change! This is called "neuroplasticity" and just because believers may show neural differences with these tasks, it doesn't mean they can't train themselves to be more comfortable with analytic thinking and not see as many "signs," for example. A really cool (and probably impossible) study could look at how believers and nonbelievers brains change over time. I used to be very religious, and I wonder how the make-up of my brain has changed over time, reflecting my movement toward atheism?

Psychology can correct some misconceptions about religion

Finally, I'd like to briefly use psychological research to correct two myths about religion. One such myth that spreads around secular circles is that religion is a mental illness, and I definitely do **not** want these studies to perpetuate such nonsense! Mental illness is by definition maladaptive and abnormal. We have shown from just a few studies that religion taps into our normal, adaptive psychology. You can read more about this in an article I wrote (Facciani, 2014) as well as an article Sincere Kirabo wrote when he interviewed many cognitive scientists who study religion about their thoughts on the matter (Kirabo, 2015).

Kirabo found that the overwhelming consensus of scientists in this area do not think religion should be categorized as a mental illness.

A second myth, sometimes spread by atheists, is that "religious people are stupid." Going into the problems with measuring intelligence would again take an entire book. Essentially, it's important to understand that intelligence involves multiple dimensions of cognitive ability (Neisser et al, 1996) and the tests are often culturally biased (Flynn, 1987). Furthermore, these intelligence tests are often from a US context where there is a strong link between religiosity and socioeconomic status (Schieman, 2010), creating a severe confounding variable.

Even if we can agree on a working definition of analytic intelligence, Miron Zuckerman, the lead author of a recent meta-analysis (Zuckerman et al, 2013) investigating the relation between intelligence and religiosity, is quite explicit in stating, "It is truly the wrong message to take from here that if I believe in God I must be stupid." Zuckerman explains his position by saying "The [anxiety relieving] functions we cover imply that in many ways religious people are better off than those who are nonreligious," and "There are things about self-esteem and feeling in control and attachment that religion provides. In all those things, there are benefits to being religious, and that is the take-home message for those who are religious." Thus, these findings do not suggest that religious people have less ability, but rather people who fall under their definition of "intelligent" have less of a need for religious belief and its practices.

Conclusion

Religion is an incredibly complex, yet influential phenomenon in our society. It impacts so much of our culture, from politics to ideas about sexuality to how we explain why certain events occurred. Psychological science provides some insight as to why religiosity is so prevalent, and also how it can be beneficial sometimes. So while religion can be very harmful when believers use their beliefs to justify terrible behavior, we can also see some psychological benefits to religiosity as well. If atheists hope to prevail in the marketplace of ideas, they perhaps need to work out how to fulfil these functions in a secular manner.

Religion appears to benefit from established psychological processes such as our propensity to seek agency and meaning in our world. When such beliefs provide some explanation to our chaotic world, it also can reduce anxiety and uncertainty. We can see such effects on a neural level as well. Atheists may have some cognitive differences from religious believers, but it doesn't mean religious people are mentally ill or more stupid.

Again, this chapter is meant to merely be an overview of some studies about religion that I enjoyed reading about and thought others may find interesting as well. It is by no means exhaustive and only scratches the surface of what we know about religion. Despite how much we have learned about the psychology of religion, there is still so much to learn. It's an exciting time for scientists interested in belief systems and we can all look forward to learning much more from their research!

References

Asch, S. E. (1955). Opinions and social pressure. *Readings about the social animal*, *193*, 17-26.

Blass, T. (Ed.). (1999). *Obedience to authority: Current perspectives on the Milgram paradigm*. Psychology Press.

Facciani, M. (2014). Why Religion Is Not A Mental Illness. http://www.patheos.com/blogs/wwjtd/2014/12/guest-post-why-religion-is-not-a-mental-illness/

Facciani, M. (2015). The Neuroscience of How Religiosity Reduces Anxiety. http://bulletin.equinoxpub.com/2015/02/the-neuroscience-of-how-religiosity-reduces-anxiety/ (this chapter used a few paragraphs from this article)

Farias, M., Newheiser, A. K., Kahane, G., & de Toledo, Z. (2013). Scientific faith: belief in science increases in the face of stress and existential anxiety. *Journal of experimental social psychology*, *49*(6), 1210-1213.

Festinger, L. (1962). *A theory of cognitive dissonance* (Vol. 2). Stanford university press.

Flynn, J. R. (1987). Massive IQ gains in 14 nations: What IQ tests really measure. *Psychological bulletin*, *101*(2), 171.

Gervais, W. M., & Norenzayan, A. (2012). Analytic thinking promotes religious disbelief. *Science*, *336*(6080), 493-496.

Good, M., Inzlicht, M., & Larson, M. J. (2014). God will forgive: reflecting on God's love decreases neurophysiological responses to errors. Social cognitive and affective neuroscience, nsu096.

Gray, K., & Wegner, D. M. (2010). Blaming God for our pain: Human suffering and the divine mind. *Personality and Social Psychology Review, 14*(1), 7-16.

Hajcak, G., McDonald, N., & Simons, R. F. (2003). Anxiety and error-related brain activity. *Biological psychology, 64*(1), 77-90.

Hill, J. P. (2014). Rejecting evolution: The role of religion, education, and social networks. *Journal for the Scientific Study of Religion, 53*(3), 575-594.

Hogg, M. A., Adelman, J. R., & Blagg, R. D. (2010). Religion in the face of uncertainty: An uncertainty-identity theory account of religiousness. *Personality and Social Psychology Review, 14*(1), 72-83.

Hogg, M. A. (2014). From uncertainty to extremism: Social categorization and identity processes. *Current Directions in Psychological Science, 23*(5), 338-342.

Inzlicht, M., McGregor, I., Hirsh, J. B., & Nash, K. (2009). Neural markers of religious conviction. *Psychological Science,* 20(3), 385-392.

Inzlicht, M., & Tullett, A. M. (2010). Reflecting on God Religious Primes Can Reduce Neurophysiological Response to Errors. *Psychological Science,* 21(8), 1184-1190.

Inzlicht, M., Tullett, A. M., & Good, M. (2011). The need to believe: A neuroscience account of religion as a motivated process. *Religion, brain & behavior,* 1(3), 192-212.

Kahneman, D. (2011). *Thinking, fast and slow.* Macmillan.

Kay, A. C., & Eibach, R. P. (2013). Compensatory control and its implications for ideological extremism. *Journal of Social Issues, 69*(3), 564-585.

Kay, A. C., Gaucher, D., McGregor, I., & Nash, K. (2010). Religious belief as compensatory control. *Personality and Social Psychology Review,* 14(1), 37-48.

Kapogiannis, D., Barbey, A. K., Su, M., Zamboni, G., Krueger, F., & Grafman, J. (2009). Cognitive and neural foundations of religious belief. *Proceedings of the National Academy of Sciences, 106*(12), 4876-4881.

Kirabo, S. (2015). Why You Sound Ridiculous Claiming Religiosity is a Mental Defect. http://www.patheos.com/blogs/notesfromanapostate/2015/09/why-you-sound-ridiculous-claiming-religiosity-is-a-mental-defect/

Lindeman, M., Svedholm, A. M., Riekki, T., Raij, T., & Hari, R. (2012). Is it just a brick wall or a sign from the universe? An fMRI study of supernatural believers and skeptics. *Social cognitive and affective neuroscience,* nss096.

McCauley, R. (2013). *Why Religion is Natural and Science is Not.* Oxford University Press.

Miron Zuckerman interview: http://archive.sltrib.com/story.php?ref=/sltrib/lifestyle/56744346-80/religion-religious-zuckerman-faith.html.csp

Neisser, U., Boodoo, G., Bouchard Jr, T. J., Boykin, A. W., Brody, N., Ceci, S. J., ... & Urbina, S. (1996). Intelligence: Knowns and unknowns. *American psychologist*, *51*(2), 77.

Pargament, K. I. (2002). The bitter and the sweet: An evaluation of the costs and benefits of religiousness. *Psychological inquiry*, *13*(3), 168-181.

Park, C. L. (2005). Religion and meaning. *Handbook of the psychology of religion and spirituality*, 295-314.

Riekki, T., Lindeman, M., & Raij, T. T. (2014). Supernatural believers attribute more intentions to random movement than skeptics: An fMRI study. *Social neuroscience*, *9*(4), 400-411.

Salsman, J. M., Brown, T. L., Brechting, E. H., & Carlson, C. R. (2005). The link between religion and spirituality and psychological adjustment: The mediating role of optimism and social support. *Personality and social psychology bulletin*, *31*(4), 522-535.

Saroglou, V. (2002). Beyond dogmatism: The need for closure as related to religion. *Mental Health, Religion & Culture*, *5*(2), 183-194.

Schieman, S. (2010). Socioeconomic status and beliefs about God's influence in everyday life. *Sociology of Religion*, *71*(1), 25-51.

Sherman, D. K., & Cohen, G. L. (2006). The psychology of self-defense: Self-affirmation theory. *Advances in experimental social psychology*, *38*, 183-242.

Stroop, J. R. (1935). Studies of interference in serial verbal reactions. *Journal of experimental psychology*, 18(6), 643.

Thompson, A. (2011). Why We Believe in God(s): A Concise Guide to the Science of Faith

Whitson, J. A., & Galinsky, A. D. (2008). Lacking control increases illusory pattern perception. *science*, *322*(5898), 115-117.

Yeung, N., Botvinick, M. M., & Cohen, J. D. (2004). The neural basis of error detection: conflict monitoring and the error-related negativity. *Psychological review*, 111(4), 931.

Zuckerman, M., Silberman, J., & Hall, J. A. (2013). The relation between intelligence and religiosity: A meta-analysis and some proposed explanations. *Personality and Social Psychology Review*, *17*(4), 325-354.

Using Common Sense to Not See God

Bob Seidensticker, Cross Examined

My passion is the apologetics debate—the arguments for and against Christianity. Atheists often focus on rebutting arguments put forward by Christians in favor of Christianity, such as the Design Argument, the Moral Argument, the Cosmological Argument, and so on. Let's take the road less traveled and focus on, not rebuttals against these popular arguments, but arguments *for* atheism. I've picked seven of my favorites. They're short and easy to understand, they're not widely known, and they should provoke any opponent to think, which is the mark of a productive debate.

The Map of World Religions

Almost everyone is familiar with maps of world religions with colors showing the religions that predominate in different parts of the world. Have you ever wondered why you never see a Map of World Science? Imagine such an oddity. Over here on the map is where scientists believe in a geocentric solar system, and over there, a heliocentric one. This area is where they think that astrology can predict the future, and that area is where they reject the idea. Intelligent Design thinking reigns in the crosshatched area, and evolution in the dark gray area. Naturally, each of these different groups think of their opponents as heretics, and they have fought wars over their opposing beliefs.

This is nonsense. A new scientific theory isn't location specific, and, if it passes muster, it peacefully sweeps the world. Astronomy replaced astrology, chemistry replaced alchemy, and germ theory replaced evil spirits as a cause of disease. One scientist should get the same results from an experiment as another, regardless of their respective religions. Evolution, germ theory, Relativity, and the Big Bang are part of the consensus view among scientists, whether they are Christian, Muslim, atheist, or other.

Sure, there can be some not-invented-here thinking—scientists have egos, too—but this only slows the inevitable success of a new theory that better explains the evidence. Contrast this with the idea that Shintoism will sweep across America or Europe over the next couple of decades and replace Christianity, simply because it's a theory that explains the facts of reality better. It works that way in science, not religion.

Let's return to our map of world religions. Religions claim to give answers to the big questions—answers that science can't yet give. Questions such as: What is our purpose? Or, Where did we come from? Or, Is there anything else out there? Or, What is science grounded on? But the map shows that the religious answers to those questions depend on where you are! Take the question, What is our purpose? If you live in Tibet or Thailand, Buddhism teaches that we are here to learn to cease suffering and reach nirvana. If you live in Yemen or Saudi Arabia, Islam teaches that we are here to submit to Allah. If you live in the United States, Christianity teaches that our purpose is to praise and worship God.

We ask the most profound questions of all, and the answers are location specific? What kind of truth depends on location?

For discovering reality, religion comes up short. Next time someone nods their head sagely and says, "Ah, but Christianity can answer life's Big Questions," remember how shallow that claim is. Sure, Christianity can answer the Big Questions. Anyone can, but are those answers based on anything? Are they worth listening to? The inability of religion to advance from its squabbling, multicolored map of world religion to science's consensus view of reality overturns Christianity's claim to have the one correct view.

The First Commandment Defeats Christian Claims

Let me propose this principle: a human-invented religion will look radically different from the worship of a real god. Human imagination or longing for the divine will cobble together a very poor imitation of the real thing. Supernatural reality is likely far more marvelous than whatever humans could dream up.

But religious historians tell us that the Yahweh of the Old Testament looks like just another Canaanite deity such as Asherah, Baal, Moloch, Yam, or Mot. What else could he be but just another invented god? The Bible itself admits this similarity. The book of Exodus gives God's demand that the Israelites avoid foreign religions when they returned to Canaan. The first

Commandment says, "You shall have no other gods before me." God had to make sure that his people weren't corrupted.

But wait a minute—how *could* they have been corrupted? The Israelites enter a land full of foreign gods—invented gods, obviously—but God had made plain the correct religion. How would those made-up gods look next to the real deal? The Hebrew religion, the only one that worshipped a real god, would be a stunning and brilliant jewel compared to the other religions' tawdry plastic beads.

Think of it this way. Imagine that God provided Disney World for the Israelites but warned against moving into the filthy trailer park across the street. Why bother with the warning? How could anyone possibly be tempted? Similarly, with the Israelites given the correct religion, the only one that worshipped a real god, why bother with the first Commandment? How could God have ever been worried that another religion would be the least bit compelling?

Things are clearer once we realize that their religion *didn't* look special. The prohibitions made sense because proto-Judaism looked similar to all the other Canaanite religions. Yahweh was the god of Israel just like Chemosh was the god of the Moabites and Moloch was the god of the Ammonites. The people in Israel knew that Chemosh and Moloch existed, they just didn't worship them.

The Bible's own prohibitions make clear that the god of the Old Testament was just another god not fundamentally different from any other god of the region, which means that Christianity's own book defeats its claim of a single god, with all other gods invented, imagined, or false.

Christianity versus Mormonism

Many Christians declare that they don't hold their religious beliefs just because they were born into a Christian environment. No, they believe because of the evidence.

Let's test that claim. If they believe because of evidence, they should accept claims that are better evidenced than those of Christianity such as those of Mormonism. The claims of Mormonism have just such a historical record. Compare that against conventional Christianity to see the many areas where the quality of the Mormon record beats that of Christianity.

Number and breadth of documents. The Christian apologist may say that the New Testament story is supported not only by the books of the New Testament but also by writings of non-Christians who lived within a century of the death of Jesus. But Mormons point to newspaper articles, diaries, letters, and even court records documenting the early fathers of their church, a far broader record than that of the New Testament. Some of these accounts of the events in the early Mormon church were written within days or even hours of the events.

Time gap from original to our best copies. The first six words of the Gospel of John 1:1 are, "In the beginning was the Word," but how do we know that? Our oldest Greek copies of this passage are two papyrus manuscripts from roughly 200 CE, which leaves a century from the original authorship of John in about 90 CE to our best copies. And that's about as small as the gap gets—it's two or three centuries for much of the New Testament. That gap from original to our best copy means a long dark period during which undetected "improvements" could've been made to the text. The apologist will talk about the tens of thousands of New Testament manuscript copies, but the vast majority are from medieval period, which does nothing to enhance claims of biblical accuracy. The books of Mormonism were written after the modern printing press, and we have many early, identical copies.

Cultural gap. The Jesus story is from a culture long ago and far away, and the gospels were originally written in Greek. They can only document the Christian tradition within *Greek* culture, a culture suffused with tales of dying-and-rising gods, virgin births, and other miraculous happenings. This makes the New Testament's original books already one culture removed from the oral Aramaic Jewish culture of Jesus. In Mormonism, we can read the accounts of the participants in our own language.

Oral history gap. The apologist will talk about how little time elapsed between the events and the documentation of those events—perhaps forty to sixty years for the gospels. That's not bad compared to the biographies of other important figures of antiquity, but Mormonism spent no time in the limbo of oral tradition. The Book of Mormon was committed to paper immediately, which means no time for the story to grow into legend with the retelling.

Eyewitness accounts. The four gospels don't claim to be eyewitness accounts. We don't even know who wrote them—Matthew, Mark, Luke, and John are merely the names assigned by tradition to the four gospels. Within Mormonism, twelve men saw the golden plates. Testimony from those men is presented at the beginning of every copy of the Book of Mormon.

Provenance. The New Testament books were written by ordinary people, not by God himself, or even angels. Joseph Smith, the founder of Mormonism, was told by an angel about the golden plates, from which the Book of Mormon was written. That his source document was vetted by an angel says a lot about the quality of what he started with (or at least it beats the claims of traditional Christianity). You might say that the Joseph Smith story is just that—a story. Why trust it? That's a reasonable concern, but it applies just as well to Christianity.

Who would die for a lie? Christian apologists ask this question and then point to the martyred disciples of Jesus, but the historical evidence documenting the disciples' deaths is contradictory. Besides, the likeliest explanation isn't that the gospel story is a lie; it's a *legend*. It wasn't deliberately cobbled together by pranksters; it simply grew over decades of retelling. **Even if we accept weak claims for disciples dying to defend the truth of the gospel story,** Mormonism can brag about the same thing. The Mormon inner circle put themselves through much hardship, including death in at least the case of founder Joseph Smith. If Christian apologists claim that this is strong evidence for Christianity, it must be for Mormonism as well.

Naysayer hypothesis. Christian apologists say that if the Jesus story were false, naysayers of the time would have snuffed it out. A false story wouldn't have survived to be popular today. This naysayer hypothesis crumbles under investigation,[1] but if apologists want to advance it, Mormonism comes along as well. If its story were false, those in the inner circle would have shut it down, right?

---

[1] Bob Seidensticker, "13 Reasons to Reject the Christian Naysayer Hypothesis," *Cross Examined,* July 6, 2015, http://www.patheos.com/blogs/crossexamined/2015/07/13-reasons-to-reject-the-christian-naysayer-hypothesis.

Point by point, using the arguments Christians themselves use, Mormonism beats Christianity. If Christians actually took their own argument seriously, they would find Mormonism far more convincing. Does this mean that *I* find Mormonism convincing? Of course not—it's just that you can't dismiss Mormonism for lack of evidence without more forcefully dismissing conventional Christianity as well.

There's one more lesson to draw from the unique weaknesses of Mormonism. The Book of Mormon makes claims that archaeology, genetics, and even linguistics don't support such as modern Native Americans descending from people from the Ancient Near East who sailed across the Atlantic about 2500 years ago. These visitors were supposed to have brought to the Americas horses, elephants, wheat, steel, and other goods that history tells us only arrived with Europeans.

Christianity doesn't make claims that are so specific and testable. A win for Christianity? Not at all—its lack of evidence becomes an advantage since it can't be caught in a lie, though that's not much of a slogan to put on the sign in front of a church—"Christianity: you can trust it because it's vague and untestable!"

The Monty Hall Problem

I first came across the fascinating Monty Hall problem twenty years ago. Suppose you're on a television game show, and host Monty Hall gives you the choice of three doors. Behind one door is a new car, but behind the others, nothing. You pick a door (say number one), and the host, who knows what's behind the doors, opens another door (say number three), which is empty. He then says to you, "Do you want door number two instead?"

Most people think that there's no benefit to switching, but they're wrong. To see that, let's push this problem to an extreme. Imagine that there are not three doors but three hundred. There's still just one good prize with nothing behind the other doors.

So you pick a door—say number 274. There's a 1 in 300 chance you're right. Remember this: *your guess is almost certainly wrong.* Then the game show host opens 298 of the remaining doors: 1, 2, 3, and so on. He skips door 59 and your door, 274. Every open door shows nothing.

So should you switch? Of course you should—your initial pick is still almost surely wrong. The probabilities are 1/300 for #274 and 299/300 for #59.

Not Seeing God

Another way to look at the problem: do you want to stick with your initial door or do you want *all* the other doors? Switching is simply choosing all the other doors, because (thanks to the open doors) you know the only door within that set that could be the winner.

Perhaps you've already anticipated the connection with choosing a religion. Imagine you've picked your religion—religion #274, let's say. For most people, their adoption of a religion is like picking a door in this game. In the game show, you don't weigh evidence before selecting your door; you pick it randomly. And most people adopt the dominant religion of their upbringing. As with the game show, the religion in which you grew up is also assigned to you at random.

Now imagine an analogous game, the Game of Religion, with Truth as host. Out of three hundred doors, behind each of which is a religion, the believer picks door #274. (More likely, the believer was *assigned* door #274 by the accident of his birth.) Truth flings open door after door and we see nothing. Hinduism, Jainism, Sikhism, Mormonism, Scientology—all empty. As you suspected, they're just amalgams of legend, myth, tradition, and wishful thinking.

Few of us seriously consider or have even heard of the religions Winti, Candomblé, Mandaeism, or the ancient religions of Central America, for example. Luckily for the believer, Truth gets around to those doors too and opens them, showing nothing.

Here's where the analogy between the two games fails. First, Truth opens *all* the other doors. Only the believer's pick, door #274, is still closed. Second, there was never a guarantee that *any* door contained a true religion! Since the believer likely came to his beliefs randomly because of the culture of his upbringing, why imagine that his choice is any more likely than the others to be true?

Every believer plays the Game of Religion, and every believer believes that his religion is the one true religion, with nothing behind the hundreds of other doors. But maybe there's nothing behind *every* door. And given that the lesson from the three-hundred-door Monty Hall game is that the door you randomly picked at first is almost certainly wrong, why imagine that yours is the only religion that's right?

Finding Jesus through Board Games

Here's my version of an insightful argument from the Atheist Experience show. Imagine a board game called "Monopoly Plus," an updated version of the popular board game. There's a track around the perimeter of the board that's divided into cells. Each player is represented by a token on the board—a dog, a car, a top hat, and so on—and each player in turn rolls dice to see how many cells to advance. You start with a certain amount of money, and you can buy the properties that you land on as you move around the board. Players who land on owned properties must pay the owner rent, and the owner can pay to improve properties to raise that rent and increase their income.

Here's the object of the game: you must accept Jesus Christ as your lord and savior.

Yes, that's a pretty bad game. The motivations within the game have absolutely nothing to do with how you win.

Now take that idea about a million times larger, and we have the game of Christianity—ordinary reality filtered through a Christian worldview. It's far more complicated than any board game. In the game of Christianity, there are good things (love, friendships, possessions, accomplishments, experiences, personal victories) and bad things (illness, death, sorrow, financial difficulties, disappointment, personal defeats), and players try to maximize the good things and minimize the bad. Immersed in this huge mass of complexity, we're told that, in the big picture, none of that matters. To win the game you must accept Jesus as your lord and savior.

Wow—who invented the rules of *that* game? And why is the game of Christianity any more in touch with reality than the game of Monopoly Plus?

Christianity Can't Be Deduced from Nature

Albert Einstein once said, "I know not with what weapons World War III will be fought, but World War IV will be fought with sticks and stones." Suppose Einstein's catastrophic World War III happens and civilization is destroyed. A thousand years pass, and civilization returns to roughly our level of scientific awareness. After losing all knowledge of optics and thermodynamics and gravity, this naive society has re-discovered it—the very same laws of optics and thermodynamics and gravity that we have now. Ditto for Relativity, or $e = mc^2$ or $f = ma$, or any other scientific law or theory.

Obviously, these post-apocalyptic humans would have different terms and ways of representing things—consider how mathematical symbols, numbers, punctuation, paragraph breaks, and even spaces have evolved over the centuries. But whatever notation they invent would be synonymous with our own since they would simply be descriptions of the same natural phenomena.

Now imagine that all knowledge of Christianity was also lost. A new generation might make up something to replace it, since humans seem determined to find supernatural agency in the world, but they wouldn't recreate the same thing. There is no specific evidence of the Christian god around us today. You can't deduce Christianity from reality, and the *only* evidence of God in our world is tradition and the Bible. Eliminate those, and Christianity would be lost forever.

There would be nothing that would let this future society recreate Christianity—no miracles, no God speaking to people, no prayers answered, no divine appearances (unless God decided to act more overtly than he does today). Sure, there would be beauty to wonder at, great complexity in the interwoven structure of nature, frightening things like death and disease for which they would need comfort, riddles within nature, and odd coincidences. People then, like they do now, would likely grope for supernatural explanations, but starting from scratch you could invent lots of religions to respond to these things. There is no evidence or observation that would guide future societies to any specific supernatural dogma that we have today, except by coincidence.

Christians today come to their beliefs because someone initially told them of Christianity. If no one told you, you couldn't figure out Christianity on your own, which is quite the opposite from how science works.

The Bible comments on our thought experiment. It claims:

> "Since the creation of the world God's invisible qualities—his eternal power and divine nature—have been clearly seen, being understood from what has been made, so that **men are without excuse**" (Romans 1:18–20).

And yet, without God informing humanity of his existence, Christianity would never be recreated. Worship of some sort of supernatural, sure, but not Christianity. This means that there is nothing inherent about *our* world that supports the claims of Christianity. We have just the Bible and tradition, both works of Man.

Here's a variation on this thought experiment. Imagine the future post-Christian society comes across a library from our day in which they find information about twenty religions that are popular today. This information spreads, and civilization gradually adopts these new religious options. What is the likelihood that Christianity would come out on top again?

Let's acknowledge that Christianity is sticky. If its message were a dud—that is, if it didn't give people what they were looking for—it would have faded away. But now we've turned away from the question of truth and find ourselves squarely in the domain of marketing, considering which features of religion satisfy people's emotional needs and which are turn-offs.

This is religion as breakfast cereal. Some new cereal brands last for a few months and are then withdrawn, while others remain appealing (often adapting to changes within society) for decades. Christianity is simply the Cheerios of religion. Like any successful brand in the marketplace, Christianity has spun off many variants—as if Lutheranism were the equivalent of Honey Nut Cheerios, Mormonism as MultiGrain Cheerios, and Pentecostalism as Cinnamon Burst Cheerios.

What can you say about a religion that cannot be recreated from evidence at hand today? About a religion whose god is knowable only through tradition? You can say what applies to all religions: we can't prove that it is manmade, but it gives every indication of being so.

Highlighting Christianity's Exponentially Increasing Claims

To grasp the enormity of the Christian claim, let us see it as part of a series of exponentially increasing claims. (This is my variation on an argument put forward by historian Richard Carrier.[1])

Suppose that each step in a series exceeds its predecessor simply in degree. For example, "I have a yellow car" is a more specific claim than "I have a car." It is different in degree simply because there are fewer yellow cars than cars of any color. Let's call this a *linear* progression.

More dramatic are steps that are different in kind, an *exponential* progression of steps. This is admittedly a sloppy use of "exponential" and "linear," but it suggests the magnitude of difference between changes in degree and the more dramatic changes in kind.

---

[1] Carrier, Richard (2011), *Why I Am Not a Christian: Four Conclusive Reasons to Reject the Faith* (CreateSpace) pages 35–9.

Not Seeing God

Here are five steps in an exponential progression. Claims at each step become increasingly unlikely.

1. Claims that are common such as, "I own a car." In parts of the world where car ownership is common, this is not a surprising claim.

2. Claims that are uncommon such as, "I own a third-century Christian manuscript." This is very uncommon—there might be just a handful of individuals who can make this claim rather than the hundreds of millions who could claim car ownership—but it's plausible.

3. Claims that are unprecedented such as, "I own a 400-foot-long nuclear-powered submarine." Such submarines *do* exist and no new science would be needed for this to be a true statement. Nevertheless, the facts that (1) there is no record of a person owning such a thing, (2) they are very difficult to steal, and (3) they are enormously expensive to build, makes this claim very implausible.

4. Claims that are inconceivable today (but perhaps reasonable tomorrow) such as, "I own a time machine." These machines *do not* exist today. New science and technology would be needed to build one, if it could be built at all. On the other hand, uncovering new science and inventing new technology is what humanity does. A claim in this category might become possible in the future.

5. Claims that have no basis in reality such as, "A supernatural being created everything and interacts with humans on earth today." While this claim is popular, it is built on nothing. No one offers sufficient evidence to support it (witness the lack of scientific consensus for any religious claim), and it's no more respectable than astrology. There is no objective evidence of *any* supernatural being, let alone one that created the universe.

Big submarines *do* exist, so someone might own one someday. Technology *does* exist, so time machines might be built in the future, and then someone might own one. But science recognizes no supernatural claims, and there's no reason to imagine that they will become more plausible in the future. No future developments in science or technology will help God make himself more available. Perhaps only outsiders to religion can fully appreciate the enormity (and lack of precedent) for the Christian claim.

Of course, billions of people today believe in some variation of this supernatural claim, but because these many claims are mutually contradictory they do more to argue that humans invent religions than that god(s) exist. The Christians who eagerly point to the billions of people who believe in the supernatural will turn around and undercut their claim by rejecting an all-roads-lead-to-God theology.

In response to a scientific puzzle such as "How did life originate?" or "What came before the Big Bang?" Christian apologists advance "God did it!" but they ignore how far-fetched the supernatural claim is. They confuse familiarity with plausibility, and on this exponential scale, God as a category 5 claim isn't remotely plausible.

Let's review this counter-apologetics arsenal.

1. The map of world religions reveals the emptiness of Christians' claims to have the correct answers to life's Big Questions.
2. The Bible can be turned against itself. The first Commandment—"Have no other gods before me"—admits that the god of the Old Testament was just one of many gods.
3. Christians might claim that they hold their beliefs because of evidence, but why then don't they adopt Mormonism since its historical record is far stronger?
4. The Monty Hall problem, when extended to the version with hundreds of doors for all religions, highlights the unlikelihood of any religion being correct.
5. The Monopoly Plus game has its object (accepting Jesus) completely disconnected from the mechanics of playing the game. It is an illustration of Christianity's inverted view of reality, where the ups and downs of our daily activities are dismissed as meaningless in the big picture.
6. If we imagine an apocalyptic world war such that humanity had to recreate civilization, they could successfully recreate our science. But Christianity isn't derived from reality; it's all manmade. This post-apocalyptic civilization might recreate religion but not Christianity.
7. The supernatural claim made by Christianity is the culmination of a series of ever more preposterous claims. Its familiarity makes us forget how insanely extraordinary it is.

Christianity was an explanation for reality when there was nothing better. Today, however, science's confident statements about reality, backed up by evidence rather than faith, make Pierre-Simon Laplace's 200-year-old dismissal of God all the more appropriate: "I have no need of that hypothesis."

Patheos Nonreligious

Not Seeing God, but Seeing Folklore, in the Bible

Jeana Jorgensen, PhD, Foxy Folklorist

When I write that the Bible is folklore, many people would interpret that statement as an offensive one. However, as a folklorist, I specialize in studying expressive culture that exhibits tradition and variation, regardless of whether the texts in question are sacred or secular, ancient or contemporary. To say that the Bible is folklore is not an insult, but rather a scholarly categorization.

In this chapter, I follow folklorist Alan Dundes in contending that the Bible is folklore: it is a text that comes from oral tradition, with demonstrable instances of multiple existence and variation. I will summarize and build upon Dundes's arguments about the traditionality of the Bible, explaining why the Bible contains evidence of the types of creativity found in oral tradition. Further, while one goal of this chapter is confirmation of human involvement in the Bible's transmission—thus I, as an atheist-leaning agnostic, see more human than God in the Bible—this interpretation of the Bible does not negate the possibility of the Bible's spiritual importance. Rather, I assert that in order to best understand the Bible, in both religious and cultural contexts, we must comprehend the folkloric aspects of the Bible, which mark it as human more than anything else.

What is folklore?

In order to understand why the Bible might be considered folklore, we need to grasp what folklore means in its scholarly definition. As with any academic discipline, arriving at *the* definition of a field of study is tricky. If you ask any ten sociologists, or biologists, or English literature scholars, what exactly they study, you'll likely hear ten answers. However, there would be common threads connecting all of them, and I hope to highlight some of the common threads in folklore studies here.

Most folklorists cringe when we hear someone say, "Oh, that's just folklore" (or swap in "just a fairy tale," "just a myth," "just an urban legend," and so on). Folklore and falsehood may overlap, but that's not considered an official part of how folklore is defined.

Similarly, while "oral tradition" was used as a prime way to define folklore in the past, and still often springs to mind for some people, not all folklore is orally passed on. Tradition is also a very fuzzy concept, though we have trouble ditching it entirely.

The definition of folklore that I prefer to use, and which incorporates a number of formerly prevalent definitions, is one that Lynne S. McNeill published in her book *Folklore Rules*:

> Folklore is informal, traditional culture. It's all the cultural stuff—customs, stories, jokes, art—that we learn from each other, by word of mouth or observation, rather than through formal institutions like school or the media. (16)

Thus, when we study folklore, we're studying the facets of culture that are informally transmitted among groups of people.

Another key part of the way we conceptualize folklore is variation. Folklore is constantly changing, while adhering to a traditional core of coherence. This is one reason why the "oral tradition" definition sticks with people: in preliterate societies, of course the wording of stories and songs would change over time. However, we can observe variation in other realms of folklore than the verbal: customs like holidays change over time and space, as do material manifestations of folklore, like traditional crafts, body art, and foods.

As folklorist Alan Dundes notes, variation is a significant way to distinguish folklore from other modes of culture, particularly pop culture and high/elite culture. He writes:

> Almost all high and popular culture exist in fixed, unchanging form either because a novel or short story is locked into print or a television program or motion picture is locked into videotape or film. Every time one reads a Faulkner novel, it is the same, and it will be the same centuries from now; the same holds true for television reruns or movies. (*Holy Writ* 2)

In other words, variation is present in folklore in ways that it is absent from pop culture and elite culture. This includes folklore that is fairly fixed in phrasing, such as proverbs, and folklore that exists in writing, such as latrinalia and autograph book verses. Once we discard the notion that the only, or best, way to define folklore is as oral tradition, we can become attuned to folklore that happens to be transmitted through writing—as when an urban legend is reported as fact in the newspaper or in an email chain letter—and study what it has in common with other folklore texts.

Similarly, once folklore is recorded in writing, it doesn't cease being folklore. As Dundes observes, "An oral proverb once written down does not then magically cease to be a proverb. Once a proverb, always a proverb!" (*Holy Writ* 9) Keep this in mind moving forward, as we discuss why it's likely that parts of the Bible came from a thriving oral tradition.

Before moving on, I'll note some folklore studies vocabulary I'll be using here. We use *text*, *item*, and *version* interchangeably to mean a single instance of folklore that has been documented. *Context* is everything surrounding the text and making it meaningful, so that information might include when and where the text (say, a joke) was told, who the teller was, who the audience was, and so on. While any example of a piece of folklore is a *version*, it must exhibit noticeable differences from other versions to be considered a *variation*. *Variation* also holds the more abstract connotation of the dynamic impulse of folklore that keeps it ever-changing over time, while *tradition* is the static impulse of folklore that represents a coherent whole that tellers and communities often strive for in an attempt to gain legitimacy or authenticity. Any group of people with one characteristic in common, no matter how small or large or urban or rural, is considered a *folk group*, likely to have shared values as well as shared folklore. Categories of folklore that are similar in terms of their structure, content, and performance are called *genres*. These terms all apply to folklore that is sacred or secular, contemporary or ancient.

Folklore, religion, and myth

The relationship between folklore, religion, and myth is a tricky one. Folklorists claim myth as a genre that we study; religious studies and literary scholars often study myth as well, using different methods and parameters. Similarly, while religious studies scholars have religion as their discipline's main topic, folklorists also study religion, though from a specific vantage point. In this section I'll clarify the relationships between folklore, religion, and myth in order to further my argument that the Bible is folklore.

I follow Yvonne Daniel in defining religion as "the union of humans with either an omnipotent nonhuman or several suprahuman spiritual entities" (2). Noting that the English term religion is derived from a Latin word meaning to fasten, bond, or retie, Daniel makes the point that religion fastens the human world to the spiritual world, a fastening that occurs through any number of mechanisms. Some religions, such as the African Diasporic religions Daniel studies, accomplish this fastening through musical and dance practices; others, like Judeo-Christian religions, emphasize prayer and connection through institutional and textual means.

Folklorists are not interested in the whole of religion, but rather the parts of it that meet the definition of folklore: informal, traditional culture. We often identify this portion of religion as folk religion, religious folklife, or vernacular religion. Don Yoder defines folk religion as "the totality of all those views and practices of religion that exist among the people apart from and alongside the strictly theological and liturgical forms of the official religion" (14). However, contrasting folk religion with official religion risks debasing the former, implying in the words of Leonard Primiano "that religion somewhere exists as a pure element which is in some way transformed, even contaminated, by its exposure to human communities" (39). In order to combat the false dichotomy of official/unofficial religion, Primiano suggests vernacular religion as a term, which is "religion as it is lived: as human beings encounter, understand, interpret, and practice it" (44). This more inclusive definition avoids imposing conceptual hierarchies, and still lets folklorists get at what we're interested in, and what we do best: the study of human creativity in informal transmission.

The contributions that we make to the study of religion through a folklore lens are multiple, and we make them

> By not automatically privileging written over oral forms, through paying attention to different forms of narrative, by close observation of material culture and the use made of it (both formally and informally), through observing belief spilling over into diverse aspects of behaviour and by appreciating the dynamic nature of 'tradition'. (Bowman and Valk, "Introduction," 7)

In other words, folklorists get to study a lot of manifestations of informal religious culture. Primiano gives this concise list of topics we might engage with, not intended to be all-inclusive:

> ...speech, music and song, dance, mime, ritual and drama, bodily communication, the manifold uses of writing, foodways, costume, culturally encoded architecture, and the permanent and ephemeral objects within domestic and public environments". (45)

The intersection of religion and folklore is vast.

Myth sits at the intersection of many of these concerns. While the study of mythology occurs in many academic fields—classicists study Greek mythology; English literature scholars study mythology as it pertains to allusions; and so on—religious studies and folklore studies both have unique insights on myth. However, it is the approach that folklorists take that is most useful for atheists attempting to understand religious culture and the Bible, in my opinion.

Folklorists define myth as sacred narrative about the origins of the world. This is not myth in the sense of Myth-busters or "oh, that's just a myth!" Rather, as William Bascom points out, in order to define myth in contrast to other folk narratives genres like legend and fairy tale:

> Myths are prose narratives which, in the society in which they are told, are considered to be truthful accounts of what happened in the remote past. (9)

While myths account for the origins of humanity, the main characters aren't always human, but are rather gods, demi-gods, demons, animals, or culture heroes. The setting of myths does not usually resemble the world of today: the world was different back then, recently created, primordial. Or perhaps the narrative is set in another world, such as the sky or the underworld. Thus, in terms of their content (the motifs and themes that make up the main topics of the narrative), myths are a distinct genre from other folk narrative genres in existence. Sometimes God, the Devil, and saints show up in European legends and fairy tales, for instance, but they often fill generic roles as helpers or antagonists, whereas in myths their presence is significant on a cosmological and irreplaceable level.

Any discussion of myth must take into account its function, or the role or purpose it serves in society at large. According to Bascom: "Myths are the embodiment of dogma, they are usually sacred, and they are often associated with theology and ritual" (9). In other words, one function of myth is to transmit the dogma associated with a given religion. Every belief system has components that are abstract or not easy to summarize, and thus illustrating those beliefs through a story is a useful way to help people connect with the message. One century ago, pioneering myth scholars Franz Boas and Bronislaw Malinowski emphasized how myth both reflects culture and reinforces it. Malinowski wrote:

> The function of myth, briefly, is to strengthen tradition and endow it with a greater value and prestige by tracing it back to a higher, better, more supernatural reality of initial events". (Quoted in Dundes, *Sacred Narrative*, 194)

Thus, we study myth both to get a sense of what a folk group's values are, and to understand how the content of this narrative helps its tellers and believers navigate through the present day world, and create the future. Therefore, myth links past, present, and future in a way that not all folklore genres do.

The aforementioned link between myth and ritual feeds into the thorny question of how to interpret myth. Philologists of two centuries ago held lively debates about whether myths were started in one place and disseminated, or had multiple origins; whether they all reflect solar or weather phenomena; whether myth or ritual came first in a chicken-and-egg fashion; whether mythic characters are based on people who actually lived (this theory is known as euhemerism), and more (summarized in Brunvand 187-191). Contemporary myth scholars apply everything from psychoanalytic to feminist theory in order to attempt to understand the inner workings of myths, and many current myth studies also utilize ethnographic fieldwork to study living myths in the context of their folk groups and believers.

Examples of myth texts abound in religion, literature, and pop culture. While not everything labeled as a myth or mythology counts in the folklore sense of the word (e.g., much of Greek mythology has more in common with the fairy-tale plots of magically aided quests, or the hero-centered adventure narratives of epic), one can find abundant myth texts about how the universe was created in world religions. The Norse myth of the creation of the world from the body of the ice giant Ymir is one example, while the Native American myth of the creature who dove into the primordial waters to return with a piece of earth (found among many but not all tribes in North America) is another. And, of course, the Book of Genesis in the Bible is an example of a myth that has been recorded and fixed in writing.

Studying myth and religious folklore more generally is important because this is precisely how cultural values are encoded and transmitted. Of course, this task requires a willingness to engage with cultural materials that may be difficult to analyze due to how close to home they register. Brunvand encourages scholars interested in myth to consider that just as contemporary people use religious narratives such as myth and homilies to pass on meaningful moral messages, evaluate their own and others' actions, and the like, the same functions and attitudes probably existed in ancient cultures as well. Knowing that the functions of myth are similar throughout time, even as the content of the texts displays great variation, should help illuminate our common humanity, not leave us feeling attacked. Specifically, Brunvand has the following advice:

> ...it ought not to damage the religious convictions of students of American folklore to regard their own system as part of a continuum of worldwide tradition rather than a set of unique literal and inviolable truths. Only the culturally naïve could regard all of 'our' beliefs and religious narratives as literally true in every detail, but regard the beliefs of 'others' as myths, superstitions, and mere folklore". (187-188)

With this principle in mind—that we should be as critical of our own beliefs as we are those of others, or alternately as compassionate toward the outlandish beliefs of others as we are toward our own—let's delve into why the Bible is folklore, and what that means for atheism and beyond.

The Bible as folklore

All that being said, what business do folklorists have studying the Bible? Remember, when folklore that used to circulate in oral tradition or performed custom is written down or otherwise documented or archived, it doesn't stop being folklore. The same is true of the Bible, and thus we can utilize our discipline's strengths and strategies to help understand the Bible in a folkloric context.

As Alan Dundes explains in *Holy Writ as Oral Lit*, we can and should use folklore studies to illuminate the Bible's inner workings both because it was originally in oral tradition as folklore, and because the same criteria that apply to oral folklore are also present in written folklore (5), namely, variation and multiple existence/repetition. Thus, the Bible is folkloric on at least those two levels. The main ways in which the Bible's folkloric nature emerge are through variation in its content (numbers, names, and sequencing) and duplicate versions of textual fragments and formulas. Taken together, the presence of variation and multiple existence prove that the Bible is folkloric in nature.

While there is not space in this chapter to list every instance of variation in the Bible, a few should suffice. In terms of variation of number, Genesis alone contains passages with different numbers of how many animals Noah should take aboard the ark (two of each vs. seven of each), and how long the flood should last (one hundred and fifty days vs. forty days) (in Dundes 22). As Dundes explains, forty is a traditional ritual number in ancient Middle Eastern cultures, and texts where ritual numbers crop up frequently may well have other folkloric features. Names also display significant variation in the Bible, with Joseph being sold to the Ishmaelites in one part of Genesis, and the Midianites in another. Differently spelled names would also qualify as this type of variation, as in the passage in Chronicles listing the descendants of Caleb (Ephrath vs. Ephah vs. Ephratah). Finally, in regard to sequence, there's demonstrable variation throughout the Bible. This occurs during creation (who and what God creates first in Genesis), and in other cases, such as whether Hagar gave birth to Ishmael before or after her banishment and whether Jesus was robed before or after being crowned with the crown of thorns (and further, whether his robe was scarlet or purple).

The duplicate texts in the Bible also testify to multiple existence and variation, which are, again, hallmarks of folklore (whether oral or written). A number of psalms are clearly variations of the same text, but repeated with minor changes. There are at least three versions of the David and Goliath narrative (discussed at length in Dundes *Holy Writ* 67-70). The fact that there are two versions of the Sermon on the Mount, with differing content, also supports this hypothesis. The folklore genre of proverbs is especially illustrative here, as the presence of proverbs in the Bible shows that it at the very least contains folklore genres, while the variation within and multiple existence of these proverbs builds the case that the Bible is itself folkloric. While folklorists use the term "fixed-phrase" to refer to how proverb texts are often rigid in their phrasing (unlike, say, jokes, which can be told in a lot of different ways but still register as the same joke), Dundes reminds us that proverbs do indeed display remarkable variation. For example, he writes:

> "Consider Matthew 7:16: '*Ye shall know them by their fruits. Do men gather grapes of thorns, or figs of thistles?*' This is clearly a variant of

'Wherefore by their fruits ye shall know them' (Matt. 6:20). Compare these with Luke's version: *'For every tree is known by his own fruit. For of thorns men do not gather figs, nor of a bramble bush gather they grapes'* (Luke 6:44). Matthew speaks of gathering **grapes** from thorns; Luke speaks of gathering **figs** from thorns. Matthew speaks of gathering **figs** from thistles; Luke speaks of gathering **grapes** from bramble bushes, the equivalent of thistles" (*Holy Writ* 76, bold in original).

These types of discrepancies between different versions of the same story in the Bible can be read as error in one light, but are actually just normal folkloristic variation. Which version of "Cinderella" is the correct version? That question hardly makes sense; the existence of multiple versions of a text doesn't invalidate the others texts in circulation. Speaking of folktales, there are also versions of international folktale plots in the Bible (discussed in Dundes 114-115).

To draw a parallel to another literary genre, ballads (stories in song form) become illuminated when we recall that they are a living folklore genre, one that happens to be written down and treated as literature from time to time. Folklorist John McDowell makes this case:

> Scholarship normally treats ballads as literature, albeit deviant literature, marked by curious infelicities, repetitions, and lapses that can be attributed to an irregular mode of creation. Ballad scholars have pored over collections of ballad texts as their primary (sometimes exclusive) contact with these traditions. Exposure to the living ballad radically alters the picture; suddenly ambient factors leap into sight. It turns out, not surprisingly, that ballads are composed, performed, and savored by human beings who are connected in specific ways to the tradition, to the events narrated, and to the other persons active in the process. The ballad text, like other documentary records of aural and verbal performances, is an artifact, a partial reconstruction of a complex web of human action and intent. It is this reliance on texts that has perpetuated the illusion of the disembodied ballad. (50)

Sound familiar? The Bible is, as demonstrated above, the product of human oral transmission, fixed in written textual form over time. Scholars are still analyzing precisely when and why and how this happened, orchestrated by whom, but the marks of the human creative process are all over the Bible, once you know how to spot them.

Similarly, Dundes has also written a book on folklore in the Qur'an, demonstrating through multiple existence and variation of its content that it contains a wealth of folklore. Dundes focuses on oral formulas—verbal phrases that have become traditional, often with poetic features—but also documents internationally known folktale plots. Simply publishing *Fables of the Ancients? Folklore in the Qur'an* was in many ways an act of bravery, due to the hostility with which scholarly studies of the Qur'an are sometimes received. But as Dundes points out:

> The presence of ancient fables in the *Qur'an* (and in the Bible in no way diminishes the religious or moral value of these sacred documents. Quite the contrary, the presence of folklore is a guarantee of their basic humanity, and, if one chooses to believe so, their divine character". (68)

It's not far-fetched to posit that many of humanity's sacred texts have been derived from oral tradition, and thus a comparative study of their folkloric qualities is one way for believers and non-believers alike to establish a common language for discussing these texts.

What happens when we view the Bible as folklore?

The impact of Dundes's argument that the Bible is folklore is quite far-reaching. For those of us who are atheists, it is inspiring to know that a text considered one of the world's greatest works of literature is, in fact, man-made. That stands as a testament to the enduring power of human creativity.

Similarly, as atheists, it is heartening to know that there is empirical evidence that the Bible is the result of human artistry. It is unique in many of its textual, textural, and contextual features, but it has much in common with myths and religious texts all over the world. Thus, there is little reason to believe that the Bible is the singular transmission of the only real deity representing the one true religion on Earth.

In the scholarly community, folklorists who trained under Alan Dundes are familiar with the argument that the Bible is folklore. However, when I looked on Google Scholar to see who else had cited *Holy Writ as Oral Lit*, only 51 results came up. Clearly, this information needs to reach wider audiences, which is part of the reason I chose to write this chapter for this book. I also thought it was

Not Seeing God

important to spell out some of the implications of these findings, which I'll do to conclude this chapter.

Scholars of religion would benefit from regarding the Bible as folklore in a number of ways. As Dundes points out in his conclusion to *Holy Writ as Oral Lit*: "One obvious advantage of utilizing a folkloristic paradigm, for example, for those with a historical bias, is that long-standing problems or difficulties can now be seen in quite a new light" (115). Issues of discrepancy or error vanish, replaced by an acknowledgement that multiple existence and variation are just how the parts of culture we call "folklore" work. Rather than getting caught up in questions of which version is the "right" version, scholars can move toward a model wherein "each version must be understood and evaluated on its own terms" (115-116).

For atheists looking for proof that we're right, and God does not exist, you can get your own copy of *Holy Writ as Oral Lit* for the fuller version of the argument that the Bible is folklore. Enjoy the book, pass it on to a friend, and call it a day. For those of us who are still in dialogue with theists, we can use the ideas contained herein to open up conversations, and perhaps even to open up some minds. We'll have to can the snark, and not lead with "Ooooh did you know the Bible is actually folklore?!" (as tempting as it sometimes may be). As someone who has devoted her life to the study of folklore, for me to say "Hey, your religious text is folklore" means that I think it's truly fascinating and worthy of discussion. That's not an insult unless I make it one.

Still, as both an atheist and a folklorist I'm pleased to have some conceptual tools to offer as we attempt to navigate a world wherein religions of the book have a major hold on political power. Folklorists are especially keyed in to power, as our academic discipline was born in regions that have been oppressed or colonized throughout history. The Grimm brothers began collecting folktales in an effort to prove that German-speaking peoples shared a cultural heritage and thus deserved to be a nation during a time when Napoleon was running rampant; the Finns and Irish began investigating their folklore during times of colonization and built strong academic folklore programs as a result; and regions that are marginalized today, such as north-east India, are channeling their resources into academic folklore programs in an attempt to document their right to an independent existence. When the balance of power shifts from emerging nation-states, as in my examples, to theist political parties—as with the Christian Right in the U.S.—it remains important to be attuned to the underlying cultural patterns that people are using to justify their actions. And when some of these people are claiming to be carrying out divine commands on earth, based on a book that we know to be folklore, understanding that the Bible is folklore gives us one more way to engage with them and lend nuance to the conversation. Hopefully this chapter has pointed out a fruitful way to connect folklore studies and atheism, to help us navigate a world where religion and tradition can intersect in many ways.

References

Bascom, William (1984) "The Forms of Folklore: Prose Narratives." In Sacred Narrative: Readings in the Theory of Myth, ed. Alan Dundes. Berkeley: University of California Press, 5-29.

Bowman, Marion, and Ulo Valk, (2012). "Introduction: Vernacular Religion, Generic Expressions, and the Dynamics of Belief." In Vernacular Religion in Everyday Life: Expressions of Belief, eds. Bowman and Valk (Sheffield: Equinox Publishing Ltd.). 1-19.

Brunvand, Jan Harol, (1998). The Study of American Folklore: An Introduction. Fourth edition. New York: W. W. Norton & Company, 1998 [1968, 1978, 1986].

Daniel, Yvonne, (2005). Dancing Wisdom: Embodied Knowledge in Haitian Voudou, Cuban Yoruba, and Bahian Candomblé. Urbana and Chicago: University of Illinois Press.

Dundes, Alan, (1999). Holy Writ as Oral Lit: The Bible as Folklore (Lanham: Rowman & Littlefield Publishers, Inc.), p. XXX, (Subsequent citations: Dundes, Holy Writ as Oral Lit, p. XXX)

Dundes, Alan, (2003). Fables of the Ancients? Folklore in the Qur'an. Lanham: Rowman & Littlefield Publishers, Inc.

Dundes, Alan, ed., (1984). Sacred Narrative: Readings in the Theory of Myth. Berkeley: University of California Press.

McDowell, John, (2000). "The Living Ballad." In Poetry and Violence: The Ballad Tradition of Mexico's Costa Chica. (Urbana and Chicago: University of Illinois Press). 39-69.

Primiano, Leonard Norman, (1995). "Vernacular Religion and the Search for Method in Religious Folklife," Western Folklore 54.1, 37-56.

Yoder, Don, (1974). "Toward a Definition of Folk Religion," Western Folklore 33.1, 2-15.

Not Finding God in Ethics

Dan Fincke, Camels With Hammers

Conservative religious believers often claim that we need to believe in God in order to have morality. Some liberal religious believers, and even some secular apologists for religion, claim that even though religions may be a bad source of scientific truths, they are to be esteemed as indispensable moral guides. In what follows I want to give an account of how ethics comes to be, how it is to be justified, and why reason, rather than religious faith, is our best guide to ethical judgments. But first I want to counter a few of the most common and fundamental claims about why secular morality would be either impossible or suboptimal, and argue for why the best moral reasoning would actually treat God as an irrelevant consideration—even for those who believe in God. This constructive account is not merely intended to challenge theists, but to dispel confusions that even many atheists hold about whether moral reasoning can be robustly objective and make claims to truth.

As a note, throughout most of this chapter, I will use Christians as representative of religious theists generally. This is not because only Christians make the arguments I will be considering but because it allows for a simpler style to refer to one specific religion and to use examples specific to that religion than to always come up with a specific enough term to capture all the relevant religions that might hold a given position and exclude all those that don't. It's also easier to read simple sentences like, "morality cannot be based on the Bible" than "morality cannot be based on the Bible, the Qu'ran, or any other sacred text reputed to be necessary for learning about morality". So, as an ex-Christian with an expected audience that comes from Christian-majority countries, I chose Christianity to be the theistic religion I explicitly address. The arguments in most cases should easily transfer to apply to other theistic religions.

Framing the Question of Morality

The key question that needs to be answered in order to establish that morality is real is, "How can there be a human-independent fact about the nature of things that gives us compelling, motivational reasons for or against certain actions that can override any conflicting desires or disinclinations we have to do them?" Moral skeptics and skeptics of the possibility of genuine secular morality think that if naturalism is true then there are no human-independent facts about how things ought to be or what people ought to do—only facts about what is the case and what people happen to do—and that the only possible "oughts" are those given to us by our desires and what conduces to satisfying the ends they set for us. There can be no facts about what we ought to do that make no reference to what our ends happen to be. And there are no facts about what our ends *ought* to be, just facts about what they *are*.

The fallout of this is that when the atheist assures the theist that she can be "good without God," the theist who is skeptical of genuine morality without God is apt to say, "While an atheist may adhere to conventional moral standards similar to how a theist might, the atheist cannot give any cogently *moral* reason why they, or others, *must* follow them even if they did not want to."

On this view, the atheist's moral behavior can be explained entirely by factors other than moral necessity. She might have a naturally pro-social personality disposition or be actively socialized to act in morally approvable ways. Apathetic or antisocial atheists might behave morally just to avoid punishments or to manipulate others into liking them so they will do what they want. In short, the atheist might be regularly moral simply because doing so happens to serve her personal interests in any number of cases. But none of these reasons would amount to a compelling, motivational, *objectively* binding reason that can trump her contrary desires and compel her to do what she does not perceive it as being in her interests to do. And even if she happened to care about morality itself, she would have no naturalistic way to figure out that there were any moral truths. There would only be scientific facts, and moral claims are not scientific ones. She would have no objective reason by which she could judge or rebuke cruel, sociopathic, or uncaring people who callously hurt people whenever it satisfies their desires and they can do so with impunity. Nor can she have objective facts to appeal to when she wants to rationally change the moral opinions of individuals, cultures, subcultures, or religions that she finds repugnant.

Ironically, many atheists would themselves agree that they are in this bleak situation as far as moral justification goes, while some theistic philosophers think atheists can no less understand moral truths without needing to believe in God than they can study the laws of nature without believing God is their author.

But, perhaps even more ironically, theists who are cynical about morality's prospects for justification and motivational force apart from religion often betray a lack of confidence in morality's ability to actually show its truth to people or to motivate them. Such theists argue for an authoritarian picture of moral authority whereby the contents of morality must be whatever God commands us to do and our logical motivations for obeying those commands boil down to considerations of our own selfish interests rather than any love of the good for its own sake.

God's Commands: Divinely Grounded Morality

Divine Command Theory interprets morality as analogous to a system of law one would see implemented by a sovereign in an earthly polity. Following the analogy out, morality has a law*giver*. A true lawgiver has both moral authority and the ability to enforce their enactments. God is postulated as the ideal (or even the only possible) moral lawgiver. God would have the moral authority to impose His will since He is our creator and, it is assumed, creating a being gives you the moral right to dictate to it completely. God would be morality's ultimate enforcer who could remedy the central moral threat that comes from the fact that people are less trustworthy when less accountable and, therefore, more dangerous when they're not being watched. If people are convinced that they are always being watched by a sovereign, righteous, and omnipotent God, who has absolute ability and inclination to effectively enforce the moral law with punishments, it will *at all times* be in their own interests to obey His moral dictates.

But this is *not* an effective way for the theist to solve the problem that we started with: the problem of how morality can give us reasons to act morally that are not ultimately prudential. Obeying God out of fear does not amount to acting for a distinctly moral motivation to do what is right that can override our selfish desires, it rather just gives us a new selfish desire to avoid excruciating consequences meted out by God.

On the divine command theory approach to morality, the objectivity of moral laws is construed as analogous to the objectivity of the laws of a nation.

The laws in a nation are a matter of objective fact, but they are in the first place the creation of *subjective* agents who are authorized to make laws. But this would mean that morality is not robustly objective enough—in the sense of having a reality that is independent of the preferences of any subjective agent whatsoever—since it hinges on God's arbitrary will. On the worst versions of divine command theory, even the most terrible things, like genocide and rape, would be morally obligatory for people to do if only God commanded them. This hardly amounts to theists having a better grounding for an objective morality that can rule out heinous things as unqualifiedly wrong, regardless of what anyone thinks or says.

Even worse, it is morally perverse to posit that a creator being can absolutely dictate any rules whatsoever to its creatures. If the creator being was like any of countless harmful and unjust autocrats we find on Earth, we should not accept any of his evil dictates as morally authoritative any more than we would accept an earthly autocrat's wicked dictates as definitive of moral rightness. Might does not make right. Our being creations of God would not by itself give God any more right to make us suffer than we have a right to make our own children suffer.

Theists reply that God by definition is a morally perfect being who will therefore not create any laws for us that are actually immoral, unfair, or fundamentally harmful to us. But this argument abandons the claim that God's authority rests on his role as creator and instead attempts to ground the authority of God's law in the rectitude of God Himself and the character of His laws. This implies an independent standard of morality that God meets, which confers on Him lawgiving authority, and which validates His laws' righteousness. This downgrades God from the creator of morality itself to a morally perfect legislator who writes perfectly moral laws according to the independent standards of morality.

However, if we cannot use our human reason to figure out what is moral and immoral, but must trust God's acts of lawgiving to tell us what is moral, then how exactly can we know that a morally perfect God may not rightly harm us or treat us in ways that our woefully ignorant moral reasoning would take to be unfair? We cannot figure this out just from consulting the Bible. First of all, the Bible is filled with endorsements of things that our ordinary moral conceptions would judge unequivocally evil—from theocratic laws mandating the death penalty for disobedient children (Deut. 21:18-21) to divinely ordered genocides, such as in 1 Samuel 15:2-3:

> "This is what the Lord Almighty says: 'I will punish the Amalekites for what they did to Israel when they waylaid them as they came up from Egypt. Now go, attack the Amalekites and totally destroy all that belongs to them. Do not spare them; put to death men and women, children and infants, cattle and sheep, camels and donkeys.'"

This command is said to have been given to King Saul by God at least 200 years after any Amalekites would have thwarted Israeli attempts to come up from Egypt, so one cannot even say that God refrains from punishing the sons for the sins of the father. In the story, the king spared some sheep and cattle, prompting this response from God:

> "For rebellion is like the sin of divination, and arrogance like the evil of idolatry. Because you have rejected the word of the Lord, he has rejected you as king."

If the Bible's prescriptions and God's own moral example through His supposed behavior in the Bible are to be normative, i.e., a guide for how we all *ought* to act, then if truly taking the lessons of passages like these to heart we would have to adopt a morality that seems to us quite evil. At a minimum believers in the Bible routinely wind up approving of numerous great evils in principle, so long as they were commanded by God (or done by God Himself) and happened during the Old Testament times.

The Bible even attributes to God a willingness to lie (e.g., 2 Chronicles 18:22)—which is not something that morally perfect beings are assumed to do—at least not when they are omnipotent and could presumably bring out good ends without resorting to lying. But even if a clever exegete could show that the Bible never truly ascribes lies to God if read *correctly* and point to the Ten Commandments prohibition against lying, still this, by itself, would not confirm for us that lying was actually wrong. For perhaps the most moral thing in the world to do is to lie and so God, the morally perfect being, lies all the time throughout the Bible—including even when He indicated it was morally wrong to lie. In fact, if it were true that lying, betraying, and inflicting suffering were among the best of all actions, then the morally perfect God might have lied about every theological doctrine that Christians take from the Bible. God's promises of salvation to those who believe in Him could be just lies perfectly calculated to make God's betrayal of His followers all the more wrenching and their suffering all the more exquisite when in the afterlife he condemns them precisely for their loyalty. So even if we knew that a morally perfect God wrote the Bible, this would not be enough to know how morality worked. If a theist wants to respond that God definitely *would* not or even *could* not make the things that we clearly recognize are immoral (like genocide and rape) to be moral, then God's unfettered will is not the ultimate source of morality after all and the Bible is not the justification for this information about what God simply would or could not morally legislate.

Some contemporary philosophers defending divine command theory claim that God's *nature* is itself the Good and that *this* constrains what kinds of moral laws God will command. But it seems to me that, even were this the case, we would still have to be able to reason for ourselves about what the Good is and in what ways we think God's will must be restrained by it. This means theism itself offers no better guide to figuring out exactly what constitutes goodness than simply reasoning about it as an atheist can.

The vast majority of contemporary Christians, for example, sift through the Bible and use their own human reason (or the reasoning of trusted human theologians and spiritual leaders) to decide which of the heinous deeds and questionable value judgments ascribed to God in there are only "metaphorical" and are in need of drastic "contextualization," on the one hand, and which ones are to be taken as literal, authoritative, and universally applicable, on the other. So it is hard to believe them when they say they derive their moral understanding primarily from God and the Bible, rather than from reason, emotion, experience, social norms, and the arguments of those around them, just like an atheist does. It is especially implausible when they try to claim that it is impossible to morally reason without access to God's word. They apply their own at least partially autonomous moral understanding to help them decide what God's word can even be *allowed* to mean.

Theists often tout the omniscience and objectivity of God's moral reasoning as superior to merely human reasoning, which they take to be comparatively ignorant and self-servingly subjective. Atheists are accused of being pathetic pretenders to godhood for wanting to play God's supposed role of determining right and wrong for ourselves. Some will straw man consequentialist schools of ethical theory—which actually argue that morally right actions are those that maximize the good in the whole world and minimize the bad—by characterizing them as being the crudest and most amoral of all hedonisms, "do whatever brings the consequence of making yourself feel good, regardless of the consequences to others." Taunting atheists to live according to the amoral nihilism they think atheism entails, such theists will sometimes insist that if they themselves did not believe in God, they would do the most heinous things because "nothing would really matter."

But human reason is, in fact, all we have to go by. In practice, for all their claims that morality could only be known by the dictates of God, religious people are just like everyone else in actually making numerous successful moral discriminations that are never mentioned in the Bible. Everyone regularly reasons about moral problems that arise from social or material conditions unknown to biblical authors. Everyone has to apply moral reasoning to novel situations that are not covered in the Ten Commandments and for which no parable of Jesus is clearly applicable. Quite often, theists in good conscience are applying moral principles that are far more sophisticated and justifiable than any that the people in the Bible applied. Such moral judgments are informed by the centuries of moral development that's occurred since the Bible was written. And when teaching children about morality and asking them if they know *why* a bad deed they have done is wrong, religious people, just like irreligious people, make sure their children understand and can apply the standards of fairness, harm-avoidance, beneficence, gratitude, kindness, and other good things that require no particular reference to God to appreciate.

Our moral reasoning would be incredibly unwieldy were there no rationally intuited and socially developed moral rules of thumb or virtues that could guide behavior, and instead, for every particular situation we faced, we had to learn an arbitrary rule, communicated to us by an invisible and inaudible being, that our reason was incapable of deriving on its own. And in such a situation, with no inherent moral conscience worth trusting, how could we even trust our judgment in deciding that a particular religious text or institution was trustworthy in what it said about ethics or God? How could we discern what texts or self-professed prophets actually carried the moral authority of the invisible and inaudible moral lawgiver?

So, contrary to the accusation that *outside* of religion people elevate idiosyncratic individual human wisdom to the level of divine authority, it is precisely *within* religion that this is more likely. Because it is within religion that people are likely to literally mistake human prescriptions for divine ones. Embracing the moral right and the moral necessity for us to reason about ethics for ourselves is the opposite of presumptuously claiming ourselves to be our own "gods" (as believers often charge). Acknowledging that morality is a matter for autonomous reasoning is to accept the *moral responsibility* to think for ourselves, to control ourselves, to defend our moral judgments and actions with good reasons when called upon, and to change our moral judgments when we are shown we're mistaken. This is the very opposite of a license to act as unaccountable gods.

And Christians need to accept that people can engage successfully in moral reasoning without reference to the Bible since there were human societies before the Bible was written and there were civilizations that never discovered the Bible until centuries, even millennia, after it was written. And all these civilizations engaged in at least some significant amount of successful moral reasoning. And even for traditional Christian theology to be coherent, non-theists (and non-Christians generally) must be capable of moral reasoning and having genuinely moral motivations and justifications for their actions if they are to be meaningfully held accountable by God for their sins. If people who do not believe in God are incapable of seeing genuine, motivational, and rationally comprehensible reasons to be moral, and instead are only capable of seeing reasons to act if they coincide with their emotional preferences or satisfy their selfish desires, then how can they have the possibility to do genuine moral good? And if they cannot even in principle do anything morally good, how can they be morally blameworthy when they fail to do so?

The Moral Conscience

For all these reasons, and more we could adduce, it makes sense for theists to reject the notion of atheistic moral ignorance and instead adopt another commonly held religious belief; namely that God equips all of us with an innate moral capacity for discerning right and wrong and, at least potentially, being motivated to do what is right because it is right. On this thinking, just as we can successfully investigate the natural world with the reason God gave us, even if we do not believe in God, we can successfully discern moral truths with the conscience God gave us, even if we do not believe in God. Some theists who hold this position still insist that we must obey commands from God since God, being a morally perfect being, will never give commands that deviate from what our moral conscience, properly used, could approve of anyway.

But, under these circumstances, it would be superfluous and redundant for God to command us to do what we can already reason out for ourselves that we ought to do, thanks to our basically reliable moral consciences. God's commands would seem not to be relevant to morality except, perhaps, for giving us special commands to do things or refrain from doing things that go beyond the scope of morality proper. But then everything that we would need to know about God and His commands would only be relevant for *religious* reasons, which is not the same thing as requiring knowledge of God or His commands in order to have *morality*.

And if our moral consciences are basically reliable, we can use them to assess the religious texts for ourselves to make sure they really are good moral guides. This makes texts like the Bible subject to a kind of moral falsification. If we can figure out for ourselves what is moral and immoral, then we can figure out whether the things the Bible says about morality are correct or not, and whether the god described in the Bible is actually a morally perfect being at all. Since the god of the Bible, Yahweh, does things that are *unambiguously* wicked, like command genocides and issue numerous legal decrees that we would unqualifiedly denounce as evil were they suggested by contemporary lawmakers, we can safely decide that we have sufficient evidence to judge that Yahweh is not a morally perfect being, whether or not he exists. We can further adduce that if God, as we are so often told by philosophers and theologians alike, should be defined as being a morally perfect being, then Yahweh, even if he exists, cannot actually *be* God, as philosophically and theologically understood. At best, the Yahweh, if real, would have to be some other sort of super-powerful being like a demigod or an alien. And, of course, there may still simply be neither any Yahweh *or* God at all. If Christians try to avoid this conclusion by insisting that humans cannot use their moral reasoning to question the Bible, then a central question reopens: if we humans cannot use our reason to assess the Bible's morality, how can we trust it to be a moral source at all? And what good moral reason could we have to accept the moral authority of a document that does not merely surpass our moral comprehension but repeatedly shows itself to be in outright contradiction of fundamental, non-negotiable, moral truths like that slavery and genocide are immoral?

So much for theistic attempts to make God the guarantor of ultimate moral justification and motivation.

What Can God-Neutral Reason Bring to the Table?

Can the atheist or the rationalistic theist do any better in establishing sources of moral legitimacy? If we can only rely on human reason and experience to develop our moral understanding and our moral motivations, can this pair succeed in providing real reasons that are objectively true and capable of motivating us to override our desires in the way that we require of a true morality? In order to answer this challenge, I'm going to very briefly sketch my account of how ethics can be grounded rationally and answer potential objections, as I've developed it through long study of the wealth of secular-friendly moral philosophy that already exists (some of key parts of which were even developed by philosophers who happen to be committed theists) and which converted me from a convinced moral nihilist to a moral realist in the decade after I became an atheist. There is no reason that the ensuing account need be rejected by theists as it's perfectly compatible with also believing in God. I just hope to make clear that it can be successfully made without any reference to God.

Before getting into the legitimacy of morality specifically, I will start with an analysis of value, or goodness, that is morally neutral. Then we can see how moral good, or moral value, can be specified within the context of what makes things good, or valuable, in general.

First, I want to distinguish that at least one connotation of the word good is uncontroversially factual in character. Goodness is a synonym for the word effectiveness. When a doctor investigates how good your eyes are, she is looking to determine how effective they are at performing the characteristic tasks that make eyes eyes from a functional perspective. Namely, she's checking to see how well they see, as assessed by a variety of metrics by which we can measure good vision. We can regularly define things as the kinds of beings they are by the way they function. Even where eyes in different species have different shapes and sizes and have different material properties, they nonetheless are eyes at all because they see. There is a very real sense in which a blind person can say they "have no eyes" if their eyes are not working, since being an eye is not just a particular configuration of matter structured in an eye-like way, but is also a way of functioning. The blind person has eyes in the material sense but not in the functional one. Every way a thing can function is a way it can be. Every way a thing does function is a way it is and a kind of being it can be said to be. To the extent it functions effectively at the characteristic activities that make it a particular kind of functional thing, it is that kind of functional thing. Things which perform multiple functions at the same time realize multiple kinds of being at the same time, one for each of the respects in which they function.

Good as Functional

When we ask about a thing how good it is, we can ask either or both of two objective questions about its effectiveness relationships. (1) How effectively does it perform the functions that define it as the kind of functional being that it is? (2) How effectively does it function for some further purpose that it might serve (or that someone is presently putting it to serve)? Notice, thanks to the discovery of evolution by natural selection, we do not need to posit that there is any intelligent mind that selects functions for natural beings to have. Through the undirected process of natural selection, beings all the time *come* to function in ways that no intelligent agent first decided they should. A great deal of evolutionary biology concerns looking at the component parts of organisms and figuring out what functions they might have served that accounted for them, or their ancestors, having a competitive advantage in reproducing. So functions are real, factual parts of nature, integral to good science. And, while on the topic of evolution, it is important to stress that while many functions are the product of natural selection, functions can be understood conceptually apart from the natural selection processes that help account for how they came about, got preserved, and became standard parts of organisms in the first place. What it *is* to function well according to a kind of possible functioning is a distinct question from what *use* a function has served in making an organism more likely to reproduce.

Since we regularly twist natural things to our purposes and so design them to accomplish a particular end we set for them, it is tempting for us to imagine that there are no functions in nature except those we give things when we put them to use for our purposes. But even when we designate something to be for a purpose, we are only able to do so when we recognize in the first place that it already *can* function that way if configured properly. For any given thing we consider, it has an enormous number of ways it can function if put in different situations or arranged with other things. The functional possibilities within nature are not made up by us. When we invent things, we are only harnessing nature's functional possibilities to make things that nature always had it within itself to manifest—were natural selection processes or animals like us, ones capable of doing intelligent designing, to come along and tinker with them enough.

In this context, I want to argue that being a human is, in the broad sense, a way to function. More precisely, human beings have a wide array of functional capacities through which we exist. We have organs and limbs that function in various ways to give us our organic existence. But more than that, in early childhood, we start developing the functional capacities that constitute and manifest personhood. These functional capacities need not be unique to human beings. Other organic life—and perhaps even inorganic beings for all we know—could in principle develop personal traits. Personal traits are various functional powers; that is, ways of being in the world. Our functional powers include our various rational powers, emotional powers, social powers, artistic powers, sexual powers, physical powers, creative powers, technological powers, and other powers we might enumerate. This is not an exact taxonomy but a rough guide to the definitive powers that I think *constitute* us as persons. We do not need to possess all of them, or to actualize all or most of them in a superlative degree, in order to meet thresholds of personhood and count as people. But it is through some mix of capacities and exercises of these powers that we have our being as persons. Each of the broad powers I've already listed comprise a number of more specific subpowers. And throughout our lives we regularly coordinate our powers in order to function in complex ways that constitute even more sophisticated powers.

I think that through understanding ourselves definitionally as both organic human beings and as persons, where a roughly ascertainable cluster of powers define what being a person is, we can understand our objective good. The more effectively we function as the kinds of beings we are, the more we realize our own being. This is inherently to become greater at being what we are. This is fundamentally good for us *as* the kinds of beings we are. Remember the eye. An eye, as the kind of being it is, intrinsically realizes itself well insofar as it functions well at seeing. Effectively seeing makes it a good eye. Similarly, for us, to effectively function according to our natures, is to function well according to our constitutive human powers and, so, to realize ourselves well.

Up to this point, I have not been specifically talking about moral goodness. I think a big mistake that most people, even many philosophers, make is that they do not delineate moral good as a subset within the larger class of things that are good. The word good, in the larger sense, has many applications that are not at all about morality. What makes for a good pulley or a good spleen is not a moral question. We can talk about good and bad nuclear weapons in terms of how well they can function as nuclear weapons even if it would be immoral to ever set one off. We would intelligibly and rightly call a defective nuclear weapon that could not explode a bad nuclear weapon, even if it turned out that it would be morally ideal that all nuclear weapons turn out to be bad nuclear weapons so that no one ever died from them.

I think that because our objective good is in our self-realization of our powers, we have an inherently rational reason to support and bolster our psychological preferences towards our objective flourishing in our abilities. Intersubjectively all people desire the kinds of powers that I mentioned above. Despite great disagreements between differing cultures, religions, and eras about *how* best to flourish, nearly everyone recognizes in broad outlines that being smarter—all things equal—is better than being less smart. Being emotionally stronger—all things equal—is better than being emotionally weaker; however we work out exactly what that means. We all understand that being faster and stronger, more creative, more capable of manipulating the world for technological purposes, etc., are *prima facie* better than being less capable in all these areas. And our brains are generally wired such that many of us experience high degrees of motivation to develop our powers and almost everyone finds realizing them highly satisfying. I want to go further than this to say that we *should* find exercising our powers satisfying since it correlates with, and reinforces us in, our objective flourishing in our powers.

Realizing Ourselves to the Maximal Degree

I think, based on the considerations above, that it is intelligible to say that we have objective reasons to prefer some things over others, if they will contribute to our overall realization of our constitutive powers that serve as the precondition of our very being and through which we realize ourselves to the maximal degree.

Morality comes in here.

We are a species of mutually interdependent beings. We must cooperate in order to coexist. Our formal and informal moral systems of principles, practices, attitudes, priorities, virtues and rules are integral to the social fabric that is necessary for each of us to survive and, even more importantly, thrive. It is absolutely vital to our own individual self-realizations that we participate in systems of coordinating our behaviors and attitudes so that we can trust one another and mutually empower one another. These systems must do all that is feasible to accommodate everyone's empowerment in order for everyone to maintain an objective reason to opt in to society, rather than to opt out of it and to work against it. The ultimate good that we must aim for in devising, interpreting, implementing, and adhering to our moral arrangements is, roughly, the maximum empowerment of the maximum number where even those who wind up the least powerful could, if adequately informed, recognize that all was done that was possible to include them in the general empowerment, and that alterations to our arrangements would have made them even more disempowered than they were. Each of us, in order to be rationally justified in opting into a morality, must be accounted for in that morality's considerations, or it cannot be binding upon us.

It is in our rational interest to commit to this kind of arrangement of mutual empowerment because the empowerment of other human beings is both the *precondition* and the *vehicle* for our own maximal empowerment. It is the precondition of our empowerment because other people functioning at their best creates incalculably many resources for us to grow and thrive in our own powers. Secondly, other people thriving means that there are less people who will actively seek to destroy us and thwart our thriving because of their own desperation. Finally, other people's empowerment is the vehicle of our own empowerment because of what it is to function in our individual personal powers.

All too often our language slanders the word "power" by equating it with the simple domination of others. But "power," when used in the default, should mean effectual realization of ability. The ability to dominate is just one way to effectually realize an ability; i.e., just one power among others—and it is hardly the most important one. The most powerful being would definitionally be the most *capable and efficacious* one. God, for example, is only ever conceived of as the most dominant being as a consequence of the more basic aspects of what it means to be God according to classical theism; i.e., the being with capabilities to do whatever can be done, and the most actually effectual being whose power is gloriously manifest in His efficacious creation of the world.

Similarly, functioning in our powers well means having the efficacious ability to do difficult things and the ability to exercise our powers in the most effective ways according to their natures. Our powers also function in their continued efficaciousness in the world after we actually exercise them. Merely dominating and destroying are lesser realizations of our power than actually increasing our critical thinking skills, creating things that are functional, harnessing our emotions and our social skills such that they create powerful functioning in other people, etc. It usually takes more power to create than to destroy. And even artfully carried out destruction is ultimately only worthwhile when it leads to the creation of something better in the end.

And we all can recognize, I think, that the most powerful people are the ones who function beyond their own bodies to make good things come about. When you are affected by a work of art, you can in a very true sense say that the *artist* is effective at that moment, even if the artist is not physically present with you and even if the artist is already dead. When we successfully use a technology, its inventors and implementers are being successful even if they do not know about this particular instance of its working well and their own thriving through its working. When we use the abilities that our teachers helped equip us with, they are powerfully functioning through us. The best political leader is clearly not the one who is merely able to subjugate people, but the one whose powerful skills as a legislator or an executive leads to flourishing functioning in her people, ideally for ages to come. Our greatest potential for power comes from our ability to empower others. When we empower others, we grow in power by spreading our power so that it is part of their power. Power, in this way, for persons such as we are, is not a zero-sum game. Power is not a thing you get more of by taking it away from others. The more you empower others, the more you function powerfully through your influence on them, the more powerful you are yourself.

From the perspective of our macro-level, long term, and enlightened self-interest, anything that morality genuinely demands of us should be justifiable to us if we are being completely honest about what is fair and if we are completely informed about what practices, attitudes, behaviors, and empirical contingencies go into the mutual empowerment of the greatest number, where the empowerment of all is genuinely aimed for. Any morality that could not justify itself on this ultimate level would not be rationally justified in compelling us to adhere to it.

But in many cases our unenlightened, short term, micro-level self-interest may lead us to see enticing material or social gains from opting out of what we recognize as the moral. In those cases, we must overtly be motivated by an appreciation of moral principle. While we are often motivated to what is morally right for other reasons than because it is morally right, sometimes the recognition of something's rightness *is* the best explanation of our behavior and sometimes the wrongness of an action is the best explanation of why we refrain from it. This is most clearly seen in cases where we feel strong desires or preferences that we reluctantly reject because our perception as to what is right or wrong compels us more strongly.

Similarly, just as oftentimes our minds refuse to let us believe something that we would prefer to believe because it is contradicted by what reason or our senses reveal to us, I also think that our minds can perceive that there would be something *contradictory* about acting in a certain way and be compelled by that rational perception not to act that way. When we judge that it would be unfair or unequal or inconsistent to treat people who are the same in morally relevant respects differently, we are using our reason. And when this compels us to alter our behavior, I see this as just as much a matter of reason motivating us as when we acquiesce to what reason shows us about facts and submit our minds to believe accordingly. And fundamentally I think personal moral motivation often boils down to such rational responsiveness to considerations of consistency by which we implicitly recognize that it would be inconsistent for us to violate moral systems we depend on so existentially and benefit from so routinely.

For all these reasons, I think we have a rational reason to say that we objectively must do certain things. It's not entirely human-independent in that this objective ought comes from what is objectively involved in our own thriving. But what is involved in our objective thriving is itself a factual matter, since we comprise a set of powers and they factually can be effectively realized to a greater or lesser degree as a factual matter that can be assessed according to any number of objective metrics. To the charge that somehow this would make morality insufficiently objective because objective facts can only be about things that would be the way they are even if people didn't exist, I answer that plainly many obviously objective facts require people to exist. The objective facts about human anatomy depend on the nature of the human. So do the objective facts about what kind of arrangements are rationally incumbent upon human persons, given the combination of our constitutive personal powers and our circumstances as human organisms in particular material and social circumstances.

Moral Pluralism, Not Relativism or Subjectivism

I consider the account of morality I just gave to be an account of an objective morality even though it lacks several features some people want to claim a morality must have. First, I didn't argue that all true, objectively justifiable moralities are *identical*. As far as I can tell, moralities are, at their core, simply those patterns of thought and practice that help us coordinate with one another for our mutual empowerment even when that means sometimes having to sacrifice particular benefits for the greater good for the greater number (which is also our *own* greater good). This does not mean that the same moral arrangements would work the best in every social group. Some fear that this entails a kind of relativism that would threaten objectivity in moral matters, but it does not. It's a kind of rational, objective pluralism. Just because medicinal practices might need to be different when treating different populations of people because they have different physiological conditions and needs, so might moral practices need to vary because people have different social and material circumstances that affect what will help them thrive maximally in their powers or not. That's not to say that either medicine or morality are either "relative" or "subjective." In both cases, there are objective metrics. There are metrics of physical health (in the case of medicine) and there are metrics of effectively functional thriving in one's constitutive powers (in the case of ethics). We can objectively assess whether given moral practices are actually empowering people or not in a comparable way to which we can assess whether certain medical practices are making people healthy.

Morality is best understood as objective in a comparable way to an applied science such as medicine or engineering. It involves considering objective facts about the states of affairs in the world to determine how best to empower people, but figuring out what the right rules and practices are is a matter of figuring out both what works most effectively in general and also sensitively reasoning through highly specific problems that arise in unique situations. That does not make it relative or subjective, again, because, like in medicine or engineering, there are clearly objective metrics for success in human thriving.

Now, in medicine, engineering, and morality, there are sometimes serious problems whereby two goods might be equally *prima facie* justifiable but they cannot both be attained and so it's up to agents to have to choose among them. But that does not mean that medicine, engineering, or morality are subjective matters *tout court*, it just means that sometimes two or more outcomes can both have objectively good rational support in their favor and we can let our subjective preferences break the tie. It would be a huge misrepresentation of the nature of morality to extrapolate from the case of "ties" in our judgments in cases like these to saying that the entire endeavor of moral reasoning is through and through subjective or, at least, revealed to be *fundamentally* subjective. That obscures the relevant reality that even as two, or a few, options may be equally good, countless more can be objectively eliminated as not good. Even the good options are recommendable in the first place because they exhibit rationally defensible merits—not just because they were idiosyncratically emotionally selected.

Morality and Evolution

Finally, let me conclude with a word about evolution and its connection to morality since many theists and atheists alike think that the acceptance of the combination of atheism and evolution should significantly impact our ethical views. I want to stress that while many of our powers were shaped by natural selection processes, assessing what it is to flourish according to our powers is not the same thing as asking what purpose they served for our ancestors that helped us survive. For example, our ancestors did not need to do very complicated mathematics in order to survive. We judge what it is to thrive in our potential to do math by standards of high functioning mathematical reasoning, not standards that limit mathematical excellence to our ancestors' uses for it. The same can be said of morality. We may be able to infer that selective pressures equipped us with brains inclined towards certain kinds of moral priorities and categories of reasoning. But moral reasoning is not merely about trying to live and think like our ancestors. What justifies it for us today is how it contributes to our objective thriving. So we can improve our moral understanding with critical reasoning. Similarly, just because survival pressures shaped our moral evolution in prehistoric times means neither that we have an overriding moral imperative to reproduce nor that all of morality should be judged by how it would help or hurt our personal reproduction. What is good for reproduction is good for our genes but not always for *us*. We are not our genes. We are the organisms that our genes construct. We have our own objective interests, distinct from theirs. Where reproduction is good for us it proves itself by reference to how it contributes to our thriving.

It's completely backwards to conceive of it the other way around and think that our actions only have value by how they contribute to reproduction. People are the ultimate end for themselves and for each other. Reproduction is highly valuable as a means to create *more* people. But it is not what the people themselves are *for*. And we certainly need not be beholden to a simplistic ethic of "survival of the fittest" whereby the only ethical rule is to outcompete and dominate others. For the reasons I have already detailed, our thriving as people in relations of mutual dependence, for both our minimal well-being and our maximal empowerment, requires that we maximize cooperation and mutual empowerment wherever possible.

Seeing God in the Bible as Ridiculous

Andrew Hall, Laughing in Disbelief

Back in the days of the Book of Genesis, the world still had that fresh, tasty smell you get after unwrapping a *Five Guys* burger. The Fall of Man took a lot off the shine of the planet. However, only the harshest critic would rate the planet less than five out of five stars. Humankind had not yet filled the land with fast food wrappers. Global warming was limited to where the Sun was shining at that moment.

East of the Garden of Eden, lay a humble mud hut. It was on a hill. This is not the inhabitants' first house. After their eviction for violating the Eden rental agreement, the couple moved to this area due to its closeness to drinking water. After building Mud Hut 1.0 on low ground, they discovered water runs downhill and rivers overflow their banks. Mud Hut 2.0 is far dryer.

At a safe distance from the river is a small fruit and vegetable farm. By today's standards, it's not much. There are no superfoods that affluent shoppers in organic supermarkets would pay top dollar for. On the other hand, every food that keeps you from starving to death in the ancient world *is* a superfood. Garden variety carrots are things of wonder.

The King of Mud Hut 2.0 ambles out. Adam stretches his weary bones in the morning light. He likes to use this quiet time to reflect on life. Once the family is awake, it's go, go, go. It's been years after *The Incident* that led to his and his wife's eviction from the Garden. All in all, he's adapted well to the situation. Take the mud hut. It's an engineering marvel. There was a steep learning curve on how to handle mud proficiently. After all, there were a few nights when he woke up due to collapsing walls. Hunting and trapping animals was another toughie. Immediately after *The Incident*, animals and he just hung out together. All of that ended when Adam discovered fire and how good roasted chicken thighs taste. It didn't take long for animals to figure out they were on the menu and now they avoid him like the plague. He thinks the animals look at him with a sense of betrayal. He's right.

What does he miss the most about Eden? Not having to wear clothes.

"Being naked was easy back then," he muses out loud to no one. "Now you can't turn around without stumbling into prickly prickles."

Oh, he misses his six-pack abs, too. God is a righteous God. God saw fit to strap on twenty extra pounds right to Adam's midsection after *The Incident*.

Shaking those disturbing thoughts out of his brain, Adam switches into business mode.

"Family meeting! It's time for a family meeting!" he cries out.

His wife Eve is the first to answer the call. She's normally calm and the emotional rock the family relies on. This morning is different. Adam disturbed her dreaming of those long lost six-pack abs.

"Oh, it's too early for this, Adam! I wish I could use the second person of the Trinity's name in vain, but I have no idea that God has, in fact, three distinct personalities!" she says.

"His ways are mysterious."

That does not make her feel better. She sits down on the earth.

Favorite son Abel walks out after his mother. He's in his early twenties, has a Channing Tatum look and a *Someday all of this will be mine* attitude.

"Dad, I had this dream last night that I was the favored son, and look, it's real! Praise be!"

Adam puts his arm around his boy. "Hallelujah and praise the LORD, Favorite Son Abel," he says.

Adam and Abel sit down in their respective spots. The head of the house clears his throat, "OK, let's begin!"

"What about me?" Cain stands in the doorway. He's a year younger than his brother with twice the angst and at least three times the brain power. Under one arm, Cain is carrying a wooden wheel. He ambles over and sits down.

"Look, it's not-Abel. Good to have you here. What do you have there? A wooden circle?"

"I'm very excited about this. I've been working on it for days. I call this the *wheel*."

"I like triangles," Abel chimes in.

Everyone except Cain agrees that triangles are vastly superior to circles. Why would he build a wooden circle, anyway?

"A wheel wouldn't work if it were a triangle. I want the wheel to go around and around and around." Cain makes his point by standing and moves the wheel around the group.

"Why would you want to do that?" Eve asks. It seems like a lot of work to push the thing around.

"I say it's unholy and blasphemous. If the LORD wanted us to have wheels they'd be growing on trees like apples," Adam announces

"Honey, we agreed never to use the "A" word," his wife reminds him.

"Oh, right. Sorry about that. Favorite Son Abel, break it down after the meeting so we can use it for the fire tonight!"

Cain's face is awash with other people's arrogant stupidity. He sits.

"First order of business, Favorite Son Abel, nice work on the sacrifices to the LORD. I've heard from a very high source that He is pleased with you," Abel says.

Abel sees his chance to play up the role as favorite son. "I don't know how I would've been able to deal with it if God didn't like it. It would've been the worst day ever."

Eve shoots him a look, "Sweetie, you have no idea what a bad day is."

A fair amount of air gets let out of Abel's balloon. While he seems to shrink a little, his brother sits a bit straighter. Seeing Abel get dumped on brings a rare smile to Cain.

"Hey, you shouldn't be schadenfreuding over there, mister! Your brother did good. You? Not so much," Adam observes.

"I sacrificed! My fruits and vegetables I dedicated to the LORD were fresh. My snow peas snapped! My zucchini firm! The elderberries worthy of Methuselah."

"God likes to smell fat burning. You can't make the LORD a vegetarian. This is a competitive world. Sacrifices have to razzle and dazzle. I got to where I am today by lighting up the grill and barbecuing high-fat meats for God," Adam says.

"It's a competitive world? You and Mom were the only ones around for years!"

Sometimes not answering your children is winning the argument Adam reflects.

"OK, onto new business. God has told me we need to be more proactive with being fruitful and multiplying. It turns out we have not been multiplying since not-Abel was born," Adam announces to the team.

Eve and Abel don't seem to understand the full import of this newest directive from God. Cain, however, can see the train coming down the track and suspects he's tied to the rails.

"God is going to make us more women? Because He's God, he can just whip up more women," Cain points out.

Adam ignores his son's attempts to question the way of the LORD. "OK, here is the schedule."

"Schedule? We don't need a schedule. I have plenty of ribs that God can make more women out of." Cain is fighting a losing battle, but gosh darn it, he's bringing his A-game.

Adam completely ignores him.

"This week, Abel is with his mother Monday, Wednesday, and Friday. Not-Abel, you're in the batter's box on Thursday."

It slowly dawns on Abel what divine family planning looks like. He looks at his mother in a whole new light. A way reminiscent of how a middle school boy looks at a Victoria Secrets catalog. "I get to be with Mom–"

"Biblically," Adam answers.

Cain mounts his last and best defense. "How is this OK? I don't think animals do this kind of thing. Back me up on this Abel! Isn't this wrong, wrong, wrong?"

His brother is silent—icky silent.

Adam hates talking to not-Abel, but you do what you have to do in the service of the LORD. "God is giving us a free pass for a few generations. There's going to be some freaky shenanigans going on. You don't want to know what the deal is going to be between Lot and his daughters."

"Look at Abel. You like Abel. If my ribs aren't good enough for God, why doesn't He pluck a few out of Abel?"

Abel offers up some sage wisdom, "They'd still be related to you."

"THEY WOULDN'T BE MOM."

Eve hopes to calm things down a bit. She's always been the peacemaker of the family. "Schnooky, if the Almighty said it's OK, then it has to be moral—divine command theory and all."

Cain can't believe what he's hearing. "Divine command theory?"

"Whatever God does or orders must be moral because He is the source of all that is good," Eve says to Schnooky-not-Abel.

Abel sticks out his chest and holds his chin up high. "If that's the way it has to be, then I'll do my absolute best."

This is all too much for his brother. "You are such a suck up." A second passes and Cain makes yet another disturbing realization. "Why does he get three days and I only get one?"

"Like I said, your sacrifice was lacking. God wants his sacrifices to smell like the annual Memorial Day Church Cookout. Maybe you amp your game up, and you will be the one with three nights with your mom," Adam points out.

"What about Saturday and Sunday?" Abel asks.

"Saturday is your parent's date night. Sunday is the LORD's day."

Cain gets up. He grabs his wheel and stomps away.

Despite everything that's happened, Abel is still positive. "I think he'll come around."

***

A day later and Cain is basking in the early afternoon sun. He stands on a hill and gazes on the field of crops. It's a humble farm. There's a stone fence encircling it. To his left is a good-sized two-wheel wooden cart. It's full of fruits and vegetables that he has painstakingly plucked.

Abel sneaks up behind him. With a swift movement honed from hundreds of attacks, Abel dope smacks his brother on the back of the head.

"Owwwwwww!"

"What's up, loser?"

This is Cain's favorite place. It's where he goes in dreams where no one is around to tell him his inventions are stupid or make fun of his sacrifices. Right now, though, he just wants to run away from his idiot brother.

"Nothing much. I'm just on my way back to the mud hut." And with that, Cain grabs the cart.

"Hey, aren't you going to ask Big Bro how his big date went last night?"

Cain had successfully repressed yesterday's family meeting so far down that there was a distinct chance he'd poop it out with last night's corn. Despite his best efforts, his brother has been able to ruin his best-laid plans.

"You mean your alone time with Mom?"

Abel's chest puffs out a bit more than usual. "Yeaaaaaahhh"

"Please save me the details, you inbreeding Casanova, I've got business to do."

Abel doesn't like the sound of that. He can't go around boasting about Eve-time with Adam. That leaves his brother as the only person on Earth to talk to. In a fit of irritation, Abel changes strategy and goes with what he does best. He knocks the cart out of Cain's hands.

"Whatcha got there? One of your stupid wheels?"

"No, it's two of my stupid wheels attached with a rotating column I call an axle. Together with this containment unit I call the machine a cart."

"So you can carry your stupid carrots and stuff that God doesn't want!"

Cain grabs the cart again. Abel knocks it down again, this time spilling all its contents out.

Cain takes a deep breath and starts gathering the nutritious and delicious produce. He looks up from the ground and sees his brother sitting in the cart. Abel is looking down the steep hill. It doesn't take a rocket scientist to see what the idiot is about to do.

"The cart isn't designed for that. That right there? That thing you're doing? It's going to end up catastrophically failing."

"Cain, you were second born and a first rate loser. Watch how a man lives his life in the here and now!"

As soon as those words leave Abel's lips, he pushes the cart down the hill. Wow! It's fast!

He's probably setting some speed record for humanity. Someday, Mom's and his kids will talk about the time Abel went really, really fast on Uncle Cain's Idiot Machine of Idiocy.

Those were the last thoughts Abel had before smashing into the stone fence surrounding his brother's farm. Cain sadly notices he was right all along. His brother's head has a lot of similarities with a pumpkin.

He had never seen anyone die before. In fact, his brother is the first person to die. Ever.

Stuck in a mental miasma, he lies down on the grass and stares at the sky.

Cain takes a few moments in silence and thought about the good times and the bad times he and his brother shared. There weren't a lot of good times. It was more a case of bad times and worse times. But he never wanted Abel to end up like this. Cain always assumed he would be working with his plants and tinkering while Abel occasionally rained down smack talk and low-intensity physical abuse. It would be like that until Abel came to his senses and settled down.

Note: Settled down with someone other than a close relative.

Cain didn't know what happened to you when you died. God hadn't told Dad anything on that front. Maybe the Almighty let that slip His divine mind. That was okey-doke with Cain. He never mentioned it to anyone, but Cain secretly thought God's plan with a capital "P" seemed a bit, well, disjointed and erratic.

A gust of wind pulls Cain back to the real world. There, standing in the tomatoes, is the LORD. God had only appeared to Mom and Dad. This couldn't be good. Even though his brother just became the first Darwin Award recipient, what Cain cares about right then and there are his delicate tomato plants.

"Hello, LORD, can you just whisk yourself out from those tomatoes? I raised them from seeds, and they are wonderful manifestations of your benevolence." Cain understands he couldn't just tell the LORD to shove off. He hopes that *manifestation of your benevolence* line is enough flattery to avoid a tomato patch disaster.

God doesn't move.

"I don't have to tell you, seeing that you know everything, how great those beefsteak tomatoes are going to be in a few weeks. Um, standing there is OK if you don't move about."

God takes a step towards Cain. One plant gets stomped by a heavenly foot.

Cain is at his wit's end. However, he's not a quitter. "OK, if you have to move how about going in between the rows? That should limit the damage –"

"WHERE IS YOUR BROTHER ABEL!" God bellows.

God's voice is deep and very godly. The LORD's fluffy beard waves in the wind. His garments are as white as His beard. God seems to care a lot about matching colors.

Cain, confident he had done nothing wrong answers calmly, "My brother Abel took a ride in my cart and got himself killed, LORD."

God takes a step and crushes another beautiful tomato plant in the prime of its life. Maybe Cain could reason with the LORD before more destruction occurs.

"Am I my brother's keeper, LORD?"

That was *not* the right thing to say.

"WHAT HAVE YOU DONE?"

"First, I made the first wheel. Then, seeing that I was on a bit of a roll [Cain makes sure he doesn't laugh at his pun] I made a second wheel and hitched them together–"

"YOUR BROTHER'S BLOOD IS CRYING TO ME FROM THE GROUND." And to bring that point home, the LORD took a divine foot and stomps another plant.

"I did try and stop him. In retrospect, I should've used smaller words."

"I AM GOING TO BANISH YOU FROM THIS PLACE FOREVER."

"Wait, what? What's my crime? Inventing the wheel or starting the Agricultural Revolution thousands of years before its time?"

"YOU WILL NEVER SEE MY FACE AGAIN."

Cain wonders if that just may be a blessing.

"YOU WILL LIVE IN THE LAND OF NOD AND THERE YOU WILL BE FRUITFUL AND MULTIPLY!"

Everything was moving very fast for Cain. However, he did pick up on the tidbit that God wants him to multiply. How was he going to do that when he could never see Mom?

"Who am I going to multiply with, LORD? Are you making me a woman?"

"THERE ARE PEOPLE IN NOD. FIND A CISGENDERED WOMAN OF YOUR OWN RACE IN THAT LAND."

And there the two stood. God in the tomato patch. Cain standing on the outside. It took a second for Cain to piece it all together. He'd never have to see God again. That was a plus for any future gardening. Two, he wasn't going to have to have sex with his mother to make babies. That seemed like a double-win for Cain.

And he couldn't help but think that the people in Nod are probably nicer.

"OK, LORD, you're right. I've been a naughty, sinful boy and I'm going to leave right now." He looks down at his cart. While Abel didn't fare well with the ride down the hill, the cart was intact. Cain looks at the angry LORD and realizes he should just bug out. He could make more carts.

Cain cautiously walks away. He prides himself as a pragmatic sort of fellow. While his parents and Abel spent their time gossiping about intrafamily politics, he kept himself focused on real world problems. No matter how pragmatic he is, his heart burns with a question for God. If there were more people within walking distance, then why the heck have his brother and he have sex with their mother? It didn't make any sense.

Knowing he was putting himself in jeopardy, he knows he has to know why. It had to be for a good reason, right? Otherwise, something was very wrong. Very wrong, indeed.

Regardless of the consequences, Cain takes a deep breath and turns around.

Something very wrong is going on. God is still there. His back is to Cain. He is gingerly stepping around the plants in the garden and holding up his robes.

And then God falls face-first into the watermelons.

Cain rushes over. There is God, face-first in a watery melon, arms and legs splayed out. He rolls God over to His back.

"Dad?"

God's beard was stuck in the fruity flesh, revealing Adam's angry face.

"You weren't supposed to look back!"

Cain stands up. He has a thousand questions. And like many people who will be the victim of gaslighting in the future, Cain figures out the only way to win that game is by not playing.

"Screw this. I'm heading to Nod." He walks away.

"I'm going to write this all down in my memoir!" Adam screams. "You're going to look like a schmuck!"

"No one's going to read your stupid book!"

Cain doesn't look back.

Patheos Nonreligious

Rationally Not Seeing God: Being Born Again. Again.

Jonathan Burrello, Blinky & Sal

Part of the Flock:

I never thought I'd be a non-believer.

I was raised in a healthy and stable Christian home. I remember asking Jesus to come into my heart as a kid (over and over again for fear of it not sticking). I remember a traveling evangelist telling me, "One day God's gonna use you." I remember that overwhelming sense of guilt welling up to induce tears at the altar multiple times. I spoke *in tongues*. I prayed several times every day and read my Bible each morning. I shared my faith with friends at school. I was baptized at age 9. Later, I would go on mission trips to the Dominican Republic and Northern Ireland. I played cello every Sunday on the stage with my family. I debated my teachers and friends whenever they brought up evolution, homosexuality, or a host of other buzzword topics.

Along with this tremendous sense of identity, there was also, however, a sickness. Constantly being told how sinful and undeserving you are can't be all good, right?

When I was a child, I made up prayer requests to fit in. In a sanctuary of hundreds, I faked being *slain in the Holy Spirit* to not be the odd man out at church camp. I could muster tears, laughter, unconsciousness, or convulsions if the conditions were right. At one point, at a very young age, I feigned seeing visions for approval. The adults were pleased. On one occasion, after a woman had prayed over me and asked if I could feel Jesus coming into my heart, I told her I had. Then she asked me what it felt like. I told her it felt like a warm octopus tickling my insides. Despite knowing how manufactured many of these experiences were, I still convinced myself they were all genuine.

At my darkest, I fantasized about killing myself so I could be in heaven with Jesus. I often wonder how common that is among young Christians. At my weirdest, I would wake up in the night and anxiously check to make certain my sleeping family members had not been *Raptured* away without me. I would physically punish myself for having lustful thoughts. There was even a time when I thought demons haunted my room.

I was going through all the religious motions, hitting every mark, and making the adults pleased with my spiritual development. As I grew, that desperate need to please the adults eventually faded away and was replaced with a desperate need to please God; a god who was, by definition, outside the realm of my comprehension and whose demands of perfection I, by design, was incapable of approaching. But I knew that all I had to do was trust, love, and believe in Jesus. Or rather I knew I had to trust, love, and believe what I was told Jesus was and believed Jesus to be. In my experience, everyone sort of defines their object of worship differently. Jesus has at least as many faces as he does subscribers, even if the differences are subtle. Maybe everyone is really just worshiping themselves; or rather, their ideals. I wonder.

Not Seeing God

After high school, I attended Central Christian College before transferring to Biola University. I read the Bible multiple times all the way through and I took classes studying biblical theology, all from a Christian perspective. After graduation, I found a church and was active in Bible studies and community outreach. I was even working as a speech coach and adjunct professor at Biola. I was happy overall, with my sense of belonging and sense of destiny encouraging me every step of the way. Sure, I found the Bible's slavery, misogyny, genocides, tribalism, barbarism, capital punishments for seemingly absurd trifles, animal and human sacrifices, and copious military campaigns over "holy" real estate somewhat bizarre and troubling, but these were common stumbling blocks for many Christians who had read the Bible. My job was to simply trust God even when I didn't understand and I could do that. At least for a time.

A Change of Heart:

So what happened?
It was not a sudden transition. It took years. And they were frustrating. And confusing. And they hurt. In many ways, I'll probably always be reeling from the paradigm shift.
One of the more depressing things about losing your faith is what some Christians say to you. They keep trying to tell me what I did wrong or guess at my story. They've all been wrong so far, and most, though well-intentioned, come off as condescending rather than compassionate. Worse, I frequently hear, "You were never a real Christian." I know the verses they glean this doctrine from, but I don't know how else to break it down for them. I believed it all. It was a crucial part of my identity. I loved my faith and Jesus and my church

community. I saw God's hand in everything. I believed I had communicated with the creator of the universe every day for most of my life. I had desperately wanted to be a Christ-like person. If walking away from one's faith was proof one had never believed, then what was the litmus test to determine if any current believer wasn't just now kidding themselves deep down and would change their mind later on?

What did happen was what happens to everyone: a compounding of a lifetime of events, information, and experiences. All of it quite humbling.

In elementary school, I learned there were other religions. In high school I learned that Christianity was far from the first religion. In college I made my first LGBT friends, who forever transformed my previously held negative perceptions of them. When my college girlfriend's grandmother was dying, she asked if she would be going to hell. Her grandmother was a Buddhist. I didn't know what to say. I wanted to believe God was at least as understanding as I was but, in light of the words of scripture, I wasn't sure.

On two Christian college campuses loaded with pastors, missionaries, theologians, apologists, and authors, I learned that—at least to my understanding and probably against the intent of my mentors—the bulk of Christendom, both contemporary and of antiquity, was quite human, hostile, and forged more by geography, politics, and culture than any unifying omnipresent spirit. I felt disheartened reading the words of Lewis, Craig, Lennox, Grudem, and a host of other respected Christian voices, and finding that, while as a Christian I had to agree with most of their conclusions, their reasoning was unconvincing, incomplete, and deliberately aiming at a presupposed target. Many of these authors were lauded as intellectual giants and I was boggled by the glaring flaws in their logic.

This is not to say that brilliant people cannot have religious convictions. What I mean to say is that the most brilliant people still have yet to present a compelling reason for their religious faith. To my satisfaction anyway.

Now, it would have been presumptuous and paranoid of me to think I was just some quiet genius who could somehow see through all these phony arguments that were bamboozling a desperate and stupid flock hungry for confirmation bias. I assumed I must have made a mistake and that my earthly pride was trying to separate me from God. The most celebrated theologians could be wrong, but not God. I kept quiet and kept believing.

My mantra was, *I am a believer and I have experienced God all my life and nothing can shake that faith.* But had I really experienced God? What was it like? Was it joy? Was it peace? Was it seeing events unfold in a seemingly coincidental fashion? And couldn't people experience joy and peace and be the recipients of serendipity without God?

I gradually admitted to myself that I was maybe not being intellectually honest. I had been actively resistant to new or contrary claims, yet I demanded openness of everyone else. Since that time, I have grown to become highly suspicious of stubborn certainty in any ideology. I felt that if I was to be honest with myself, I had to be open and follow the Truth wherever it led. At the time, I believed it would lead to an affirmation of my beliefs so there was nothing for me to fear.

The Beginning of the End:

I had been taught to believe that:

a.) Every Muslim, Mormon, Jew, Hindu, Buddhist, Wiccan, etc. were all deceived or deluded and they were damning themselves by not being open to the Truth and accepting my religion. Their motives may have been pure, but nothing more than misguided cultural indoctrination.

b.) As a 20th century American Protestant Christian, I just got lucky because I happened to be born into the right religion.

I forget how old I was when this struck me as oddly convenient. Too old.

If I could write off all the religious experiences and detailed histories of others as understood sociological effects and legends, then I had to turn it on myself. Was it possible my own religious experiences could be psychologically prompted and my own religious texts be merely the stuff of Bronze Age myth?

I had never considered that question before and it really was all it took. The house of cards fell, over the next few years.

What seemed more likely?

a.) Another ancient group of people created another god whose face changed with the tides of the ever evolving culture of which it was a part. (Something you really notice about God in the Bible—from Genesis to Revelations and then subsequent councils, schisms, and reformations—is how much he changes over the thousands of years it was written, and it always perplexed me).

b.) Magic was real, sometimes, up until ~2,000 years ago and anyone who doubts that is a fool worthy of death (thus saith the Lord).

The first proposition seemed to have a lot more explanatory power and appeared much less reliant on suspension of disbelief and vengeful threats.

I was fresh years out of college and still reading my Bible every day, but suddenly I was no longer simply presupposing its inerrancy. Suddenly I was reading the Good Book with the idea that it was possibly the mythology and politically-influenced historical accounts of a superstitious, tribal people in a pre-scientific age who fashioned a deity in their image, composited with other contemporary gods of the region. I had been trained to regard all other religions as such already. It was utterly shocking how much more sense the entirety of scripture made to me, as well as the entirety of history. So much of the confusion I had had, concerning so many passages, were explained so well with this hypothesis. And it was only a level of scrutiny I had already been quick to apply to all other sacred texts previously.

I got hired to teach in South Korea. I packed up my belongings in Buena Park, California and started my long solo drive to my parents' home in upstate New York to say goodbye. I also revisited my old alma mater in McPherson, Kansas. I had heard stories of atheists being converted to theism simply from beholding a majestic waterfall. I was overwhelmed by the beauty of Monument Valley in Utah. At sunset it was breathtaking. "What difference would there be to this landscape if there were no God?" I thought to myself. I couldn't think of anything. Even as a Christian, I had a basic understanding of how rocks and mountains formed. "How would humanity be any different today if there were no God in control of it?" Even harder. No way to tell. I had heard it said that there would be no morals, but even as a Christian, I understood the survivalist and societal advantages of cooperation and reciprocity and had observed both extensively within the animal kingdom. Morality seemed to be a very human construct anyway, as evidenced by the fact that there was no set standard of morality across cultures or millennia. All the morals that **had** culturally overlapped more frequently were logical, tangibly beneficial, and designed to continue. The development, flux, and resilience of morality actually presented an elegant portrait of cultural evolution.

Once in New York I hinted to my father that I was experiencing "agnostic days." I decided to withhold more detail as he was going through the process of becoming an ordained minister at the time. Secretly, my doubts were greater.

I had been taught that God answers prayers in three ways: yes (it happens), no (it's not God's will so it doesn't happen), or wait (it happens later—on God's timeline). Coincidentally, those are the exact same and only three possible outcomes if you don't pray. Praying did not increase the chances of any desired result. Was it possible things were just happening at random and everyone was just interpreting events through their pre-adjusted religious lenses? I already believed every non-Christian was operating under this bias. What made me so different?

What all pious folk know is that good and bad circumstances befall believers and non-believers alike with seemingly random dispassion. True, we all will assign different meaning to our misfortunes based on our worldviews, but beyond that could anyone really say that the actions of an incomprehensible and unpredictable god were in any way distinguishable from the expressionless whims of a weather system?

Many ancient gods, including the Abrahamic god, were endowed with authority over the weather. It seemed that in our yearning to find meaning and fairness in a pitiless universe we could not understand, many ancient societies personified the elements as gods—in many cases man-like and displaying their cultures' prized attributes—and devised ceremonies and sacrificial rites to try and appease and somehow control nature or supplicate themselves to it. I had already believed this of every other religion and culture. What reason did I have to make an exception for the religion I happened to be brought up in and indoctrinated in before I was old enough to understand it?

Was it possible I had been innocently brainwashed?

Belief is not some arbitrary choice. If it were, its morality and rewards system would be even more nonsensical. Even for the most devout, they were either indoctrinated when they were young or they simply found it convincing at a later time. Do any of us truly have the capacity to choose what we believe? Can we flip a switch in our brain and believe that elephants are doorknobs? What if there were a threat of bodily harm or death attached to the doorknob-elephant claim? Would that make it more reasonable or even possible to start believing it to be true...or would it cast further doubt on the claimant? What if the claimant insisted they loved you? How would that matter to the claim's validity or feasibility?

Facing the Music:

All these questions wrecked me from the inside. I was deathly afraid of not believing. Everyone I knew was a believer. For a few years, to quell my doubts and anxieties, I privately sought counsel from pastors, theology professors, apologist texts, online resources, the Bible, and, yes, genuinely and tearfully praying to God for many nights. I asked God for faith, guidance, forgiveness, answers, mercy, understanding, hope; anything he could spare for a sinner like me. The human help was depressingly bad and incongruous and God remained as silent as ever. No dew for my fleece. Who would I be without belief in God and my presumed relationship with his son? How would this effect my relationship with my family?

When I was younger, my father had told me that the only way I could make him sad or disappoint him was if I turned away from God. That thought echoed in my mind for years. It made me hate myself for having doubts. I loved my father and disappointing him would hurt. And I could not vilify him for saying that. I knew all too well where those feelings came from.

I had never seriously considered the atheist perspective or read any atheist literature. I thought if the bad arguments for Christianity were enough to make me doubt, maybe the worse arguments of atheism would bring me back. It was not the case. I found myself nodding to the beats of their logic too much for my own comfort. The infidels had some good points, dammit.

I had no experience with *de-converted* people. The idea was alien to me. It was only after hearing the stories of former Christians' de-conversions that I was able to admit to myself that I no longer believed and there wasn't much I could do about it. I think I cried. It was helpful to know I was not alone. But, boy did I feel alone. It frightened me.

I had lost my comforter, but I had to come to grips with the fact that the truth is not contingent upon our preferences.

The next few months or so were absolute hell. The paradigm shift proved to be a traumatic transition. I had never been more depressed in my life. I remember the first morning waking up and realizing that I was truly and utterly alone. There was no cosmic father figure watching over me. There never had been. I had imagined it and it had been reinforced daily by a steady regimen of spiritual aphorisms stitched into throw pillows and influential figures closing their eyes as they lifted their hands to the ceiling. I gazed upon everything with despair and contempt. I was tormented with feverish nightmares. I was in spiritual withdrawal. What was worse, I couldn't tell anybody.

At that point I was living alone in South Korea, more miles from the familiar than I had ever been. I stayed out of the country for five years, too afraid to return. Terrified of looking my deeply religious grandmother in the eye. I knew it would hurt her too. It did. Their tears still break my heart every time they surface.

I kept it a secret from my family for over a year before I finally told them. I wish I had waited longer. I wish I could take back all the emails I sent to my dad. I wish I could have just said, "Dad, I don't want to disappoint you and I know we will always love each other, but I just don't know that I believe this stuff anymore." I should have ended it there. He didn't want to hear my thought process and incendiary remarks about the thing that was so real and integral to who he was. And I was in no place to effectively communicate what I was going through.

I can only imagine what I put him through; what I'm still putting my whole family through—knowing I am 'in rebellion' against God, soaking in my unwashed sin. I know some probably shrug it off as "a phase" and feel that I'll "come to my senses" eventually. They always remind me that they're praying for me. It may be condescending, but I believe it is a necessary comfort for people who hold the beliefs they do. In any case, I'd rather them say words in the dark for me than take me to the edge of town to stone me to death before the whole community.

I have been very fortunate, actually. My family still loves me and we talk. We talk a lot actually. They may not support my opinions on the supernatural, but they don't have to. I know many who have not been so lucky under similar circumstances. I am extremely grateful that I was not disowned.

Religion will always be a touchy topic, but the good news is most of it doesn't matter. If personal mental conclusions are more important than actions and consequences then maybe we have our priorities out of order. Folks may think I'm evil for not sharing their beliefs, but I do not have to extend them that same discourtesy. He may not have been the first one to say it, but if Jesus got one thing right it was the Golden Rule.

Onward:

There's something refreshing about not having to rationalize or defend the more horrific passages of the Bible or the obtuseness of many church doctrines

Not Seeing God

anymore. The universe is still mysterious, but I do not feel the need to morally justify how it works.

For those who were never a part of this world, it may seem easy to be dismissive of the mental struggles of others and faith in general. My thinking may seem obvious, but it really was a very taxing journey to reach the conclusions I did. Those with sincere faith do not shed it lightly, nor do they seek to.

The weirdest thing is that losing my faith and old notions of a soul, afterlife, spirits, and gods has had very little impact on my personality. I'm still pretty much the same guy. Maybe a little more curious and skeptical, but essentially the same. And the world didn't explode either. Many times when people give accounts of their conversion or de-conversion to or from any religion, they say how much better everything is now that they've found the "truth" and their eyes are open. I'd rather not make that claim. Emotions are fleeting. Some days I have a far more positive outlook than others. It would be disingenuous to pretend otherwise. I'm still the same silly, little man...who probably thinks too much. And I like me.

People might feel that my experience was not *experiential* enough, but I feel that that is part of why it is so personally compelling for me. Experiences are fickle, unverifiable, and have resulted in conversions to every mutually exclusive religion, ideology, or movement under the sun. I think because this was a very slow, thoughtful, and honest endeavor, it was maybe more meaningful. Personally, I would rather have a deliberate intellectual process that I can admit to possibly being in error over a subjective personal experience that I rigidly believe to be unimpeachable.

The smoke is still settling and I suppose I'm what you'd call a skeptic, but I hardly hope that is the most interesting thing about me.

I still wrestle with myself about what to say or not say to my family. Their religion is still a very integral part of their identity. It gives them what they need, it makes their world make sense, and I for one would not wish them to lose the thing that brings so much to their world. If it is a delusion, hopefully it remains a harmless or maybe helpful one. While it has the potential for harm (as all human institutions do), I still would not want to put them through what I endured.

My family and I may never be on the same page again and this has been the biggest and saddest loss to me, but we are separate creatures on our own paths. I have to respect that. All I know is that I am an ever-evolving organism who is capable of change and no longer afraid of where my questions take me or if I never get the answers I'm looking for.

I have a lot of regrets about the way I treated people and the way I thought about people when I was a Christian. I cringe to think of it, but perhaps it was a necessary stage in my development as a person. I also deeply regret the people I "brought to Christ", knowing what it did to their family relationships now.

Despite what I was told, it is not wicked rebellion or a desire to sin that has led me to the conclusions to which I have arrived. Either:

a.) I have simply not found sufficient reason to follow the crowd and found serious reason to question the motivations and psychological amenability of both crowds and myself as an individual.

b.) I have been legitimately deceived by some supernatural force into believing proposition a.)

In either case, a god that would eternally punish me or anyone else for an honest, thoughtful mistake is not really worth worshiping, in my opinion. If there truly is a god or gods out there in some unprovable realm, then I hope they are a good deal better than the ones humanity has devised thus far.

It's not a happy ending where everything suddenly clicks and just works out. And most religious people will tell you the same thing for their personal conversions too. We may change throughout our lives, but life itself continues

Not Seeing God

to go on. Sometimes merrily, sometimes with great suffering. Whether our joys and pains have any ultimate cosmic purpose is perhaps only for the individual to guess. The answers to all of life's puzzles may continue to elude our species until the sun flickers out, but there's something sort of exciting about knowing we're all on the same mysterious journey together, spinning on a colossal, wet marble suspended in an impossible void that dwarfs even our egos. I find it spooky yet comforting to believe that even the wisest among us is still just making it up as he goes.

Patheos Nonreligious

Part Two

REFLECTING ON GODLESSNESS IN MODERN SOCIETY

"Modern society" is in an ever-changing state of flux, and covers a multitude of nations, geographies and peoples, as well as sub-peoples, rules, ideas and cultures, institutions and organizations. Again, as with the last section, we offer you a hand-picked selection of humanist offerings from around the world. From Ghana to Iran, the UK to the US, and some Latin America thrown in, humanism and atheism means different things to different people. Okay, so not believing in God is pretty one-dimensional as a proposition, but the ramifications that the professing of such a simple statement garners is hugely varied.

It's not just a geographical thing, either. Within established societies, what does atheism look like, or how does it prevail or manifest itself, in terms of different societal "areas"? How does atheism look in the military or in education? How do people come by their atheism, and how does it affect them?

Atheism is at a crucial stage (as if it can easily be seen as a singular "thing" or a movement...). Atheist and humanist organizations have had some decades to mature (and, indeed, go through some growing pains). Now it's a case, in some areas of the world, of sending down deeper roots, and starting to think about flowering, to create fruits for new plants for successive generations.

Success, in terms of time and influence, is about how atheism is represented, and how it can be normalized. These steps seem to take so very long, but in the context of the history and marketplace of ideas, perhaps we are actually moving at good pace. There are many of us, I am sure, who have seen atheism as being a wholly more accepted worldview when publicly professed to. Indeed, the whole religion versus atheism debate seems almost ubiquitous these days, with media outlets running commentary on a consistent basis. Though we

Patheos Nonreligious

may hate FOX News for the way it might characterize atheism, the fact that is characterizing it so often in public is arguably a great sign of its normalization.

As far as this section is concerned, this is what atheism means to some of us. Come join us in our adventures. It's not always easy, but, looking to the future, it is so very important.

Not Seeing God in the Mind

Nail Carter, Godless in Dixie

I wasn't active in the skeptic movement long before I discovered how different my perspective on religion was from that of other atheists. In time, I came to understand that people who have never been religious come to the subject as outsiders who cannot always sympathize with those who formerly were.

But I most definitely was religious. Except I never would have used that word to describe myself. In fact, I would have recoiled from that word as I had been thoroughly indoctrinated against accepting the label by years of hearing that I was "spiritual but not religious." What I enjoyed was not a religion, you see, it was *a relationship*.

That's utter nonsense, by the way. It most definitely *is* a religion. But Christian exceptionalism has always been a key component of the evangelical faith, and ironically I don't think they are exceptional in that regard, either. I believe a majority of world faiths harbor the notion that they are uniquely authentic while all other faiths are dim reflections of the truths of which they themselves are the sole proprietary owners.

That said, my religion was absolutely *relational*. For me, the Christian faith was best summed up in that statement of Jesus in John 17:3 where he said:

> "This is eternal life, that they may know You, the only true God, and Jesus Christ whom You have sent."

That's the lens through which I was taught to view my religion—I viewed it fundamentally as a relationship with a living person who was to be known and experienced in daily life just like any other person would be. Well, not exactly in the same way, I suppose, since this particular person was invisible—detectable only to those who believed in him. In this relationship, one must come with a sincere expectation that God is real and that he can indeed be known by those who want to know him. As another key verse, Hebrews 11:6, explains:

> "Without faith it is impossible to please Him, for he who comes to God must believe that He is and that He is a rewarder of those who seek Him."

So that's exactly what I did. I came to my faith, and to the Object of my worship, in as full a confidence as was humanly possible that he was real and that I could know him in daily experience. More than that, even, as a diligent student of the apostle Paul, I believed that this confidence and that faith could only be supplied by an act of grace—it was a gift of God (see Ephesians 2:8-9) since human beings are so helpless in matters of the spirit that they can only believe if God enables and empowers them to believe.

I believed all of this sincerely. Although I was raised in an evangelical church (Southern Baptist) in the Deep South, I didn't really "get it" until my teen years, at which time I had what I viewed at the time as a conversion experience. I "got saved" during a youth evangelism conference at age 15 and I hit the ground running. I immediately began devouring books of the Bible, reading books on theology for fun and even dabbling a little in comparative religion until apologetics had become a hobby more enjoyable to me than swimming or watching movies. I was that kid.

I spoke at evangelistic meetings, revivals, and youth retreats. I taught Sunday school for nearly ten years. I minored in Bible at my Baptist college and then earned a Master's degree in biblical studies from a Reformed seminary not too far from where I grew up. I was as devoted to Jesus in word and in deed as any other person I knew, and I held nothing back. I ultimately maintained an active faith for 20 years of my life until I reached my mid-thirties, at which time I began to realize that the faith of my youth would no longer fit the adult I had become despite having invested so much of my time and energy and passion into it all those years before.

Looking back on those years today, I now believe that those who handed down the pietistic tradition I received made a crucial mistake in teaching me to believe that God was a person who could be known and experienced just as any other person could. My favorite writer at the time, A.W. Tozer, put it this way:

> …God is a Person and, as such, can be cultivated as any person can. It is inherent in personality to be able to know other

personalities...In making Himself known to us He stays by the familiar pattern of personality. He communicates with us through the avenues of our minds, our wills and our emotions. The continuous and unembarrassed interchange of love and thought between God and the soul of the redeemed man is the throbbing heart of New Testament religion.

This, I've come to believe, was their biggest mistake. They taught me to expect a God who can be known. But there's one key problem, one confounding variable in this equation: You yourself have to create this person in your own mind in order to "know him." That becomes simultaneously this faith's greatest strength and its greatest weakness.

To the surprise of no one who knows me well, the best way I know to explain this dynamic is by referencing three movies that I feel capture what I am trying to say: *A Beautiful Mind*, *Castaway*, and *Nim's Island*. Spoilers will follow, by the way, so reader beware.

Creating Our Own Reality

In *A Beautiful Mind*, the protagonist, John Nash, spent a significant portion of his adult life relating to three individuals who we learn only later in the film are figments of his own imagination. Besides being a brilliant mathematician, Nash is also a paranoid schizophrenic. He sees and hears things that aren't really happening, and he detects intelligible patterns in random arrangements of letters and numbers which no one ever intended them to have (Bible code, anyone?).

It takes Nash until much later in his life to figure out that these people whom he has grown to love and respect don't even exist in real life. Other people tried to tell him so, of course, but he couldn't accept their opinion because he could see these fictitious people with his own eyes and hear them with his own ears. Thanks to his atypical neurochemistry, he himself was creating these people with his own mind. Consequently, no one but he himself could discount their existence. It ultimately fell to him to figure it out in his own way.

I believe an individual's experience of God works the same way. Those of us who were taught to believe in God in time learned to create our own experience of him. This is why I don't spend a great deal of time trying to deconvert people who sincerely believe that God exists. I know better. I know from my own past experience of the divine that this person doesn't only exist as a social convention in whom they believe merely because other people tell them they're supposed to believe in him. They create their own experience of him through their own belief in him.

Which isn't to say it is of no use telling people they are fabricating their own experience. In *A Beautiful Mind*, multiple friends and loved ones tried warning Nash that he was imagining situations and people that weren't really there. At first their admonitions went unheeded as Nash convinced himself they were part of the conspiracy against him. But in time their words found root in his consciousness, and a traumatic event snapped him out of it long enough to figure out for himself that he himself was the sole creator of his own implausible adventures.

Which incidentally reminds me of yet another favorite film analogy: the moment in *Toy Story* when Buzz Lightyear finally figured out he's only a toy—a child's plaything—not an intergalactic space ranger sworn to protect the galaxy from the evil emperor Zurg. A commercial helped him see the reality of his situation, but it cannot be overlooked that Woody had already told him hours before that it was all just his programming.

Woody sowed the seeds of doubt, or perhaps I should say self-discovery, which eventually produced the self-awareness Buzz needed to accurately ascertain his situation. Granted, the paradigm shift took its toll, and momentarily threw Buzz into depression. It's a hard pill to swallow realizing your entire life was built upon a narrative based in little more than the collective imaginations of opportunistic marketing specialists. But he soon figured out there were more immediate, and more real, challenges to face.

My point here is that each of us possesses our own beautiful mind capable of creating beautiful internal stories, some of which may include imagined relationships with people who aren't even there in real life. They can be fun. They can even be fulfilling in their own ways, meeting emotional needs that we have so that we never want to let them go. But we and we alone can pull back the curtain on our own imaginations to see how much of our own experience we create ourselves, perhaps with a little help from institutions that have been enabling people to do this for nearly two millennia.

Making Love Out of Nothing at All

In the movie *Castaway*, Tom Hanks plays Chuck Noland, an overly anxious FedEX executive whose plane crashes into the ocean near a deserted island on which he learns to live completely alone for a period of four long years. Not long after washing ashore on the remote island, he discovers a volleyball amongst the wreckage and soon gives it a name. Wilson soon became his best (and only) friend for the duration of his stay on the lonely island.

Chuck knew good and well that this volleyball wasn't a real person, but he just didn't care. He was lonely, and he needed somebody to talk to, so he painted a face on the ball and created a companion for his seemingly endless exile in the South Pacific. He eventually got off the island, thanks to some creative engineering using only what he could find growing on the island, and in the process he lost his friend in a storm that nearly ended his own life.

Losing Wilson was gut wrenching for him. It was for me, too. I cried in the theater, knowing as well as Noland did that this hollow leather sphere never heard a word he said because it wasn't a sentient being at all. But for him it might as well have been, and the loss of it/him was devastating.

Losing God can be just like that. By the time you finally let him go, you know good and well that you are saying goodbye to someone who was never really there in the first place. He existed only in your own imagination. But it doesn't dull the pain to know this. You are still losing a friend. You had a constant companion, a witness to all of your struggles, losses, and victories, and now he is just gone. How can it not be painful to let that go?

I know some people learned to worship a different kind of deity, but the one I grew up with was highly personal, and like Wilson was crafted to be exactly what I needed at the time. Losing sight of that brought its own peculiar sorrow, and the adjustment to life on your own can take some getting used to.

Becoming Our Own Heroes

To be sure, the movie *Nim's Island* garnered far less attention than the two or three films I've already mentioned. It's nowhere near as well-known, but it captures something about losing God that I don't think I have seen portrayed so clearly anywhere else.

Jodie Foster plays a multi-phobic writer named Alexandra who lives in self-imposed solitary confinement in her own apartment where she dreams up adventures she herself will never go on. Instead she puts her adventurous alter ego, Alex Rover, through every conceivable perilous situation because he can do things she could never do. Where she is weak, he is strong. Where she is afraid, he is brave. Where she can't touch dirt or germs, he dives into the pit of snakes or whatever and always manages to save the day.

In time, though, Alexandra has to learn to face her own fears and leave her safe, antiseptic apartment when she receives a distress call from a little girl out in the middle of nowhere who needs her help. Alexandra decides to overcome her limitations at the encouragement of her imaginary friend, Alex, who coaches her through her challenges and pushes her to accomplish things she never thought she could do without dying of fright.

Alexandra does such a good job of overcoming her own fears that, in time, her imaginary friend decides it's time for him to exit stage left, leaving her all alone to face the challenges that lay ahead of her. She was terrified and heartbroken by his departure, but the truth is that she no longer needed him. It turns out that it was she and she alone who ventured out into the unknown, taking on the big bad world in order to become the hero she previously only wrote about in her novels.

Like the intrepid Alex Rover, whose existence was confined to a work of best-selling fiction, our gods can be viewed as collectivized forms of wish fulfillment. In time we learn to encapsulate our own fears and dreams into personifications of all that we wish we ourselves could become. We praise them and emulate them as if they weren't merely fabrications of our own imaginations, but in time the process has a way of producing in us the very traits we previously could only project onto our invisible creations.

When that time comes, we will see that we never really needed our objects of worship at all. Or perhaps it would be more accurate to say that we did need them for a time, but that eventually our goal should be to wean ourselves off of these temporary placeholders for our own aspirations because it ultimately falls to us to become the heroes in our own stories.

Our religions may very well have been the only way we knew how to preserve and transmit our noblest dreams to successive generations. But if we can manage this time of transition, we may find that the time has come to pack them away into our box of memories because their time has run its course. Now it's our turn to do what needs to be done.

Switching Movies

Each of these stories captures a different aspect of what it's like to lose someone who was never really there in the first place. The fact that these loved ones were never real to begin with doesn't really matter. As human psychology goes, the pain of loss is still just as real even in those instances wherein we know it's all just happening inside our own heads. Somehow that doesn't dull the pain at all.

Those imaginary companions served essential purposes for us, and their disappearance can be traumatic. Many of us go through periods of depression upon realizing someone we cared for, and who cared for us, was never really there. The emptiness that leaves behind can be devastating.

And I suppose I should interject here that I realize not everyone who leaves their faith (or rather has their faith leave them) will be able to relate to this emotional dynamic. Not everyone was taught to believe in a personal God who wanted to walk with and talk with them through the mundane events of their daily lives. But I was taught that, and I internalized it thoroughly.

I also should add here that some people are not as good at conjuring their own personal deities as others of us are because they lack the requisite imagination to make it feel real. People like me, on the other hand? We excelled at it. For us, God was very real. In the fertile soil of our active imaginations, we conjured some of the most enamoring personality traits for our deities so that the loss of them truly broke our hearts.

That is something I've always had difficulty getting my never-religious friends to understand; namely, that it isn't only the most gullible who are taken in by the claims and promises of this religion. Highly intelligent people can cling dearly to their religions as well, even into old age. It turns out the smarter you are, the better you are at rationalizing your beliefs, immunizing them against falsification so that almost nothing will ever change your mind.

Those of us with rich, fertile imaginations dreamed up gods who were far more inviting and believable than the ones our friends saw fit to leave behind so many years sooner than we did. Sure, we were only falling for a lie, but in our minds they became beautiful, captivating lies capable of fueling our entire lives, at times enabling us to achieve our own dreams.

Like Dumbo's magic feather that wasn't really magic at all, what some of us needed was a convincing placebo to capture our imaginations and coax us out of our shells, goading us on to become what we never even knew we had inside us. Gods can be that for people, and that explains at least some of the draw of religion.

In the end, we had to become the heroes of our own stories. But until that time, our eyes were trained on the objects of our worship so that we could learn what it was that we ourselves needed to become. This is what I think our religions were meant to produce in us. Now it's our turn to become like our gods and create a world we want to live in.

Patheos Nonreligious

It Started with Yoga: Unravelling the Threads towards Not Seeing God

Suzanne Titkemeyer, No Longer Qivering

If there is a God, then he really doesn't give a crap or intervene in our day-to-day lives like I was taught during my years as a sold-out Christian. I have recently moved from the idea that there might well be a god, in an agnostic sort of way to going that one god extra.

Back in my earlier inquisitive days, the question I'd been wondering about and had to ask my friend and blogger, Bruce Gerencser, at the time of my burgeoning skepticism was what was the first thing, the very first thread pulled from the tapestry of his faith, that caused it to completely unravel. Was it a slow process or all at once? Bruce was kind enough to answer my question. Indeed, he concluded[1]:

> I went through what I call the stages of deconversion: Evangelical Christianity to Liberal/Progressive Christianity to Universalism to Agnosticism to Atheism. This path was painful, arduous, contradictory, and tiring. I spent many a day and night not only reading and studying, but having long discussions with Polly about what I had read. In November of 2008, I concluded, based on my beliefs, that I could no longer honestly call myself a Christian. Since I no longer believed the Bible was an inspired, inerrant, infallible text, nor did I believe that Jesus was God, rose again from the dead or worked miracles, there was no possible way for me to remain a Christian. At that moment, I went from believer to unbeliever. I call this my born again atheist experience.

---

[1] Gerencser, Bruce (2015). "Question: Was My Deconversion Gradual or Instantaneous?", https://brucegerencser.net/2015/04/question-was-my-deconversion-gradual-or-instantaneous/ (Accessed 06/18/2016)

> So, my deconversion took a long time, but there was also a moment in time when I went from believer to nonbeliever.
>
> If I had to point to one thing that most affected my deconversion, it would be learning that the Bible was not an inspired, infallible, inerrant text. I suspect this is the case for many Evangelicals turned atheist. Bart Ehrman is a good example of this. The belief that the Bible was a perfect text written by God and absolute truth from the hand of God himself, was the foundation of my system of belief. Remove this foundation and the whole house comes tumbling down.

His answer made me start thinking about where exactly that point was in my own journey where the first thread was pulled and the tiniest seed of doubt sprang up.

My moment of thread pulling occurred because of yoga.

At some point in the early 2000s, we were all handed a paper booklet and told to pray, then fill out the book. It was a spiritual inventory list: all the sins you'd done, things you'd done that might open the door to Satan, etc. It was a self-shaming checklist catalog that was a companion to the book we were fixing to study. I no longer remember the book name or the author but some of the questions on the inventory still stick with me, like having to admit to and renounce bathing in urine to glorify the devil.

I had no problem checking off the standard boxes on those things everyone knows is a sin: things like lying or stealing. But all the things on Satan worship and the lists of normal ordinary things they were trying to say were sin, such as watching television or practicing martial arts, were extremely off-putting to me. I could not see what the sin was in certain types of exercise.

One of the biggies in the exercise-sin category was yoga.

Yoga?

Now *that* I really could not fathom because I'd practiced yoga off and on for years, starting in the late 1970s when my oldest child was a new born. Every afternoon and morning, religiously you might say, I put my baby in the baby swing, took off my shoes, switched on the local PBS station and did yoga along with Lilias, host of the yoga program on PBS.

I was trapped in a bad marriage with a man I should never have married, home all day with a new born, trying to regain my pre-baby body and deal with the stress of a mother-in-law who lived next door and who happened to hate me merely for marrying her own son. My twice daily yoga was a ritual that helped me cope with the hopeless situation I was living in. I kept up my yoga practice through the divorce but at some point stopped doing yoga more than once in a while.

The poses helped with my stress levels and the breathing exercises helped the asthma. It was a win-win in my eyes.

So when this spiritual inventory book went around the church and we started going through the booklet, talking about the sins, one by one as a group, I could not help but very timidly ask why yoga was on this list. It had helped me and I felt no need to repent from it, and didn't think it should even be on the list.

Up until that moment, I'd been a true believer, *Kool-Aid*-drinking, Qivering momma. I believed that every word of the Bible was true. I understood that believers would never lie to further their own agendas. And that there was a demon under every bush.

For those of you unaware of Qivering, let me briefly explain. The Patheos blog, *No Longer Qivering*, was chosen as a name by Vyckie Garrison because there is no "you" in "Qivering". "Quiverfull" is a term to represent the growing evangelical movement of pro-life home education. As she states on the blog:

> **Quiverfull** ~ is the idea that truly godly families will "trust the Lord" with their family planning. Children are viewed as unmitigated blessings ("As arrows in the hand of the mighty man, so are the children of one's youth, happy is the man who hath his quiver full of them") and as such, the couple is willing to have as many children as the Lord chooses to bless them with. Artificial or chemical birth control such as the Pill or IUDs are equated with abortion ~ the sin of murdering your own offspring. "Natural" birth control such as Natural Family Planning is not actually "natural" because a couple must abstain at the very time of the month when the woman is naturally more desirous of physical intimacy. All methods of "conception control" is considered a lack of trust in God to provide for the "children of the righteous."
>
> Here's how I described "Quiverfull" back when I still believed it:
>
> ***Radically Pro-Life*** – A.K.A. "Quiverfull," "allowing the Lord to plan our family," or "trusting God with our family planning." It is this ideal which has resulted in our having quite a few more than the average number of children. Why do Christians seek to limit the size of their families through the use of chemical birth control? The truth be told, our reasoning generally parallels that of the abortion culture – additional children will cause inconvenience, financial hardships, lifestyle constraints – all this coupled

with the desire to separate sex from procreation. How can the Church expect to speak with any moral authority on the evils of abortion when we ourselves are guilty of the very anti-life values fueled by the family planning mentality?

That was where I was. For fifteen years. Fifteen long years.

But back to yoga. When I voiced my concerns about yoga, I was told that yoga was a sin because you had to chant the names of demons while doing yoga. Yoga opened a door to the demonic realm and I had better repent and ask God's forgiveness as quickly as possible.

There was something about that I just could not accept. I'd done many hours of yoga and, in my spirit, I felt that what this leader said was very wrong indeed.

I didn't dare talk back but… I shrunk down in my pew and thought about this list and yoga. I could not ever remember doing any chanting in my yoga practice, certainly nothing 'demonic.' So I kept my mouth shut; but I did start thinking for the first time since we joined that church that someone was spewing bullshit about something they knew nothing about.

Later that day, after we arrived home from our usual five-hour Sunday church service, I pulled my ancient and yellowing copy of 'Lilias, Yoga and You' from the bookshelf and started reading through it. I noticed in the very first chapter that the author referred to their faith in Christ and practice in yoga. This was confirmation of what I thought: that yoga was simply a harmless gentle exercise that held no religious connection in the way I'd practiced it. I realized for the first time, as a Christian, that sometimes people put additional rules onto believers that had nothing to do with Christ, reality or faith.

Once that first thread was pulled out, others followed, until the big messy tangle of threads that was my leaving the old church unraveled.

Funny how some small thing can start your journey in an unimaginable direction.

Yes, I still do yoga, but I stick with the water version now. If you lose your balance in the Warrior Pose and fall down, it's much gentler to fall into the arms of water than the cold hard floor of the gym.

I vividly remember the last two years before I walked away from my old church. Every Saturday night or early Sunday morning, I would have a nightmare involving church. They always involved church. For example, it might be something like the pastor calling me out for some imagined sin from the pulpit and the two of us fighting in the sanctuary. One time, I dreamed that my home was filled with an abundance, a crazy wild abundance, of things, like opening the bread box to have three fresh loaves leaping out instead of one, or opening the silverware drawer and finding set after set of silver in the drawer. That dream was terrifying because I was attempting to get my pastor to see the heaping helpings of abundance everywhere I turned in my home, and he was scoffing, saying hateful things.

It wasn't only the pastor I dreamed about. Church members whom I knew to have issues or to be a bit on the hateful side featured prominently. I woke up one Sunday morning horrified that I'd dreamed of beheading a fellow parishioner in the chapel out back. Church does funny things to you. Religion does funny things to you.

But occasionally the dreams would not feature anyone I knew. I dreamed one morning that I was walking down a dark country road, late at night, and I spied God coming down from the heavens like a white-robed wraith. I ran to him, calling out, screaming that He was all I wanted. As God drew near to me, I could see him instantly change from the Almighty to a dark demon, a demon who grabbed my hands and would not let go.

The nightmares stopped as soon as my husband convinced me to go with him to a local mainstream United Methodist church. I've not had another nightmare involving any church or pastor or churchgoers again.

Some ten years away and I've come to conclude now that it wasn't 'the devil' making me have all these horrible dreams. I was told when I timidly asked about nightmares at the old church that I was under direct attack from Satan in order to stop me going to church. But that wasn't it.

I think now that it was my subconscious screaming at me to wake up and run! What I could not perceive as unhealthy, twisted and cult-like while I was awake (because I was in denial, brainwashed even), my inner mind knew was bad. All stimuli had to be switched off for the message to make its way into my active mind. The inner parts screaming at me to run away as quickly as possible, to protect myself and go.

Starting to know that I had to leave wasn't hard. But what was hard was the *actual* going, the giving myself permission to leave a toxic environment for a healthier future. After what I went through leaving my old church, I think I now have some small inkling on a very primitive level why abused women stay with their abusers. Giving yourself permission to leave is hard. It requires that you recognize and admit to yourself, that regardless of how hard you tried to make things work, that it was never going to work. It's admitting a failure, even if that failure isn't caused by you. It is hard to give up a dream, a vision of how things really should be, and to finally be able to take a long hard look at the reality of your situation.

It goes well beyond the practicalities of detangling yourself financially and physically from a religious organization. It involves almost amputating yourself from the body, sometimes in a radical and bloody way. But it's worth it, after you finish licking your wounds that is. Because no one else at the place you're leaving is going to give you permission to go. They're going to insist you don't have that right, or that you are deceived, to please stay because it is 'God's will.'

Let's get one thing straight, if you are being spiritually abused, none of the abusers has the right to stop you from leaving. However, they will try their darnedest to stop you and insist that they are doing it out of love.

Even after ten years, there are still people I run into from the old church who insist I'm sinning by having left, or that I'm going to hell for working at *No Longer Quivering*, or they think I'm running around doing 'UnGodly' things. You know, like yoga. They don't understand that I hold all my own power and their attempts to control me are like mosquitoes trying to bring down a Harrier jet.

You don't owe them explanations.

You don't need them to give you permission to leave.

You don't have to keep allowing them to try and make you feel guilty.

You are strong.

You are enough.

Science and Medicine: Not Seeing God in Your Prayers, Thank You Very Much

Kevin Davis, SecularVoices

The following letter was posted to SecularVoices on May 27, 2015—exactly one month after my youngest son, Grayson, was unexpectedly born 3 months early, at 27 weeks, weighing 2 pounds, 7 ounces. Grayson would ultimately spend over 2 months in the neonatal intensive care unit, making steady progress with just minor setbacks along the way, as close to a best-case-scenario as we could have hoped for, but still testing our mental and emotional strength while inspiring us at the same time. After sitting next to Grayson's bed in the NICU every day during the first month, the emotional roller coaster my wife and I found ourselves riding was beginning to calm down and I began using this time watching over him as an opportunity to think about what we've been through as a family, reflecting on our relatively unique situation—atheist parents with a sick child, surrounded by believers offering their prayers. This was something we found little value in aside from a nice gesture of verbal support. As more and more of Grayson's progress was attributed to a deity rather than the well-trained and skilled doctors and nurses assigned to him, my frustrations grew and I decided to use my blog as a way to loosen the release valve and allow some steam to escape. What I didn't expect was the widespread attention the piece would draw, as well as the reactions I would observe from both the atheist and religious communities.

An Atheist's Open Letter to Those Praying for His Son

As many of my readers have noticed, I haven't posted anything in about a month. That's because on April 27, my life got exponentially busier, when my wife went into preterm labor and delivered our son 12 weeks early. Grayson now lies in the local neonatal intensive care unit, where he's been since he was born. He's doing well and continues to grow and gain weight, but the experience has been draining—physically, emotionally, and financially. As things normalize and he comes home, activity on the site will resume and most likely increase, since the field of GOP presidential hopefuls is an ever-expanding source of church/state separation editorial fodder. I don't normally post personal stories such as this, but since I've found myself in a situation that has caused monumental frustration—with my only true sympathetic outlet being my wife (who is probably tired of hearing my rants by now)—I've decided to turn to the loyal audience of my blog. I hope that you'll read this, and more importantly, share it with believers, so they better understand what goes through an atheist's mind when we hear, "Sending you prayers," or something similar.

The following open letter may upset you. You may feel insulted because when it comes to matters of faith, people are more apt to take criticism personally and react defensively when their religious beliefs are brought into question. Please know it is not my intent to offend, because, as I said earlier, I am truly grateful for the offers of support and kind words from family and friends. But sometimes we're faced with emotional situations that escalate to a boiling point. I'm at that point, and it's time to open a vent.

I'd like to open this letter by acknowledging and thanking those who have shared that they're praying for my son, who was born prematurely and since then has resided in our local neonatal intensive care unit. I realize your intentions are good and that you believe your prayers are helping him grow stronger. By appealing to a deity that you believe exists and listens to your pleas, you feel you're offering your support and contributing to my son's cause in some way. Because I realize you believe you're helping, I thank you for doing what you feel will help my son get healthy and strong.

However, my wife and I are atheists. We don't believe in the supernatural, and we have good reasons for that, but that's a topic for another day. We have placed our trust in science and modern medicine, and we are absolutely amazed at what is possible, thanks to medical research and man's advanced understanding of biological sciences. In fact, if we had not placed our trust in medicine, or lived in different times, or belonged to a religion that frowns upon fertility treatments or medically assisted conception, we would not have any children at all.

If we left it to a god to decide, our 4-year-old son, Ryan, would not exist. He would not have been conceived without modern science and fertility doctors. And if we had become pregnant on our own, he very well could have died in childbirth without the intervention of doctors and nurses, as my wife had to have an emergency C-section after a difficult attempt at childbirth that put Ryan at risk. If we left it to a god to decide, our 4-week-old, Grayson, would not exist. He also would not have been conceived without modern science and an IVF procedure. And if we had become pregnant on our own that time, he would have died shortly after being born prematurely, without the intervention and constant care of doctors and nurses. Thanks to medical breakthroughs, **not miracles**, we have two children and get to experience all of the joy, pride, love, and everything else that comes with raising them—all of which would have been replaced with sorrow and heartache had we left it to a god to decide. We would have had no children, and like many of the religious, would have attempted to rationalize this in an attempt at comforting ourselves by saying it was god's plan, or that everything happens for a reason.

So should you be appealing to that same supernatural entity to help protect my son—a child that he never wanted to exist? Does that make sense to you?

There's a reason that the sick go to hospitals full of doctors and nurses when they need healing, instead of seeking out faith healers or priests, or staying home to pray as their only means of treatment. It's because most believers realize that prayer isn't an effective cure for anything. Even so, the religious are so quick to thank their god when they or loved ones recover from illnesses rather than show their gratitude to the men and women who made it their life's work to treat the sick. Let's be honest, if an all-knowing, all-powerful and all-loving god wants to heal the sick or let them die, what's your prayer going to do? Aren't you just telling him something he already knows? Aren't you asking him for something he already knows you want? Isn't your god going to do what he wants despite your pleas? Isn't that your rationale when your prayers aren't "answered"... that it was "God's will"? So really, what's the point? And that's ***IF*** (a monumental IF) a deity exists and you're praying to the right one, out of the >2000 that have been worshiped throughout human history.

So now you're thinking, "So what? What does it hurt that I want to pray for you?" It's not that it hurts anything or anyone directly. Your prayers are your prerogative. By telling us you're praying, you're saying to us that you want to do something to help, and that's appreciated. But the avenue of assistance that you've chosen is one that we feel is an ineffective one. You're telling us, "I'm going to do something for you that has no value to you. I'm really doing it to make *me* feel like I'm helping." If you want to help a religious person who believes that prayer actually does something, then by all means, pray until you're hoarse. But if you want to do something in your power to help a family who places their trust in the doctors, nurses, medicine, and technology that heals the sick and is the reason my son is alive and sleeping in my arms as I type this in the NICU, then do something tangible. Donate to families in need or medical research. Contact your representatives when a vote comes up that might inhibit scientific advancement. Call a friend or family member who's in crisis and be a compassionate ear. Volunteer with a local group without an underlying agenda (like preaching to those benefiting from their good deeds). There are so many things you can do that are infinitely more effective than talking to a god who already knows what you're going to say and will do what he wants anyway.

So when you tell me you're praying for Grayson, I'm going to be gracious and say thank you. But know this—your gesture does more to make *you* feel better than it does to comfort me or help my son fight for his life in his incubator. Everything does *not* happen for a reason, and my two children are anything *but* god's plan. I feel grateful every single day for mankind's scientific and medical advancements.

***

After it was posted, the letter made its rounds among atheist and secular social media pages and was shared a great deal. Commenters began sharing their support and asking what they could do to help. Shortly thereafter, a fundraising page was set up to help with Grayson's medical costs. The fundraiser was a huge success, thanks in large part to the secular community, as well as some religious folks who understood my viewpoint and why I wrote the letter. Thanks to the way Medicaid works for newborns, as well as the Affordable Care Act, Grayson had little out of pocket medical expenses while in the hospital, so some funds received were donated to a charity who helps families in similar (and much worse) situations than ours, and some were put away toward his future education.

During our time in the NICU with Grayson, we became friendly with some of the nurses who cared for him regularly. I never expressed to anyone there what my views were on religion, and I didn't openly scoff when I overheard other families around us thanking God for their child's progress. As far as I knew, no one was aware we were atheists. But a few days after the letter was posted and took off, one of the nurses quietly pulled me aside. She started by saying, "A few of us have read the letter you wrote." Here we go. Immediately my mind is telling me, "This is going to be so awkward." She continues, "I just wanted to say thank you. Sometimes it's so frustrating to us when we work so hard for these kids because we love what we do and we love these kids. And then they thank God for saving their kids. We don't do this job for the accolades, but it's nice to be recognized for the work we do, because we really do work very hard and this job is emotionally draining." Sigh of relief. I just smiled, with tears in my eyes—they seemed to always be there, just on the cusp of falling down, through the sixty-plus days in the NICU—and thanked her again for her work and dedication. Caring for kids who are barely clinging to life, many hooked up to machines bigger than they are, while standing next to their worried parents, has got to be one of the most difficult careers possible. NICU nurses are part caregiver, part counselor, part teacher, and part coach. They're amazing.

Unfortunately, though, not all readers responded with empathy and love. About a week after the letter went viral in the secular community, it seemed to be making the rounds among the religious. When that happened, the comments section exploded. I would estimate that more than half of the comments from Christians were an attempt to either explain the purpose of prayer, teach me about their religion, or explain God's plan for me and my family.

Thanks, but no thanks. You missed the point.

The rest of the comments from Christians were a combination of respectful acknowledgements of my situation peppered with an assortment of very angry outbursts telling me what a terrible person I am. And that's when some of the most heartless comments I've ever received on the internet started coming in.

"My logic and scientific knowledge do not allow me to give you my hard earned money. Logically it would not benefit me."

"What a total bitch."

"This is just a rant to rally the non-believers behind you to get money for your kid. Anyone who doesn't agree with you is 'missing the point' or a 'religious fanatic'- that's simply not true. However- I can say this, Kevin I think you're a dick."

"Oh I'll find this fucker."

"I hope your stabbed you dumb bitch."

"They will find you! Lol but seriously it has happened I'd be careful."

And then this gem:

"You and your family will get what they deserve, trust me. People are going to retaliate and it's not good to put out information anybody can easily find you just through a search."

Did he seriously threaten a baby in an incubator? Feel that Christian love pour over you.

I'm not the type of person who lets these types of comments get to me. Many people on the internet like to take advantage of their perceived anonymity and remove their filter, showing the world how vile they are. That's their problem, not mine.

A lot of Christian commenters tried to make the common argument that God gave doctors and nurses the skills and knowledge, or ability to learn those skills, to save Grayson's life. That doesn't make sense to me either. If God knows how to heal the sick and possesses our medical knowledge before we discover it, then why didn't we have this knowledge thousands of years ago? Why did so many humans have to die from curable diseases throughout history just so we could make these discoveries in very recent times? Why did thousands of parents in my situation watch their children arrive prematurely only to see them die hours later because modern neonatal care didn't exist yet? Why did so many men and women remain childless because of biological flaws that were no fault of their own? Is that a benevolent god? No.

Some others even attempted to make the mean-spirited argument that my wife and I had so much trouble conceiving because we were atheists and God didn't want us to bear children. Well that's just stupid. If that were true, then no atheists would be able to conceive. And if God didn't want us to have kids, and we conceived anyway, then what does that say about this omnipotent god? We won? Humans are now more powerful than God?

So the question remains, is Grayson a "gift from God" or a "miracle baby" like our religious friends and family members believe? Or is Grayson the child God didn't want us to conceive in the first place, tried to take away with a premature delivery, but was made possible through man's discoveries in fertility research and saved by neonatal medical advancements? Has our progress in modern medicine outlasted our psychological need for prayer? Now that we have the knowledge and skill to solve many of the medical problems we used to beg a deity to cure, have we outgrown this phase of humanity? I think we're moving in that direction.

It's time we take back the power we gave to imaginary gods in the sky and shift our efforts from kneeling with hands clasped to standing with our hands ready to assist.

Not Seeing God through Celebrations in Life

Galen Broaddus, Across Rivers Wide

In January of 2017, I got to experience something that not a great number of people get to experience: I saw a decision come down in a federal lawsuit, finding a state statute to be unconstitutional, with my name on it as a plaintiff.

The lawsuit, which was brought by myself and the Center for Inquiry (CFI), directly challenged the marriage statute of my home state of Illinois, which gave the legal authority to solemnize marriages to select classes of individuals, most notably judges and religious officiants—but not secular celebrants wholly unaffiliated with any religious organization. CFI, as a nonreligious organization certifying celebrants, and myself, as a CFI-certified secular celebrant, brought the suit in order to secure the same right for secular celebrants, and fortunately we were able to prevail in federal district court.

Despite my confidence that the court would see reason on this point, given that we were merely asking for equal treatment under the law, I found myself afterwards reflecting on just how strange it was that, only a mere five years after casting off religion in my own life, I would be in a place where I would not only be serving in such a role as a secular celebrant but actively advocating for it.

How Religion Helped Me See the Importance of Ceremony

It was five years ago, as of the time of this writing, that I had a moment of clarity where I realized that a long period of reflection, deep intellectual study, and engagement with atheists on the Internet had led me to reject the religious beliefs I had been taught during my childhood as the son of a Baptist minister in rural Illinois. Because I had spent a substantial amount of time engaging with the ideas of atheism and freethought generally, I had some foundations on which to land when I finally hit this realization, which cushioned my "fall from grace" a little.

That childhood did leave a number of indelible marks on me, of course, some of which I have had to learn to cope with and retrain my thoughts to eliminate. Not all of those experiences left me wishing that I could have been spared that exposure, though.

As a PK—a "preacher's kid," although the nomenclature is somewhat flexible—I had a front row seat for virtually all of the facets of the life of the many Baptist churches my father ministered in, from my infancy through my teen years. Although we would have never dared to couch them in terms of "sacraments," that dirty *Catholic* word, there were of course many regular rituals that were part and parcel of the religious community of the church. The most significant, naturally, was baptism, a rite performed by immersion on any individual who could demonstrate an understanding of the basic doctrines of Christianity and a procedure that would signal that individual's full entrance not only into the fold of Christendom but also into the full life of the church community as well.

I remember well the feeling of seeing individuals—often children, but also frequently adults—stepping into a baptistery, answering a few questions from the minister to confirm their full understanding of the rite itself, and then, "in the name of the Father and the Son and the Holy Spirit," being dunked and coming up to exclamations of delight from the congregation. (Indeed, I remember my own baptism at the age of eleven and how ecstatic that feeling of validation and acceptance was.)

This is not to say that I was successfully indoctrinated to be a full-fledged believer in the rightness of ritual. There were plenty of ritualistic elements of my upbringing that I recoiled from or even rebelled against, such as the ways that these evangelical churches would force displays of patriotism into religious contexts. (Pledging allegiance to the US flag, the Christian flag, and the Bible in succession during Vacation Bible School every summer always struck me as very odd.) But these rites did instill in me the conviction that ceremony had a function and a role in the lives of individuals and communities.

As I grew older, I began to have more of a personal role in some of these functions as a musician. It was here that I first began my involvement with the most ubiquitous ceremonies of life: weddings and funerals. I started playing piano when I was around four years old, and I was playing hymns in church essentially as soon as I was musically conversant enough to handle them. Music would eventually become my primary involvement in churches, but outside the regular activities of church life, beyond the Sundays and Wednesdays, family and church members had needs for a pianist.

It was here that I really recognized what ceremony could do: It could bring together a group of people for the celebration of a milestone of life, whether that was the celebration of a new union or a life lived or the entry of a member into a community (as with baptism). Having grown up with a father who facilitated these ceremonies as part of his pastoral duties, I now found myself fascinated by my own ability to help make them possible, to play a vital role in marking these moments of life.

So it didn't take me long, once I found myself on the outside of religion and its own particular ceremonial turns, to consider the inevitable question: Is this something that atheists, agnostics, secular humanists, and non-religious people still find useful?

Why Ceremonies for People without Dogma?

One of the most common remarks I hear when I talk about the idea of secular ceremonies is that they just flat-out aren't necessary. "Secular people," they might say, "don't need to have ceremonies that replace religious ones. Civil authorities can provide the basics where needed for legal unions and such."

That, however, is not how matters have largely turned out where religion has been on the decline. The British Humanist Association, which has been lobbying for a number of years for humanist weddings to be legally recognized in the whole of the United Kingdom, has noted an increase in such weddings in England, Wales, and Northern Ireland since 2012 despite an overall decrease in weddings, and in Scotland (where these unions *are* legally recognized), humanist weddings have now overtaken both the Catholic Church and the Church of Scotland in numbers.[1] In Australia, since the advent of Civil Marriage Celebrants in 1973 as an alternative to ministers and official marriage registering authorities, civil ceremonies have overtaken religious ones, surpassing them in 1999 and constituting 70% of all marriages by 2011.[2]

---

[1] "Humanist weddings continue to surge in number, bucking national trend." *British Humanist Association*, April 28, 2016.
https://humanism.org.uk/2016/04/28/humanist-weddings-continue-to-surge-in-number-bucking-national-trend/. (Accessed 04/02/2017)

[2] "Losing My Religion?" *Australian Bureau of Statistics*, last updated March 17, 2014.
http://www.abs.gov.au/ausstats/abs@.nsf/Lookup/4102.0Main+Features30Nov+2013. (Accessed 04/02/2017)

The US, which has also seen its overall religiosity waning, is beginning to see similar trends. It isn't entirely unsurprising, though—after all, even people who leave religion don't necessarily stop caring about marking these moments, and when they do so, they are going to seek out alternatives to traditional religious ceremonies if they can. (This is even true for people who fall away from religion but not from theism. One individual who discussed the matter with me said that they would feel hypocritical running back to the church just because they wanted to get married, like they only needed God for their big day and not so much before or after.)

So if it's true from an empirical standpoint that decreased religiosity doesn't necessarily result in apathy toward ceremonies, *why*?

I think my own interaction with religion bears out one reason: *Ceremonies bring together a group of people for the purpose of sharing in an act of meaning-making.*

One of the benefits of a secular celebrant for secular people—and particularly for atheists, agnostics, and secular humanists who generally have certain shared views about the universe (for instance, a lack of belief in the afterlife)—is that they can have an individual who also shares similar beliefs and values help them facilitate such a milestone. Yet, like most secular celebrants, I don't typically perform "atheist ceremonies," *per se*, ones where the beliefs of an atheistic worldview are laid bare for all to see. Nor do I only perform such ceremonies for non-theists.

There are of course several reasons for that, the most important of which is that seldom are all of the participants non-religious, let alone non-theists. (I work out of central Illinois, which isn't quite "Bible Belt" but is certainly Bible Belt-adjacent and thus still fairly religious.) Secular ceremonies have an advantage to religious ones in this regard, since ceremonies that aren't religious in nature don't inherently exclude anyone—they just don't center religion by giving it a vital place. My experiences with wedding ceremonies in particular have been that religious people in attendance hardly even notice; they enjoy the parts that resonate across lines of religion, the parts that talk about the joy of two lives becoming one and the importance of human connection and community, and it isn't even important that these ideas are being couched in entirely non-religious terms.

That itself might be the most powerful aspect of secular ceremonies: *They are a way to demonstrate how shared meaning can be celebrated without ever invoking God or the supernatural.* In unions, we exalt the joy of love, commitment, and sharing ourselves with another being; in memorials, we celebrate the ways in which our lives, regardless of any potential hereafter, can touch those around us and leave an impact that long outlasts our own short existence.

And this meaning-making is not limited to these two ubiquitous events. There are also coming of age ceremonies, in which we recognize the path from childhood to adolescence or adolescence to adulthood and how it symbolizes the way in which we all must grow as individuals and cultures. Some individuals even choose to mark the entry of new lives into their families, such as children newly born or adopted, and their own expansion of their familial sphere to incorporate more people in their love and connection.

These are not religious values in the strictest sense, they are *human values*, rooted in our need for social connection and existential understanding. Yes, religions do try to address those needs, and for that reason, rituals constitute a significant part of their function and their persuasive power. But the core of that is something that exists outside religion and cannot be contained by it.

On a personal level, I take great joy in helping facilitate these moments. The part about rituals that often bothered me profoundly was how impersonal they felt, as though they were more about going through certain motions than trying to bring out some genuine meaning. With secular ceremonies, there is no liturgy, no sequence of actions to act out with little thought about their importance. Not every moment has to be treated with a cookie-cutter approach. I can craft a ceremony for an individual or couple that meets their specific needs, that expresses their own beliefs and values, in a ceremony that really does end up being a participatory act of meaning between individuals and those who share in their moment.

Not every non-religious person is going to feel this way about secular ceremonies, to be sure, and there are certainly many secular individuals I've met who have expressed absolutely no interest in ceremonies of any kind, either out of apathy or out of a rejection of the idea because of experiences with religion. Far be it from me to dissuade them about their own convictions. But there is a wealth of evidence that this is not likely to be the general outcome as religion fades in societies, and more and more, people will look to individuals like secular celebrants to fill that role.

And even those who are personally indifferent to the idea of secular ceremonies should remember that in a good many countries, even ones that are becoming increasingly secular, these are not live options, either because of legal inequities in permitting secular or humanist celebrants to perform ceremonies that have equal legal standing to civil or religious ones or because religion has crowded out their secular competitors in these terms. You may not have any desire to have a non-religious memorial service, but someone else—even an otherwise religious person—may want that, and when it is not made available, they may instead settle for a religious ceremony that does not respect the wishes of the deceased and may in fact cause more pain to the grieving.

It is the mark of a civilized society that we support the availability of institutions and practices that we may never personally benefit from, if they provide a tangible social good. Secular ceremonies, I would contend, are such a good, and access to them helps promote secularism and offer an alternative to religious ceremonies so that no one feels obligated to set aside their apprehensions in order to find closure or mark an important life event. Supporting their equal access under the law is not only a just action but also a significant way for secularists to put their convictions about church and state into action. Advocating for their widespread availability normalizes secular living and further erodes religious privilege.

Secular ceremonies are not going anywhere anytime soon. They serve an important role in the lives of many, and their existence is itself a sign of progress toward more open and secular societies. Perhaps even more importantly, though, they allow us to demonstrate how we make meaning in the face of claims that we cannot intelligibly do so without God.

And that alone is something worth celebrating.

Not Seeing God at the Movies

Andrew Spitznas, Atheist Cinephile

"Poetry is a making oneself at home in the world, of showing how we share the world."[1]

Hans-Georg Gadamer

"There's no eye in the sky
Just our love
No unobstructed views, no perfect truths
Just our love"[2]

"Unobstructed Views," Death Cab for Cutie

"Where do you get your morals from, if you don't believe in God?" As atheists, we get used to answering this question, each in our own idiosyncratic way.

When asked, I reply that I find guidance from a mixture of common sense, compassion, philosophy, and the arts. Music plays a small part here, as I find useful morsels in songs by the likes of Peter Gabriel, Rush, and Death Cab for Cutie (as quoted above). The 20th Century German philosopher Hans-Georg Gadamer (again, cited above) named poetry his guiding star.

As a lifelong film lover, and now, as a film critic, I look to the best of cinema as a source of knowledge, wisdom, and moral guidance. To borrow again from Death Cab for Cutie, movies are not sacred texts, nor repositories of perfect truths. Instead, I look to them as generations from centuries past would've regarded Aesop's Fables or narrative paintings, offering insight through their composition, plot, and characters.

---

[1] Watson, Peter (2014). *The Age of Atheists: How We Have Sought to Live Since the Death of God* (New York: Simon & Schuster), p. 505.
[2] Death Cab for Cutie. "Unobstructed Views." *Codes and Keys*, Atlantic, 2011.

In the course of this chapter, I would like to walk you through a gallery of my most prized films from around the world. Not only are these movies admirable works of art, but they illustrate eight key aspects of atheism and secular humanism.

Rejection of the Existence of God

It is self-evident that atheism would begin with the assertion that God is a fictional construct. For me as a film critic, it was less obvious where to turn to illuminate this notion.

As a lover of intelligent science fiction, I was tempted to dig into Spielberg's *A.I.* or Alex Garland's more recent *Ex Machina*. With their stories of human beings crafting and then lording it over sentient machines, both films compellingly persuade the viewer that a powerful creator is inevitably fickle, manipulative, imprisoning, and cruel. Even if it's not quite science fiction, Peter Weir's splendid allegory *The Truman Show* makes the same points.

But for this section, I would prefer to highlight the work of Swedish director Ingmar Bergman (1918-2007). Over the course of his 57 year directing career, Bergman molded demanding, emotionally intense films that contemplate darker aspects of existence and human relationships. I'd like to consider two of them briefly.

Bergman's 1963 film *Winter Light* unfolds during a dreary Sunday in the life of Pastor Tomas Ericsson. It opens with Ericsson presiding over a joyless, sparsely attended morning service, and then concludes with his going through the same motions in the evening at a second, empty church.

In between, Pastor Ericsson attempts to counsel a despondent fisherman, ironically named Jonas. Rather than fleeing God like the biblical Jonah, this fisherman is seeking God but coming up empty. The well is just as dry for Ericsson, who fails to provide Jonas with spiritual comfort. Reflecting upon a Europe that has suffered through two world wars, Pastor Ericsson hasn't abandoned belief in God, but has concluded that the deity must be a remote, monstrous being.

A later Bergman film, *Fanny and Alexander*, is a richer human drama than *Winter Light*. Replacing the unrelentingly grim visages and depressing black and whites of the earlier film, *Fanny and Alexander* uses a more varied palette of human emotion and color.

Fanny and Alexander are the son and daughter of an exuberant theater family in early 20th Century Sweden. The film opens with their parents taking part in a Christmas drama, in which their father Oscar proclaims that God the Father protected the infant Jesus. Oscar then concludes their play with a benediction for God's protection of them all.

Sadly, Oscar's blessing goes unfulfilled. Soon after a Dionysian holiday dinner, he takes ill and dies. His grief-stricken wife Emelie rushes into remarriage with the local bishop, who turns out to be as monstrous as the God of *Winter Light*. Bishop Edvard sadistically abuses Alexander for his youthful defiance and demands that Emelie shed all external trappings of her earlier life.

Bergman and his longtime cinematographer, the legendary Sven Nyqvist, are hardly subtle in contrasting the before-and-after quality of Emelie and her children's existences. Whereas their home with Oscar was gaudy and baroque, "home" with Edvard is grotesquely austere.

The helpless suffering of Fanny and Alexander perfectly illustrates how the problem of evil makes implausible the existence of a benign deity. And how ironic that their life is made worse under the shepherding of one of God's supposed ministers!

Bergman drew here from his own childhood as the son of a Lutheran minister. No doubt young Alexander was also the director's mouthpiece when he says, "If there's a God, then he's a shit, and I'd like to kick him in the butt."[1]

A Critical Eye on Man-Made Institutions, Including Religion

For me, being a freethinker implicitly involves striving to be a critical thinker on all issues. Emerging from a background of religious belief, I first had to apply close scrutiny to my Christian faith.

For this section, the easy path would've been a shout-out to the 2016 Oscar winner for Best Picture, *Spotlight*. While this dramatization of *The Boston Globe*'s uncovering of priestly pedophilia deserves every plaudit it's received, I've elected to turn my attention to the efforts of director Alex Gibney.

Gibney has been working like a man on fire lately, making over twenty documentaries since 2005. His films have smartly covered subjects as diverse as Steve Jobs, American torture tactics, Al-Qaeda, and Lance Armstrong.

His 2015 film, *Going Clear: Scientology and the Prison of Belief*, offered skeptical viewers plenty of gratification in seeing smug Tom Cruise and sleazy David

---

[1] *Fanny and Alexander*, directed by Ingmar Bergman (1982; Janus), DVD.

Miscavige receive some well-deserved, unfavorable exposure. I would argue, however, that *Mea Maxima Culpa: Silence in the House of God* is Gibney's most important documentary to date.

Like *Spotlight*, Gibney's 2012 film focuses upon the sexual abuse scandal within the Roman Catholic Church. Unlike *Spotlight*, however, *Mea Maxima Culpa* extends its view beyond New England to the Catholic Church worldwide.

Like a lawyer masterfully building his case from scratch, Gibney starts with a single instance of a pedophile priest before moving outwards. Father Lawrence Murphy was the headmaster of a Milwaukee-area Catholic school for the deaf from 1950–1974, preying upon countless vulnerable boys during that time.

Using interviews with a handful of his victims, Gibney shows how these former students, once attaining adulthood, attempted to obtain justice and prevent further molestations. Despite lobbying two archbishops, the police department, and a district attorney, these men were met with inaction and indifference.

Gibney then broadens his scope to reveal convincingly that priestly predation is a worldwide phenomenon. Whether in Boston, Ireland, or another school for the deaf in Verona, Italy, the pattern of abusive priests and institutional inertia remained the same for decades.

Not satisfied to stop there, *Mea Maxima Culpa* draws from interviews and the historical record to demonstrate that Popes Paul VI, John Paul II, and Benedict XVI were fully aware of this problem, but were disgustingly negligent and enabling in their responses. (Being made in 2012, Gibney of course has nothing to say about Pope Francis, who came to power one year later.)

Most damningly, before rising to the papacy, Pope Benedict (as Cardinal Ratzinger) was head of the Congregation for the Defense of the Faith. In this capacity, Ratzinger was the church official most aware of the prevalence of pedophilia within the priestly ranks. Despite this, when a Milwaukee archbishop (Rembert Weakland) finally decided to act upon the allegations against Father Murphy, instead of praising Weakland, Ratzinger chided him for his lack of docility.

A viewer of *Mea Maxima Culpa* cannot fail to be sickened by its narrative. By bringing to light the Church's longstanding pattern of shuffling pederasts to unknowing parishes, paying off victims for their silence, and favoring abusive priests over congregants, Gibney's documentary is a fatal indictment of an entire institution.

Early in his film, Gibney's camera lingers on a statue outside the Milwaukee school, a portrayal of Jesus compassionately laying his hands upon two children. *Mea Maxima Culpa* shows us a religious reality that is far different. Like a polluting megacorporation, the Church is far more interested in image, profit, and perpetuating its cultural dominance, and comparatively doesn't give a damn about its rank-and-file customers.

An Embrace of Naturalism

In rejecting the supernatural, atheists affirm the reality that only natural forces are at work in our universe. As such, the scientific method is one of the crucial ways to comprehend the world around us.

Many great movies buttress a secularist's fascination with nature and science. *Particle Fever*, the exuberant film that shows us experimental and theoretical physicists discovering the Higgs-Boson Particle, immediately comes to mind here. So do the documentaries of Chilean director Patricio Guzman, whose recent films *Nostalgia for the Light* and *The Pearl Button* combine a curiosity about astronomy, archaeology, anthropology, and recent South American history in a gorgeous feat of poetic alchemy.

However, no director melds artistry with a scientist's curiosity more consistently than German-born Werner Herzog. Whether considering the psychology of a failed actor who lived and died among Alaskan wildlife (*Grizzly Man*), the history and future implications of artificial intelligence (*Lo and Behold, Reveries of the Connected World*), or the research of biologists and geologists in Antarctica (*Encounters at the End of the World*), Herzog never fails to kindle wonder and curiosity.

With his 2010 film *Cave of Forgotten Dreams*, Herzog takes us inside the Chauvet Cave in the south of France. Closed to everyone but a few select scientists, Herzog and a minimalist crew were granted brief access to create his documentary.

With cave paintings that are an estimated 32,000 years old, from a time when Neanderthals and *Homo sapiens* still co-existed in Europe, the huge number of pristine polychromatic works in Chauvet are twice as old as any other known paintings. Smartly choosing for the first time in his 50+ year directing career to use 3D technology, Herzog demonstrates how these Paleolithic artists used the natural curves of cave walls and stalactites to add perspective to their paintings.

Plenty of the run time of *Cave of Forgotten Dreams* is rightly and simply devoted to the contemplation of this prehistoric art. With such images as an open-mouthed horse, caught mid-exertion, it is hard to imagine anyone leaving this film unimpressed with the craft on display. The artists even painted bison with eight legs and rhinos with multiple horns to signify movement, resulting in what Herzog aptly describes as protocinema.

As in his other documentaries named above, Herzog mingles unforgettable imagery with interviews with knowledgeable scientists, conducted in his inimitably off-beat style. In the midst of witnessing cutting-edge mapping technology that captures every millimeter of the cave, we learn, for instance, that one of the lead Chauvet scientists was a juggler before turning to archaeology.

Other scientists show us discoveries that are contemporaneous with the cave paintings. One archaeologist plays "The Star Spangler Banner" on a reconstructed flute, while another in charmingly awkward fashion demonstrates the use of an ancient atlatl (a spear-throwing tool).

For me, one of the best measures of a movie's impact is whether it leaves you hungry to learn more. By this test, *Cave of Forgotten Dreams* succeeded marvelously, inspiring me to travel to France to observe some Paleolithic art in the Dordogne River Valley. Of course, nothing can compare to seeing strikingly vivid images of prehistoric mammals firsthand, but Herzog's film is the next best thing.

A Realistic View of Humanity

When I deconverted from Christianity, a major piece of baggage I needed to discard was the notion that human nature (including me) is fallen and broken, with a hole that only God could fill. How liberating to recognize instead that all of us have our share of light and darkness within. How freeing to accept that I am capable of bettering myself, that humankind can make progress as a whole towards greater goodness and kindness.

In choosing a film for this section, I felt I could go in one of two directions. First, I could've selected a movie that illustrates the best and worst of humanity. A Holocaust-themed film like *Schindler's List* or the more recent *Son of Saul* could've worked here. Or I could've chosen the Coen Brothers' great adaptation of Cormac McCarthy's novel *No Country for Old Men*, with its spectrum of characters ranging from virtuous to sociopathic, with regular corruptible people filling in the larger center.

But I'd rather focus upon a series of films by the French director Francois Truffaut (1932-1984) that concern themselves with ordinary people living ordinary lives.

Truffaut is a fascinating figure in his own right. After an extremely unhappy childhood, he found salvation in his cinematic obsession and his bond with a father figure, the film theorist Andre Bazin. As a young adult, Truffaut became an incendiary movie critic, brashly calling out established directors for their stagnant style while championing the films of Alfred Hitchcock.

Soon enough, he became a director and leading figure in the French New Wave. As a reaction against stodgy period pieces, New Wave directors like Truffaut and Jean-Luc Godard favored spontaneity, on-location shooting, and contemporary characters who spoke like typical people of their day.

Truffaut's first movie, *The 400 Blows*, was released in 1959 when the director was only 27 and brought him immediate acclaim. Earning the Best Director award at the Cannes Film Festival, *The 400 Blows* ultimately became the first movie in a series of five that followed its lead character Antoine Doinel across 20 years of his life.

The 400 Blows focuses upon Antoine as an early adolescent, giving us an intimate look at a miserable home life with neglectful, economically struggling parents. Antoine devolves into truancy and petty thievery that land him in a correctional facility for juvenile delinquents.

All of this mirrored Truffaut's own life, though by the next film *Antoine and Colette*, 17 year old Antoine's passion for music was a substitution for Truffaut's love of movies. The autobiographical tone continues into the beginning of the third film *Stolen Kisses*, which opens with Antoine's release from military prison, another experience shared by the creator and his creation.

Across the Doinel saga, Truffaut presents characters who are universal in their struggles. We see Antoine fall in and out of love, try and fail at multiple jobs, get married and raise a son.

At the same time, in their particulars, each character in these films is unique. As acted by the charmingly hyper-expressive and kinetic Jean-Pierre Leaud, Antoine is playful, opinionated, and impetuous. He has strong views on the merits of handkerchiefs over paper tissues, and both aggravates and endears himself to his wife Christine with his silliness, as when he names her breasts Laurel and Hardy.

In the totality of this series, Truffaut seems effortless in conveying psychological insight. We humans tend to repeat ourselves in our meaningful relationships, just as Antoine perpetually seeks out well-mannered young ladies to woo, while simultaneously courting their bourgeois parents in an effort to replace his own mother and stepfather.

We see in Antoine that change is possible, occurring incrementally by trial and error. By the fifth film *Love on the Run*, a thirtysomething Antoine makes an uneasy peace with his childhood and tentatively moves beyond superficial charm to meaningful intimacy with the woman he loves.

Truffaut's best movies are suffused with a warm humanism that sees beauty in the everyday. As Madame Tabard, one of Antoine's romantic obsessions in *Stolen Kisses*, tells him: "Every woman is exceptional in her turn…you're quite exceptional yourself…. We're both unique and irreplaceable…. People are wonderful."[1]

The Centrality of Individual Freedom and Universal Human Rights

Once again, there are so many options to choose from! Cinema has the potential to take us places we'll never go, to deepen our empathy and concern for people around the world.

A recent favorite of mine in this category is 2012's *Wadjda*, a movie of many notable firsts. Most significantly, it was the first film shot entirely in Saudi Arabia, by the first female Saudi director. (At the time of this writing, Saudi Arabia has only one movie theater and a miniscule film industry.)

Surprisingly, given her confidence, believability, and charm in front of the camera, *Wadjda* also contains the first role for Waad Mohammed, the child actress portraying the title character. Wadjda is a ten-year-old girl living in Riyadh, who dreams of having a bicycle of her own.

Unfortunately, Wadjda is short on cash, despite her cottage industry of making and selling bracelets to her classmates. More significantly, though, bikes are culturally forbidden to females in Saudi Arabia. Even Wadjda's normally supportive mother tries to squelch her daughter's wish, for fear that a spill on a bike could injure her hymen and nullify her all-important virginity.

As you've probably guessed, *Wadjda* is about much more than a kid who wants a bike. During the course of her film, writer/director Haifaa Al-Mansour

---

[1] *Stolen Kisses,* directed by Francois Truffaut (1968; Janus), DVD.

illustrates the indignities large and small that females suffer in Saudi society. Since women are barred from driving, Wadjda's mother must be chauffeured to her teaching job by a verbally abusive man who turns off the air conditioning at each stop, leaving his passengers to swelter inside the vehicle. Even worse, Wadjda's mom fears that her husband may abandon her for a second wife, due to her failure to produce a male progeny.

At Wadjda's school, the girls are ordered to abandon their playground, for fear that male construction workers atop a nearby building might see them and succumb to lascivious temptation. Their joylessly devout principal even tells her students to stop singing, so their voices don't tempt men outside to indecent thoughts.

For a relative novice to film-making (this is only her second feature), Al-Mansour has already assimilated the essential wisdom to show, not tell. The main danger in cinema concerning itself with social justice is becoming overly preachy. *Wadjda* never crosses that line, by giving viewers what feels like an authentic slice of life for females in Saudi Arabia.

Al-Mansour also manages to keep her movie light, despite its subject matter. This is helped in part by an airy, upbeat score; but most importantly, Wadjda is such a spunky, resourceful kid, that viewers can't help but feel hopeful that young people like her (and subtle activists like Al-Mansour) are making their world a better, more equitable place.

Expanding Our Concern for Earth and All of Its Inhabitants

Here, it's tempting to turn to Japanese anime masters Hayao Miyazaki and Isao Takahata. No-one depicts the consequences of humanity's despoiling of our planet more artfully and emotively than these two leading directors from Studio Ghibli. Even with their large doses of animism, films like *Spirited Away*, *Princess Mononoke*, *Nausicaa of the Valley of the Wind*, and *Pom Poko* are essential viewing for any humanist committed to caring for the earth.

However, since the majority of freethinkers are on board with opposing pollution and global warming, I'd prefer to focus instead upon *Homo sapiens'* relationship with other species. Atheists may have left behind the notion that we humans are the pinnacle of God's creative agency, but more often than not, we still act as if we were specially created to have dominion over other creatures.

Along with the writings of philosopher Peter Singer, films played a decisive role in altering my views on our treatment of non-human animals.

Blackfish, though not a perfect documentary, enlightened me with the insight that orcas, given their brain structure and behavior in the wild, may have a greater capacity for social empathy than humans. *Virunga*, a splendid documentary about the efforts of Congolese rangers to protect mountain gorillas, indisputably showed that these beautiful primates experience the same range of emotions as their human protectors.

Among fictional narratives, one of the best recent works to address this topic is *White God*. Defying facile categorization, this Hungarian film is an odd mélange of horror story, revenge flick, domestic drama, and child-and-pet bonding tale that nonetheless coheres satisfyingly.

In a sequence akin to the start of Danny Boyle's zombie movie *28 Days Later*, *White God* begins with a long-distance aerial view of a lone bicyclist on the empty streets of Budapest. Then, with a close-up of her stockinged legs manipulating the pedals, we realize this lone figure is a schoolgirl. Soon after, the streets behind her fill with hundreds of dogs hurtling towards her (literally hundreds: 274 dogs were employed in scenes like this during *White God*).

The film then backs up a few weeks, so we can learn more about this girl and one of the dogs in this massive pack. The girl is 13 year old Lili, and the canine sharing center stage is her beloved brown mutt Hagen.

During the course of *White God*, both Lili and Hagen begin a descent into abandonment and mistreatment. With a travelling academic mother, Lili is left with a dad she barely knows and experiments with drugs and alcohol. Her dad detests dogs, so Hagen is kicked out of their apartment, where his path then crosses with fellow strays, the dogfighting underworld, and a euthanizing animal shelter.

Courtesy of writer/director Kornel Mundruczo, the sufferings of Lili and Hagen are equated by cross-cutting through their respective narratives, as well as mixing up first- and third-person imagery for both characters.

Far more audaciously, Mundruczo allegorically compares the suffering of Budapest's canines with that of Holocaust victims. Like Jews and other "undesirables" of the 1930s and 1940s, all mutts must possess special documents, with their owners paying punitive fees. When Hagen ends up at the animal shelter, the ruthless winnowing into "survive" versus "lethal injection" categories conjures up memories of Auschwitz, especially with the nuclear cooling towers in the background bearing an uneasy resemblance to crematorium funnels.

Despite the reassuring news that all of the stray dogs in *White God* were furnished with caring homes after the cameras stopped rolling, this is still a tough film to watch as an animal lover. Without giving too much away, Mundruczo fortunately manages to suffuse some hope into his ending, holding out the possibility that human and non-human animals can find a way to coexist on our planet.

Living the Good Life

I'll let the true philosophers in this anthology fully handle the question of what a good humanist life encompasses. For this amateur philosopher, the good life includes compassion, generosity, flourishing, and authenticity. For this critic, no-one's work embodies these ideals better than that of the great Japanese director Akira Kurosawa (1910-1998).

Across 50 years and 30 films, Kurosawa's crisp editing and narrative style inspired the generation of American directors who made their own groundbreaking films in the 1970s. To their credit, when their hero fell into hard financial times late in life, George Lucas, Francis Ford Coppola, and Steven Spielberg lent their aid so Kurosawa could keep making movies, while Martin Scorsese even starred in one of Kurosawa's last films.

Not only do Kurosawa's movies serve as a stylistic and storytelling masterclass, but a humanist's heart beats strongly at their core. In his scripts (all of which he wrote or co-wrote), Kurosawa always concerned himself with how to live rightly in a scarred and flawed world. In both period pieces and contemporary dramas, whether his main characters were samurai (*Seven Samurai* and *Yojimbo*), police detectives (*Stray Dog*), doctors (*Drunken Angel*), urban bureaucrats (*Ikiru*), or corporate bigwigs (*High and Low*), they all faced relatable existential dilemmas. Like his viewers, these protagonists were challenged to use their skills and resources ethically in a world with suffering and inequality.

No doubt it's partly because I'm a physician, but for me, the most meaningful Kurosawa film is his tale of two doctors, *Red Beard*. Created when he was in his fifties, Kurosawa had moved beyond the kinetic editing that propelled his earlier movies and inspired the young American directors. Instead, *Red Beard* revels in longer takes and breathtaking chiaroscuro.

Like many of Kurosawa's stories, *Red Beard* centers on a mentoring relationship. Set in feudal-era Japan, the film opens with young Doctor Yasumoto arriving at the clinic and hospital of Doctor Niide, nicknamed Red Beard. Yasumoto, a member of the samurai class, indignantly believes that the destitute patients and austere setup of Niide's clinic are far beneath his station.

Initially, he refuses to work and chooses to make a sulky nuisance of himself, hoping that Niide will fire him. Yasumoto only awakens to his duty to serve all humanity, rich and poor, after witnessing the demise of two virtuous older men and experiencing his own brush with death.

Akin to his favorite author Dostoevsky, Kurosawa conveys his values and furthers his narratives by way of interlocking and contrasting characters. When Yasumoto first shows up at the clinic, he is guided around by a departing young doctor who can't be bothered to hide his contempt for the impoverished patients treated free of charge by Niide. Set against stirring images of the suffering masses (highly reminiscent of Daumier's classic prints of the French downtrodden), this physician loudly declaims that these folks would be better off dead. Yasumoto, on the other hand, commendably demonstrates a willingness to mend his attitude and behavior towards Niide, his staff, and the sick under his care.

The other major opposites are two female patients at the clinic, "the Mantis" and Otoyo. We learn that both of these young women suffered horrific trauma, some of it sexual in nature. The Mantis, so completely defined by her lethal behavior that we never learn her birth name, has seduced and murdered three men in the past, such that she must be kept under constant lock and key.

Contrarily, twelve year old Otoyo, rescued from a brothel when deliriously ill, elects to follow the path of aiding those who are equally needy. In one of *Red Beard*'s climactic sequences, the doctors and Otoyo gather around a gravely ill child, forming a semicircle. The camera, and by extension the viewers, close the remaining 180 degrees. It is as if Kurosawa is asking us all, "Will you lend a hand, too?"

Cultivating an Attitude of Wonder

Secular humanism and atheism substantially involve living out the concepts I've described above. But just as all work and no play makes Jack a dull boy, right notions minus a sense of wonder make for a desiccated existence. Joy and awe over the splendor of nature and human creativity complete a humanist's life.

In a parallel process, the greatest films are not merely vehicles for ideas, but display a mastery of narrative, editing, sound, and image. My favorite cinematic instance of this are the movies of Japanese director Yasujiro Ozu (1903-1963). A true Cezanne or Shakespeare among filmmakers, Ozu developed a unique visual style for his scripts that are themselves masterpieces of concision, characterization, and wisdom.

For all of these reasons, an Ozu film cannot be mistaken for that of any other director. For starters, Ozu kept his camera in a stationary position about three feet off the ground. This places the viewer in an ideal position for his contemporary domestic dramas, at eye level for the characters seated on the tatami flooring of their homes.

During scenes of dialogue, Ozu typically framed his subjects in a head-on, head and shoulders view. For moviegoers accustomed to the over-the-shoulder, "shot/reverse shot" editing that dominates moviemaking, this can be disconcerting at first. Once acclimated to it, though, Ozu's style offers an impression of intimacy, so one feels like a guest in his characters' homes or on their social outings.

Ozu consciously eschewed other standard elements of film grammar. Tracking shots, panning and scanning, dissolves, and fades are rarities in his movies. By contrast, Ozu inventively bracketed his scenes with "pillow shots," so called since they indicate a change in location, serenely cushioning individual scenes and allowing a moment of contemplation.

Just as Ozu restricted his visual style, his narratives are almost invariably domestic dramas of extended families facing transition. These tales lack heroes and villains but instead feature regular people coping with change at home and in the society outside their doors. For Ozu as well, depth of characterization supersedes plot complexity, so that most of his storylines can be summarized in a couple of sentences.

To flesh out these descriptions, let's look at one of his films in more detail, *The End of Summer*. It's not Ozu's supreme creation; that would be *Late Spring* or *Tokyo Story*, with the latter routinely topping critics' lists as one of the two or three greatest films of all time. Even if *The End of Summer*'s philosophizing is a bit unsubtle by comparison, this movie holds a special place in my heart. Each time I watch it, I am won over again by its central character—jovial family patriarch Kohayagawa—and the comical sparring between him and his eldest daughter Fumiko.

Here's the plot of *The End of Summer*, simple though it may be: Kohayagawa and his family run a small sake brewery that's being edged out by larger companies. A widower, Kohayagawa is always sneaking away from home to spend time with an old flame, spurring indignation from Fumiko. Meanwhile, two young women in the extended family are weighing marriage proposals.

Across its 100 minutes, we witness a family juggling tradition and change. Some characters wear kimonos and wooden *geta* sandals, others go out in Western-style suits and dresses. The young ladies debate whether to marry for love or accept matches arranged by their elders. This contrast between old and new also shows up in Ozu's pillow shots that alternately contain flashy neon signs in Osaka, as opposed to old-fashioned sake barrels lined against the wooden walls of the family brewery.

Though Ozu's setting is unmistakably mid-20th Century Japan, his character types are recognizable everywhere. To name just two, Kohayagawa is a mischievous older man who refuses to "act his age," while Kumiko is the adult daughter who thinks she knows what's best for her father.

Still more universal is Ozu's recognition that family structures and life itself are ephemeral. In his movies, children are always growing up, marrying, and moving away. In *The End of Summer*, mortality is emphasized even more strongly by Kohayagawa's two heart attacks. Ozu also hints nicely at life's brevity through the manifold clocks in his scene's backgrounds, pillow shots of empty hallways, and the sounds of cicadas and train whistles on the soundtrack.

Lest all this sound too heavy, Ozu handles his material lightly. I always come away from his films feeling refreshed from spending time in the company of ordinary decent people and newly appreciative of the goodness inherent to daily life. Just because a day at the museum ends or a wine bottle surrenders its last drop, their joys and pleasures are savored no less. Good memories of our relationships and wonder-filled experiences linger as long as our hearts keep beating.

Humanism and Witchcraft: Not Seeing God in Africa

Warren Alan Tidwell, Kudzu in the Pines

Humanist Service and the Problem of Witchcraft Allegations in Africa

There was a point in 2014 where I knew my lifestyle would mean I wouldn't see much of 2015. I put the bottle of wine down and left my high-paying high-stress job in sales to go to work at a local hardware store. As an atheist in Alabama, I had to be careful who knew of my nonbelief. I wanted to return to humanitarian work from years past but, without a church membership, there weren't many organizations I'd find who would work with me long term and I just couldn't fake being a Christian to be a part of someone's organization. I say that because most every disaster relief organization in my area, where I could work in my area of expertise, was led by Christians or was a Christian organization themselves.

In 2015, I found out about the Humanist Service Corps, an organization founded and managed by atheists, that was working in Northern Ghana in support of women who were victims of witchcraft allegations. Within a year of leaving my high stress job that was killing me, I applied for the organization and six months later I left my wife and son to spend a year in refugee camps of women accused of witchcraft in rural West Africa. It was a whirlwind of a time to say the least.

When I speak on the Humanist Service Corps, the question I most often get asked is what exactly does humanist service entail and, soon after that, I'm asked of the presence and makeup of atheist and humanist groups in Africa and how they are treated by the populations in each country. I can only speak of my experience in Ghana, but I have gotten to know leaders in other countries in Africa very well and now know of many groups and the issues they've faced. In the past five years, there has been an explosion of atheist, agnostic, and freethinker groups in Africa. From Ghana to Nigeria, from Kenya to Uganda, nonbelievers have started to stand up and demand to be counted as they work for progress in their home countries.

What exactly is humanist service?

The founder and director of the Humanist Service Corps, Conor Robinson, defines humanist service as "service designed by humanists as an expression of humanist principles." He goes on to say,

> Humanist service focuses not only on what resources the community lacks, but also on the emotional and psychological needs of the people involved. Humanist service seeks neither to convert nor to deconvert. Instead, it aims to connect by focusing on shared values. Humanist service emphasizes the growth rather than the sacrifice of the volunteer. Above all, humanist service empowers communities. The first way we can do this is to wait for an invitation to collaborate before volunteering in communities that are not our own. The second thing we can do is just that: collaborate. Although we may bring valuable skills, perspectives, and resources with us, this does not entitle us to dictate what solutions to implement. Even when we think we see a more efficient or effective way to do things, we must weigh that relative value against the immense value of a community's self-determination. Sustainable change occurs when community leaders develop their own skills and confidence by taking the lead in designing and implementing community-driven solutions to problems identified by members of that community.

That means, to me, service that is meaningful in expressing my values as a humanist within the context of the culture where we will be working. It is a way of working that supports and empowers others with no effort to proselytize. Humanist service allows me, as a nonbeliever, to work in the humanitarian arena free from the constraints and motives of religious groups. My atheism only says I reject the idea of a god. My humanism is how I choose to interact with the world around me. The people I have worked with in Ghana, I have learned, do not care about my lack of religious beliefs and are often taken aback that I don't have an ulterior motive of wanting to share my worldview with them. They appreciate the fact I simply want to spend time with them and work with them. Ghanaians, however, are suspicious of other Ghanaians who do not adhere to a religion. Culturally you are expected to have a religion as Ghana, per a number of polls, is one of the most religious countries in the world. It doesn't make sense to some Ghanaians that their fellow citizens would choose to be nonreligious.

What does it mean to be an atheist in Africa?

There is a growing group of atheists in Ghana and Africa as a whole. The Humanist Association of Ghana (HAG) has a healthy group of individuals who support the work of the Humanist Service Corps in any way they can. In my travels throughout the country of Ghana, I have often been given a place to stay the night. The Humanist Association of Ghana has a podcast that airs regularly and they take part in many meetings and activities in the capital city of Accra. There is push back on social media at times, but the members of HAG bravely defend their worldview when pressed. They are quite open about their atheism.

There is a very active humanist group in western Uganda, near their border with the Democratic Republic of the Congo, in the town of Kasese. The Kasese Primary Humanist School is growing in both size and number thanks to numerous atheist sponsors from around the world. In the past two years, they have moved from an abandoned rail yard to newly constructed buildings purchased by patrons from England, Australia, the United States, and Canada. Using the internet and social media, the headmaster Bwambale Robert, has been able to secure donations for a computer lab and a library. The flip side of that is that locals outside of the school have started accusing them of witchcraft and using dark magic to make their money. While there is a growing humanist community in Uganda the traditional beliefs are very strong and the associated superstitions are firmly entrenched with many in the community. The coming years will tell the story of where humanism, and by extension the school, will end up in Kasese.

Nonbelievers working in Africa

Atheists in Ghana are tolerated, but in African nations like Nigeria there is more of a hard line taken against them. A Gallup poll once reported that the nation's population is two percent nonreligious. It may be a higher number but there are apostasy laws in parts of Nigeria that would certainly lead many atheists to keep their lack of religion private. However, in March of 2017, a group of Nigerians joined their counterparts in Nigeria and founded the Nigerian Humanist Association. At the time of this writing, nearly 300 had joined in on the Facebook page for the organization. Their focus is ending the stigma of nonbelief in Nigeria and working to end witchcraft allegations against children.

In Uganda a teacher named Masereka Solomon has helped with the organization of the Kasese Humanist Primary School from its inception. Along with that, he has used the power of the internet to create a worldwide network of like-minded individuals to support his work in Uganda. Many days he posts pictures of the projects he is working on, from bee keeping to a soccer team he coaches. In doing so, he keeps people engaged with what is going on with the projects they support. He is also quite outspoken online in the forums in Uganda and often advocates for a world based in reason and rationality and not superstition. He is hoping to be a light for other Ugandans who fear coming out as a nonbeliever.

The Humanist Service Corps started out in 2015 in Ghana with five U.S. volunteers and one Ghanaian. The 2017-2018 team will consist of one United States citizen, one Kenyan citizen, and 4 Ghanaian citizens. They are supported by the Humanist Association of Ghana based in the southern part of the country. Even though the Humanist Service Corps is based in the United States, it is now staffed and supported by a majority Ghanaian group. From the beginning the focus has been on working towards ending witchcraft allegations and banishments in the Northern Region of Ghana.

Witchcraft Allegations in Modern Day Africa

Leo Igwe, an atheist and noted authority on witchcraft in Africa, hails from Nigeria. He started out as a Catholic in seminary in Nigeria and left the church after studying the tenets of humanism and rejecting the mix of traditional African tribal beliefs and Christianity in which he was raised. In Ghana, I was introduced to Leo by my fellow Humanist Service Corps volunteer, Baako Alhassan. Baako had served as Leo's research assistant in Ghana in the year of 2013. They both traveled around the Northern Region of the country to study cases of witchcraft accusations and speak with the women who were banished from their village as a result. In one case a woman was accused after a child in the village had a bad reaction to a vaccination. The woman was banished and the child eventually recovered but the woman was not allowed to return home. In another case, Leo was told a woman turned herself into an electrical current and traveled to the south to the capital city of Accra where she electrocuted her victim through an appliance.

While there is still a widespread belief of witchcraft in Ghana, it is only the northern area of the country where violence is still inflicted on the women. Men are very rarely accused and, even if they are, it is often of a benign nature. In the instances of witchcraft allegations, the overwhelming majority accused are women. Allegations can occur for most any reason. If someone has a bad dream where someone else tried to harm them, they'll accuse that person of witchcraft. If someone falls ill or dies in a village, an accusation can occur. When that happens, a woman is most often blamed and said to be a witch. Many times, the dreams are the results of things like a fever from malaria but the superstitions from the traditional beliefs dictate someone is plotting against someone else using witchcraft. The dreams, to those having them, are very real and tie in to their daily experiences.

Women have been killed and beaten as a result of these allegations in Ghana. In June of 2017, a woman was lynched and then burned in the Upper East Region of the country.

As a result of the persecution, sanctuaries for those accused have been created in Northern Ghana and are known as witch camps. As of 2017, there are seven witch camps spread throughout the Northern Region of Ghana. No one knows exactly how long they've existed, but it is before a time anyone currently alive can remember. The women are allowed to live there because the local village priests say the land takes their powers away. The camps are all set apart from a local village aside from the instance of the village of Kukuo where the women are allowed to live in homes throughout the village.

When it comes to witchcraft allegations in Nigeria, those accused can also be children. This is where Leo Igwe began his mission to end witchcraft allegations in African countries. In the beginning of Leo's work, he spoke out against certain pastors in Nigeria who claimed witchcraft is real and that children can be possessed. At a conference for human rights in Nigeria in 2009, he was attacked and beaten by members of a church he had spoken out against. The attackers also stole his possessions, including his wallet and phone. The church the members belong to is led by the controversial Nigerian Pastor Helen Ukpabio. Ukpabio has made many claims in the past that children in Nigeria can be bewitched and, as a result, many children have potentially been harmed. Leo Igwe is tireless in bringing these issues to light.

My humanist work in Ghana

I arrived in July of 2016 to Bimbilla, Ghana, a town of a few hundred people that is extremely rural, in the northeastern part of the country. It was as isolated as I have ever been. Villages dotted the landscape of the savanna and the roads comprised rocky red dirt not unlike the old country roads I grew up on in Alabama. While the southern part of Ghana is highly developed with highways, malls, and museums, the northern part of the country has been left behind in terms of development. Many Ghanaians have been led to believe it's a combination of the fact that colonial development never made it very far north before Ghana gained independence, and the fact that northern Ghanaian tribes rejected the ways of the colonial occupiers and refused to educate their children in the British colonial schools. No matter the full reason, there is little doubt that the north of Ghana is far behind the south in many metrics. There is far more illiteracy and poverty in this region than any other region in Ghana.

Belief in witchcraft is still high throughout the country, as well, but in the more developed areas, there is no real violence towards those who are accused. In the north, however, as I have written, there is a need for sanctuaries for the women.

My work began in the village of Kukuo, east of the town of Bimbilla. To get there, it was a thirty minute ride on my motorcycle and I was struck at just how isolated it was. The road was covered by water in many places and I had to walk my motorcycle through rocks in other areas. The road wound through the savanna, or bush as it's referred to by the locals, and through farms with yam mounds and rows of maize.

I met up with my contact there, Mustapha, who gave me my first tour of the place. He introduced me to women who had been sent there in the late 1950s. Most women I met had spent the majority of their lives there and most were elderly. I met women who had lived in Kukuo since they were teenagers and were now in their seventies. The women did have mud brick homes and a good deal of them were able to work local farms. Most, however, were forced to depend on the kindness of their fellow villagers for food and had to sleep on the concrete floors on a thin mat each night.

I noticed many of the mud brick homes at the edge of the village were in disrepair with caved-in walls and thatched grass roofs missing whole sections. I would learn that these were once homes to some of the alleged witches. The rocks and mounds outside of those homes marked the graves of the women once banished there. They had spent their entire lives in the witch camp at Kukuo and weren't even allowed to be buried in their home villages. It is one of the many indignities the women must endure. I met up with a woman named Fatima who, at age 83, still had to make the long trek to the river for water in the dry season, which runs for four to five months in the hottest time of the year.

Mustapha belonged to the tribal royalty of Kukuo and he worked as the liaison for the women when it comes to nongovernmental organizations working to support them. Mustapha would also prove quite invaluable when it came to our work to get some of the women home to their villages through our mediation efforts. Mustapha, being a devout Muslim much like most of the citizens of Northern Ghana, was well aware of my atheism when I arrived. He did not care. As we walked through the village, he told me that it wasn't up to him to judge me. All he could see is that I'd come half-way around the world to help strangers and he respected that. He told me that all he could concern himself with was his relationship with God and that he believed he would receive his reward in Heaven. I told him "fair enough" and we never mentioned it again. Mustapha would become one of my dearest friends over my time in Ghana.

One of the first things I learned about is that which Leo Igwe rejected: the odd merging in Africa of traditional beliefs with Christianity or Islam. Even though Mustapha was a devout Muslim he also still held the local traditional beliefs even to the point of believing in witchcraft himself. He just chose not to believe in the need for violence against those accused. I found Mustapha to be very much like my friends I made in the south. They believed in witchcraft but not the real, malignant effects that others claim to be real. They saw the women as victims and still refused to let go of the old superstitions.

In Ghana, at present, the Humanist Service Corps doesn't take an official stance on witchcraft. We don't try to debate it unless someone draws us into a debate. We only see our job as one to educate and challenge the conditions that bring about the allegations, while supporting the work and ideas of our local partner organization. To openly challenge the beliefs would be counterproductive at best. The beliefs and superstitions are just entirely too powerful.

Most of our work there entailed arranging for mediation between the families of those accused and the accuser. Mustapha, my Humanist Service Corps teammate Baako, and I traveled to many isolated villages to arrange these things. One of our focuses was to work within the context of the culture and this was a necessity as we worked to get the women returned to their homes.

There were times when we had to load our motorcycles into hand-built canoes so we could cross swollen rivers to reach the far-away villages referred to as "feeder villages". They were called that since they were sending most of the women to Kukuo. As the majority of the accusations were coming from that one area, we focused our efforts there. Since there had already been a year of visits through the first year of the Humanist Service Corps, they were much more receptive to outside visitors. We found a few who were less than willing to speak with us at times, however.

We discovered that, as time passed, people were far more open to seeing the return of the women to the villages. We made arrangements through the partner organization to support the women for a small time and we planned out livelihood options for them such as small stores where they sold spices outside of their homes. From July of 2016 to February of 2017 we were able to get fourteen women home to their villages. Sadly, two more died just before returning home.

The final ritual before the women were allowed to leave the witch camp had to be performed by the local priest. In working in the context of the culture, I would find myself as a witness to these rituals where a priest killed a chicken at the village shrine to appease the local land god to allow the woman to leave. A locally produced gin was also poured out at the shrine. Apparently, the land god likes a little booze, too.

I absolutely look forward to a day where these superstitions are no longer followed but, at this time, we must stand by if we want to help the women who are suffering in the camps. As a humanist, I want to see suffering eased and, as such, I am willing to work in a certain way in a culture that isn't counterproductive or damaging.

I am so happy to see the growth of atheism in Africa and the rejection of superstition by so many. There will be fits and starts as the movement grows on the continent, but I feel as if groups like The Humanist Service Corps are essential as people are educated (and helping them become educated) in Africa about humanism. It's one thing to explain that you are an atheist. It's quite another to show them that you can live as a caring human being as a humanist.

One other thing I've learned in my time in Ghana is that the people from my home country of the United States and those I've encountered in the world are more alike that we all realize. While there is a problem of witchcraft allegations and violence in the north of Ghana, the country is overall very peaceful. In between visits to rural villages, I was able to get online and read the news from the United States. It is in those times that I realized we United States citizens have so many problems in our country as well. Like Ghana, though, I know so many wonderful individuals who are working toward a better world. As the growth of humanism spreads throughout the world, I encourage you to support these organizations and individuals. Maybe through all our work together and through the support of humanist initiatives, we can see these superstitions die off and a more enlightened and reasonable time come about in every corner of the world.

Patheos Nonreligious

The Importance of Visibility when Not Seeing God in Latin America

Luciano Gonzalez, Sin God

In the summer of 2014 I did the unimaginable. It was a warm day in early May in Georgia and I was sitting next to my mom as she drove down the road, cars all around us as we all got closer to our destination: Fort Benning. She was talking to me about Christianity, something she believed in moderately. When she first started talking about it that day as we drove home, I knew I was going to do what I had promised myself I'd do if she brought it up first. I was going to tell her I was an atheist. I didn't look her in the eyes as I said it, nervous about her reaction. I said the words with more confidence than I imagined I would: "I'm an atheist." She stopped talking for a second, probably feeling somewhat uncertain. It was definitely a shock to her. She would accept it, more or less, by the time we got home, but I'll be the first to admit that it was an awkward drive. Later on, I'd wonder if any of the other cars on the road that day had nonbelievers having the same awkward conversation I was having with my mom.

My name is Luciano Gonzalez and I blog at Patheos as "Sin God" which I thought was clever since it could seem to mean "God of sin" in English, or "Without God" in Spanish (I know it would probably make more sense as "Sin Dios" in Spanish, but I wanted my blog to appeal to Patheos Nonreligious readers in English so that it could serve as a bridge between Latin American skepticism and freethought and free-thinkers and atheists in English speaking countries). My blog is dedicated mostly to talking about atheism as a Latin American with a few other things mixed in as well, such as talking about figures in the history of free-thought, and news affecting irreligious people in Latin America. I want to use this space in this book to motivate Latin American and Hispanic atheists to be brave and vocal. Which is a very scary request and thing to do in general, but it is also one that I believe is fundamentally necessary to overcome the Christian cultural dominance constantly visible in Latin America. If you are unfamiliar with what I mean by "Christian cultural dominance" in

Latin America, I'll give you some examples so that you can begin to formulate an idea of what I mean.

Christian Cultural Dominance in Latin America

Christian cultural dominance is more than just assumptions about religiosity based off of the fact that we are Latin American. It's more than the idea that Latin Americans believe in superstitions. It's about more than Jane the Virgin's hip portrayal of Catholicism. Christian cultural dominance is about Pope Francis's statements on marriage having importance in nations in Central-America. It's about casual statements by Latin American politicians fusing Christianity with goodness. Many of these things are present in the United States, but vocal statements of opposition by secular groups don't seem to matter as much in Latin America, which in and of itself can be seen as a small example of the Christian cultural dominance in action.

If you want to hear a rather silly example of what I mean by "cultural dominance", we're about to chat about an occurrence in Honduras which involves the police. During "Holy Week"/"Semana Santa" (March 20th-26th) of 2016, Emiliani, the local auxiliary bishop of San Pedro Sula, performed a religious ceremony for the purpose of "putting it in God's hands," which, when simplified, meant that Emiliani made it explicit that any tragic deaths that occurred during the Holy Week were due to the will of God. There are many people who won't find this interesting, but it seems to say a lot about "God's" effectiveness given that according to the vast majority of press published in English and in Spanish, San Pedro Sula is quite possibly the "murder capital of the world" (though some sources claim it has begun to get safer) and the police are asking "him" to help them police it. I actually like San-Pedro Sula, but that example always made me laugh. This example is kind of harmless but it is still a good one to illustrate one kind of cultural dominance. Honduras is not by any means a "secular" state, but this example shows just how normal Christianity can be in most of Latin America. If this was to happen in the United States, I have no clue as to how secularists there would react but I can only imagine that they would at least talk about it. Perhaps this is some sort of "normal" in Honduras, because no one was phased by it.

Another Honduran example was that time in late 2014 when the legislative branch actually considered changing adoption laws to allow adoption equality to become a reality. That didn't happen largely because Honduras's

Evangelical Brotherhood protested against it and demonized any real attempt to rationalize expanding adoption laws. Many of the examples of Christian cultural dominance in Latin America are along these lines, things that logic dictates would benefit society are denied because of hyper-evangelical Christians, but the examples I want to use are largely personal examples where names can be used and where readers can be introduced to specific people to humanize irreligion in Latin America.

A further example of the type of cultural dominance I think about when I think about Latin America and Christianity is the case of Carolina Peña, which involves how Christianity affects everyone, independent of their social standing and their own religious views. If you aren't familiar with this story, this was the case of the viral video in which a girl sang for various judges for the Ecuadorian TV show "Ecuador's Got Talent" and proceeded to be asked about her beliefs relative to God. This was a rare case of an event related to atheism and Christianity happening in Latin America and going viral in the United States as well as in Latin America. Carolina Peña stated that she was an atheist, and the judges proceeded to be condescending towards her, attempting to undermine her position by stating that she would reach a point where she would need the "love of God" in order to get through. For example, one judge stated: "There will come a time when you suffer and the only thing that can help you get through is the amazing love of God," among other such statements. It's frustrating to watch, but it's hardly the only time something like this has happened, even if it's a rare example of famous people scolding soon-to-be famous people about belief or disbelief. Carolina Peña would be seen once again at the Reason Rally where she would sing a song by Penn Jillette he named "No Martyrs No Saints" which was inspired by a conversation Jillette had with Christopher Hitchens. Hers is an inspiring story and one which could serve as inspiration for other Latin American skeptics to come out of hiding.

If you ask non-believing Latin Americans about the responses we've gotten from our families and friends when it comes to our irreligion, our responses range from the silly to the terrifying to the heart-breaking. Not every example ends as positively as Peña's did, and many right now will end sadly for affected families. Christianity in Latin America can negatively affect non-Christians, and this is just one example of that.

The last example I want to talk about in this section, to give an idea of what "Christian cultural dominance" can look like in Latin America, is the case of Miguel Trujillo. This isn't a case that had the luck of going "viral" among English-speakers, but is a case I find immensely important. Miguel Trujillo is a philosophy teacher who works at a school in Huila, a department in Colombia. Trujillo's story began to circulate a few months back in the wake of an interview by a group of atheists who live in Bogota, but at that point a couple of Colombian newspapers had already begun talking about the infamous philosophy teacher. Trujillo's story began to circulate with one title capturing part of the reason why the story was so discussed: "A professor between atheism, philosophy, and discord."[1] That alone could summarize what you need to know but this is a story worth discussing with some level of depth. Trujillo is an atheist who teaches. In all likelihood there are many other teachers in Latin America who are also non-believers. The difference between those teachers and Trujillo is that Trujillo faced harassment by parents, and that Trujillo is vocally irreligious. Trujillo's atheism is known by his students, known by parents, and known by administrators at his school. Trujillo's discussion of philosophy, his willingness to ask questions to his students, and his ability to fascinate his students with discussions of reasoning and the importance of asking questions at home, have made him the subject of discussion among some Spanish-speaking circles. Trujillo isn't a biology teacher explaining evolution, he's a philosophy teacher whose willingness to challenge opinions have made him face serious opposition in the town he teaches.

He has stated that some teachers, like him, face the possibility of censorship, and some articles about him point out that there are individuals who want him to be censored. Miguel Trujillo's story is a possible outcome (perhaps even probable) when one tries to teach in Latin America and isn't afraid to speak honestly. He has been accused of "making kids think of shit" by a parent. He is evidently seen as an opponent by people who try to "raise their children as Christians," according to another parent who accused the teacher of "making children think nonsense."

Apparently, Christian cultural dominance in Latin America is fragile enough that a single brave teacher can stand in direct opposition to it, and must be stopped, according to at least some local parents. Trujillo has faced attacks from various parents, and even newspapers (for example, in an article by a newspaper named "La Nacion"). Stories of irreligious teachers are not at all common in Spanish publications, and I would love to talk about more of them. However, this one is the only case, in Latin America, of an irreligious teacher

---

[1] Argüello, Francisco. (04/24/2016) "Un profesor entre el ateísmo, la filosofía y la discordia." *La Nacion*, http://www.lanacion.com.co/2016/04/24/un-profesor-entre-el-ateismo-la-filosofia-y-la-discordia/

that has substantial details that I know of. Indeed, in this way, Christian cultural dominance can also be seen in the *absence* of stories about irreligious teachers, because they almost certainly exist but, one assumes, refuse to speak in detail about their irreligion for fear of losing their jobs.

Standing firm by being who you are

I mentioned that I'd be making a brave request. I began this chapter by talking very briefly about the time that I told my mom that I was an atheist. I was and am lucky because my mom accepted my irreligion quickly. I am aware of my privilege. In spite of the fact that I am privileged to be an accepted nonbeliever, I need other Latin American non-believers to be vocal. Here, we need more such vocal non-believers. Stand firm and be honest with yourself. Stand firm and be honest with others. If you are an atheist or an agnostic Latin American please be vocal.

There needs to be a subtle shift in culture that reflects what is, no doubt, a movement in the demographics of non-belief. Research conducted by the Pew Research Center in 2014 demonstrated a rise in the "Nones" throughout Latin America, with numbers that hint that the "Nones" have close to doubled in size, and that in the United States nearly 20% of Latin Americans are atheists, agnostics, or "Nones."[1] In order for Latin Americans in general, but especially in Latin America (as opposed to Latin Americans in the United States or in other parts of the world) to become accepted as nonbelievers, those of us who are already open and vocal nonbelievers need help from those of us who aren't. If you are a Latin American who doesn't believe in God (or in any other deities) and you want to know what you can do to support your community, your fellow Latin Americans who practice Christianity, other faiths and none (because Christian cultural dominance doesn't just affect Latin Americans who are irreligious, it affects Latin American believers in other religions just as much) the answer is simple: you can tell people that you do not believe. By letting others know that you are a skeptic you open up possibilities for honest conversations and genuine questions which is something that many in Latin America seem to want. Believing Latin Americans all over Latin America have questions for Latin American skeptics who want to know about skepticism from the point of view

---

[1] Pew Research Center (2014). "Religion in Latin-America," *Pew Research Center – Religion & Public Life,* http://www.pewforum.org/2014/11/13/religion-in-latin-america/ (Accessed on 03/02/2017)

of skeptics. If we are willing to have genuine conversations about religion and irreligion we can and will be heard by Latin Americans both resolute in their positions and who are questioning where they stand. In Latin America being an atheist is powerful. Being a vocal atheist willing to have conversations about atheism and irreligion can be even more powerful.

It's dangerous, as a Latin American, to be willing to say aloud that you do not believe, but it is necessary. It is necessary because there are Latin American children who are skeptical of the claims made by Christianity and Catholicism but don't want to voice their doubts because they are afraid of the very real societal consequences of being an apostate. As long as Latin American societies continue to be dominated by Christians (particularly Catholics, at least presently) who pressure atheists and other non-believers into silence, we'll never truly know how many skeptics there are.

The social consequences of being a nonbeliever in Latin America are terrifying and they are often more intimate than not seeing representation on television. In order for skeptics in Latin America to transform society we must take a first step and become more visible. In nearly every nation in Latin America there are already groups of atheists, agnostics, secular humanists, and more who've already taken that first step by crawling out of the darkness and coming together to create groups and organizations dedicated to pushing back against Christian cultural dominance. If you want to learn about those groups, I'll give you some basic information I've learned after researching them: these groups are led by tremendously brave men and women who understand that in order to empower secularism in Latin America they'll have to make sacrifices, they'll have to face attempts to humiliate them, and to attack their "Latin American-ness" by other people who have conflated being Latin American with being Christian. Latin American nonbelievers who seek to become leaders among their communities will have to face comments such as "Oh I'm worried about you, you know because of your *soul*" and we'll have to accept that at times these come from people who actually mean well but who are simultaneously being immensely condescending.

Condescending Remarks and Debates

I and other vocally skeptical Latin Americans have to face condescending remarks all the time. These range from the "You need to come to God on God's terms!" to the "I'll pray for you", to the usually kinder ones (although no less condescending) like "Did you leave because you felt disillusioned with the hypocrites?"

Part of the issue in Latin America seems to be that debates don't appear to be very common. In the United States, and in Puerto Rico, debates between believers and non-believers happen fairly frequently; but in the countries I've lived in, in Latin America, public debates seem to be a far rarer occurrence. I've lived in Panama, Colombia, and Honduras, and in all three of these nations, such events don't feature on the radar. This has to do, most probably, with the far more pressing matters taking place in each of these countries, but that doesn't change the fact that debates are a fantastic way of presenting alternative viewpoints to audiences in Latin America who otherwise might not have considered various ideas and concepts. This gives oxygen to the credibility of such viewpoints. Even the very announcement of a debate can be used to present new ideas, terms, and concepts to potential audience members.

If there are any Latin American non-believers who read this book and want to hear one of the bits of advice I'd give to skeptics in Latin America who want to normalize skepticism and encourage other skeptics to be vocal and brave it'd be this: rather than staying in your groups and meeting other vocal skeptics, engage with believers in safe, and productive ways and a debate can certainly be safe and productive. A debate can allow participants to speak to diverse audiences and can be used to refine ideas. It can be the space where we, as nonbelievers, respond to comments made by believers. We can use debates to show people that our position isn't evil, or the product of a dark heart. We are human. Debates are vital because the reality is that many people in Latin America who criticize atheists and nonbelievers probably wouldn't sit down and listen to us talking to others who naturally agree with us, but they might actually listen if we engage in debates, and conversations with believers about religion and irreligion.

Debates are possibly the perfect place for nonbelievers who are talented communicators to work to normalize irreligion. In many formal debates both sides have the opportunity to speak for an equal amount of time and can advance ideas without interruption. It's a great mechanism for nonbelievers who are interested in demystifying disbelief. Another great mechanism can be conversations formatted like debates, or interviews held by representatives of both sides. It's just that individuals in Latin America who are interested in real intergroup dialogue like this don't seem to be very common. So perhaps debates would work better for achieving real communication.

Places like the United States and the United Kingdom have thriving media and social media locations where the conversations have been raging for some years now. There has been a normalization of these conversations and, therefore, the associated worldview positions. This has acted as a snowball effect in allowing other similar people the confidence to come out, growing the communities. Don't take those opportunities and networks for granted!

Leadership as a godless Latin American:

I wanted to get to this point as I feel it is very important, where I could talk about leadership as a Latin American who is godless. And if you're still here and haven't skipped to the next chapter, thank you.

Being a leader as a godless Latin American doesn't mean you appear on debates or at protests. It doesn't mean you have to be an obnoxiously vocal atheist. It means giving godlessness a face in your community and even among your family and friends. Some of those faces will be friendly, others won't be, but we all matter. What does it mean (to me) to be a godless Latin American who leads?

It means, first and foremost, that you accept something. What I think needs to be accepted is that if you are a Latin American who is godless, you are part of a family. You join a new family due to your heritage and your godlessness. And this family includes people you didn't know were in it. Like Jorge Ramos. And while you may never meet Jorge Ramos, there are members of your family that you have already met. Indeed, if you remain silent, you might not learn who is a primo or prima because they might be as afraid as you are of being vocal about their doubts. But by being brave, you encourage the other skeptics around you, motivating them by your doubts and your willingness to face the consequences that come with being a minority among your friends and family. There are Latin Americans who cannot afford to be vocal about their irreligion, who'd put their lives at risk by being vocal about their lack of beliefs. But if you can afford to be vocal, you should be. If you are able to be vocal about your skepticism towards the claims made by Christians, you become a resource. And that is something to be proud of. It's empowering to be able to inspire other skeptics to live honestly.

Being a resource means when a child begins to question the claims made by believers, they have someone they can go to with questions. It means that their questions won't be answered exclusively by people with a vested interest in keeping them in the fold of the church. That is significant. Your doubts and your skepticism matter. Being a leader means that you can engage with other non-believers and with believers. It means that you can talk about what skepticism means to you, and that can be significant. Your story is part of who you are as a leader. Your experiences can help you overcome Christian cultural dominance. Your experiences can help people overcome their biases.

In becoming vocal and visible, you become a hindrance to Christian cultural dominance in Latin America. In becoming vocal and visible you become a powerful symbol against religious oppression, even "casual" kinds like erasure and the act of denying that atheistic Latin Americans exist. In interacting with believers in Latin America you become part of the reason why demonizing irreligious people should be hard for believers. In becoming a resource you overcome perceptions held by foreigners in Latin America and our own internalized perceptions of ourselves that we are religiously homogenous. If you are a vocal nonbeliever who is Latin American, your very existence is something you can use to overcome the idea that Latin Americans are universally Christian, and that is important. Your life can be inspiration for future Latin American skeptics. If you want to be a leader who is irreligious and Latin American, you become one the minute you let people know that you are a non-believer. You don't have to go shouting in the streets that you are a skeptic. You don't have to make YouTube videos, or post on Facebook about your lack of beliefs in the divine. Believe in the importance of your story, and you start to overcome Christian cultural dominance.

You help overcome the cultural dominance that helps keep children in orphanages because they can't be adopted by would-be same-sex parents. You help overcome Christian cultural dominance that prevents thirteen-year-olds in places like Honduras and El-Salvador from getting abortions and emergency birth-control because they were rape victims. You contribute to overcoming the same dominance which prevents same-sex couples from gaining the same recognition as heterosexual couples, even if they've been together for decades. Your story has the power to transform your family. It has the power to transform your community. Your story can touch one life, or ten thousand, but that won't happen until you let people know that you do not believe. As someone who has been there, if people actually love you, even if their opinions change when they learn this, they won't leave your side.

I want to encourage you to be visible. I want you to be heard. Your story alone is enough for you to be a leader. If you are a hidden Latin American nonbeliever, please stop being hidden. I can guarantee you that if you speak up, and speak out against untrue assumptions, and if you vocalize your questions, you'll transform the lives of people in your community for the better. Be proud of your doubts. Be proud of being different. Be proud of being a non-believer. Because throughout the world there are Latin Americans with the same doubts who can't be as vocal and as unapologetic as you can.

Your story and your willingness to voice it can start conversations that lead to parents accepting children who have doubts. It can start conversations in which people learn the value of honesty and the value of questions. Be proud of that.

Politics and Religion: Not Seeing God in the Islamic Republic

Kaveh Mousavi, On the Margin of Error

The Marriage of Islam and Politics

This is the essay I'm writing for a book that collects a number of essays from the Nonreligious Channel of Patheos website. I want to use my essay to justify the main driving forces of my own blog, *On the Margin of Error*. In that blog I'm mostly concerned with two issues: ex-Muslim issues and politics. In this essay, today, I want to argue that these two issues are in the end the same thing. Being an ex-Muslim is a political act, as much as it is an act of excluding yourself from a religion. For this purpose, I will begin by showing how Islam and politics are interconnected in their shared history, and then I will show what it means for someone to be an ex-Muslim in today's world. These two facets together will reveal why being an ex-Muslim is inherently and inevitably political.

The history of Islamic jurisprudence and theocracy are intertwined in an irreversible way. Usually, when one thinks of Islamic theocracy, one's mind goes toward modern proponents such as Sunni Saudi Arabia or Shiite Iran, and many Islamic apologists want to introduce "Islamism" as a separate and modern entity, and as a new addition to the Islamic tradition.

That is not true. While one can define Islamism as "the reaction of traditional Islamic institutions to modernity" and in that way define it as a modern entity (and it would be a legitimate definition), one has to remember that the tradition of Islamic theocracy goes far beyond the modern Islamism. Theocratic readings of Islam are still the dominant readings in most sects and traditions, and for the majority of history, they were the only reading. In fact, it is the secular versions that are new, and not dominant. If one wants to understand the experience of an ex-Muslim, one has to remember that theocracy and Islam as a religion are extremely interconnected.

This is deeply rooted in the Qur'an as scripture. Show me one instance where the Qur'an addresses a Muslim as an individual, or it establishes a purely personal rule. That is right, the book never does that. The Qur'an always addresses the Islamic community, or Muhammad, as the leader of the Muslim community. The Qur'an spends a lot of time discussing social laws and completely neglects the individual laws. Indeed, it spends a lot of time detailing divorce laws, for example, but never discusses prayers. Each time that The Qur'an mentions praying, it simply says "pray", and even then you know that it is referring to prayer as a social activity. People should pray together, to show to the world that they are Muslims; prayer is a form of "uprising". Zakat (one of the pillars of Islam, compelling charity) laws are not really charity laws, they are tax laws, as the amount you must pay is based on your income and value of the possessions, and it should be ideally paid to an Islamic state. Failing that, it should be paid to the clergy. I think it is evident that with such a mentality the social position of a person is more important, and it is more important to serve the society rather than the individual.

This gives Muslims far better excuses to butt in to other people's business, and also to get more riled up when they don't get their way. The followers of all religions (and most ideologies) try to suppress what they don't like in society, but it's not simply a matter of the existence of this phenomenon; what has separated Islam from other religions is the degree of this phenomenon. Few religions and ideologies have such a strong mental and ideological backbone to justify the erasure of the individual, possibly with exception of fascism and Stalinism. All religions are against the individual, even when they are individualistic. But it is much harder to define an individual within the Islamic context.

Following on, if you want to practice Sharia, you have to have a theocracy. There is no other way. Who presides over marriages and divorces? Who collects taxes? Who punishes the criminals? Who presides over the inheritance laws? Who decides what the amount of blood money should be? Who makes sure that the banking system is working without usury? For the life of me, I can't see how you can observe these laws without a government.

I understand that Christianity was, until recently, a theocratic religion throughout history (and arguably still is in some parts of the world). But the point is that it does not necessarily have to be. Marriages and charities are things that people can observe without a government, and I think most Christians observe the laws of their religion without the need of a government. It gets trickier when it comes to abortion and creationism; this is when radical Christians try to influence the government in a negative way. But no other religion (that I know of) has these deep roots into the governmental system, such infatuation with the political and economic process, as Islam. And nowhere is this more evident than in the Qur'an. Islam is not merely a religion; it is also a political party.

History supports this claim, too. Muhammad was the ruler of his country. If you go by the Sunni religion, his four holy successors were his political successors as well, they were his caliphates. According to the Shiites, the first two major Imams were caliphates and the rest were trying to become caliphates. The early history of Islam is a history of political uprisings, wars, and power struggles. It's not an accident that Islam begins its calendar not at the birth of Muhammad but at the time of his migration to Medina, which is the time that he lays the foundation of his empire.

And from the early Islamic era onwards, there are two major dynasties, whose ruler is at the same time the emperor and the religious leader (Amir al-Mo'menin, a title which translates into the ruler of the faithful). Now, even in the heights of its theocracy, Christianity at least separated the Pope and the monarch of any given country into two separate entities (with England being an eventual dissenter of even this set-up).

And even after the downfall of these two political dynasties (the Ummayad and the Abbassid), which lasted more than a thousand years, most of the ensuing governments, up until today, have tried to implement the Sharia law and have tried to claim religiosity. The Ottoman Empire was completely religious, for example. Today, King Abdullah is both the religious and the political ruler of Saudi Arabia.

Even most of the so called "secular" regimes are not secular by any measure. The constitution of both Iran under Shah and Egypt under Hosni Mubarak included Sharia, and in almost all Islamic countries, all the Sharia laws are enforced by their "secular" governments. There are some governments in Islamic countries that go to the opposite extreme and limit religious freedoms (which is obviously equally wrong). But even in those countries, the Islamists have either successfully risen to power and have dismantled the system (Turkey and Tunisia) or are the most prominent opposition. Political Islam is not new. Politics was always the heart, the mind, the body, and the soul of Islam. All religions are political to a degree, but none as political as Islam.

I have already shown how theocracy is deeply rooted in the Islamic scripture and tradition, so it must come as no surprise to anyone that all major jurisprudence movements of Islam have been deeply theocratic too. Islam's predecessors considered blood (inheritance), tribe, and religion as the most important legitimizing factors. Muhammad and his successors changed this, and elevated religion as the main legitimizing factor for political power, although they did not eliminate the other two factors. It is due to this fact that religion has become the main justification for various regimes and powers, and that is why the clergy class has considered it its duty to grant legitimacy to them. This, then, is comparable to the Pope crowning the kings.

Muhammad and his immediate successors used a political system analogous to the tribal system of the civilization they came from, but this changed in the Ummayad period into a monarchical empire structure with monarchs inheriting the power, and this continued into the Abbassid period, including the Ottoman Empire and Safavid regime. Islamic monarchies such as Saudi Arabia, Jordan, and Morocco are the direct descendants of that same system. There have been other systems, such as Islamic Republics, as we've seen in Iran, Pakistan, and Afghanistan. We have seen people in the modern era, such as Taliban and IS, attempting to revive the same tribal regime that existed at the time of Muhammad. The important point is that all of these regimes, in spite of their differences, have one thing in common: they derive their legitimacy from Islamic jurisprudence, and from the clergy class, and all of them consider enforcing the laws of Sharia as their main duty, and, even, their raison d'etre. In that, all of these ruling systems are or were different forms of theocratic regime.

The clergy class justified the existence of Islamic monarchical empires by making the sultan the central figure of their political thought. His presence was considered the only possible way of protecting the religion from the outside world, and his reign was considered the absolute manifestation of Allah's will. Even an unjust ruler was better than no ruler at all. The ruler was a kindness that Allah had shown to His creatures. The ruler was dubbed "the shadow of Allah". Now, it was the ruler's duty, in return, to enforce the rules of sharia and fight the enemies of Islam. Of course, even if the ruler was "unjust" (that is, if he didn't abide by the laws of Islam), people still had no right to rebel against him. Even a corrupt, unjust ruler was still the will of Allah, and if Allah saw fit to punish people by granting power to an oppressive ruler, it was still His will, and therefore anything but absolute obedience toward the king was a rebellion against the will of Allah. This was the major political philosophy of Islamic jurisprudence for the vast majority of its history, and it was common within

Shiite and Sunni sects. Excepting their differences, all of the clerics during this long period of history were fatalistic, authoritarian, and theocratic, and they used these three pillars to legitimize the existing empirical regimes.

But the important point to remember is that this political thought received no real opposition during its long-lasting dominance. Islamic thought was not monolithic in its history; however, the rival movements never thought or attempted to challenge the political philosophy of the jurist clerics.

Mystics were one rival to jurists, who emphasized an internal devotion to Allah and were generally much more tolerant than the jurists, accepting different faiths and even, in some cases, unbelief. However, the mystics were also as fatalist as the jurists, and they were completely apolitical. To mystics, the only path to salvation was to completely withdraw from all worldly affairs and completely devote yourself to prayer and austerity; therefore, the issue of government had no place in mystical thought. While mystics were able to challenge many aspects of jurist thinking, they never played in the political arena, and therefore they produced no coherent political philosophy of their own.

The other major rival of jurists were "philosophers." The Muslim philosophers included such names as Al-Farabi, Avicenna, Averroes, Suhrawardi, Ibn Khaldun, Mir Damad, and Mulla Sadra. These people differed from jurists in one important way: they were deeply influenced by Greek philosophy (especially by Plato, Aristotle, and Plotinus). While the vast majority of jurists demanded blind faith and considered the study of philosophy blasphemous, these philosophers sought to find rational justifications for the existence of Allah, and therefore created Islamic theology. However, like mystics, these people also refused to compete with jurists in the political arena. All of them were the elites of Islamic society, all were very close to the sultans of their time, all of them were financially dependent on the monarchs, and, as a result, none of them were motivated to challenge the political power of their time. Most of them either completely ignored political philosophy or only talked about it in the terms of "utopia," an idealistic society that could not actually be realized. All of them accepted the theocracy of the monarch as the correct form of the government.

The final major rival to the jurists were the Mu'tazila movement. In thought, they were very close to modern skeptics. They considered reason the most important tool of humanity, and they said that even Allah and the Qur'an must be tested by reason. That is why they rejected many aspects of traditional Islam that could not be justified rationally. And in many aspects they also fought against many political positions of the jurists. They believed in free speech, allowed atheists, and didn't necessarily silence criticism of Allah, the Prophet, and the monarch. However, they, too, did not challenge the theocratic regimes of the time. Therefore, given their more liberal ideals, one could consider them reformists, trying to reform the theocracy rather than creating discursive alternatives to it. And anyway, the Mu'tazila were repressed and did not gain a great following, and were sadly eliminated from the broader Islamic discourse very soon.

All of this shows that for the vast majority of its history, a theocratic philosophy was completely dominant and utterly unchallenged in the Islamic societies. This historical background is very important in understanding the position of an ex-Muslim in today's world.

Today, in this world

In the modern era, many jurists continue the same relationship with the regimes. The Wahhabi clerics reinforce the King of Saudi Arabia, and Egyptian Al-Azhar University did the same thing for Hosni Mubarak (and now Abdul Fattah Al-Sisi). One can say that the same movement we talked about through history is still the dominant movement. Many of the rival movements are equally theocratic. One rival movement was that of Khomeini's, which tried to eliminate the middleman: instead of the king, the jurist himself should take over the government and enforce Islamic laws. Other rival movements have been inspired by people like Sayyid Qutb or The Muslim Brotherhood, who want a much more powerful theocratic system. And at the very extreme end of the spectrum are more overtly radical movements like Al-Qaeda, Taliban, and IS: revisionist movements that seek to revive the same tribal system of the early Islamic era.

Of course, we now do have influential Muslims who are indeed supporters of the secular regimes and opponents of theocracy. So the main improvement from the early to mid-Islamic eras is the fact that theocratic movements are not necessarily a monopoly anymore. However, these movements are still not the dominant ones. That said, I think all of these factors show why being an ex-Muslim is so much interconnected with politics. If you cannot separate Islam from politics, and you can't, you really cannot be an ex-Muslim without your apostasy being a political action. Your very existence, in short, is political rebellion. At the end of the day, Islam is a strict moral system (with many absolute rules in both the Qu'ran and the collected sayings of

Muhammad, the Hadith) and politics is a subset of morality. Whenever you are saying people, or society, *ought* to do something, you are making a moral statement. It is little wonder, then, that Islam ends up being so political since it demands that people, that society, should act in certain ways.

So what does it mean to be an atheist in an Islamic theocracy? It certainly means many different things. To start with, no one can talk of a universal "ex-Muslim experience"—there is obvious variation. And no one can deny the existence of the many privileges that are unfairly given to certain categories of people, by the government and by the society, in Islamic countries, and those privileges rarely extend to atheists. Let me talk about my own country, Iran: The logistics of the situation differ a lot, depending upon whether you were a man or a woman, gay or straight, cis (a person who conforms to the gender assigned to them at birth) or trans, a Persian or a non-Persian, an ex-Shiite or an ex-Sunni, if you used to belong to the right kind of Shiism or the wrong kind, if you live in Tehran or in a big city or a small city or a village, if you are rich or poor, if your family is religious or not, how pious your family is, if your pious family is among the supporters of the regime or not. And after all of these external conditions we have to consider the personality of the apostate, their mental health, and their temperament. All of these factors transform the experience.

I'm a healthy, straight, cis, middle-class, Persian, Tehrani-born male from a secular and liberal family who exposed me to a lot of books and learning. In many ways, I'm the most privileged person possible in that context. That is why I wouldn't face many repercussions that other ex-Muslims face because of the fact that so many other factors and discriminations can and do add to the burden of their atheism. My personality also helps me immensely in this regard, as well. I never had to face many of the problems and dilemmas that other deconverts have faced and face. I never had to fear losing my "community" because I had none to begin with. I didn't have to fear being rejected by people because I never cared. I never had a crisis of faith; doubt and lack of certainty were always familiar and comfortable for me. My extreme tendency towards solitude made my transition to atheism a smooth one. And when I did have problems, I suffered a lot because I came out to the last person I should have come out to: my very religious teacher. Later on in life, when I did face continuous discrimination, like a bad novel, all my conflict was external, but I never doubted myself or felt sad or lonely. And I believe that when I became an atheist, my family sighed in relief. I'm sure that they were much more concerned at the prospect of becoming a Muslim.

I believe most ex-Muslims' accounts would be much different to mine. They might include invasion of bodily autonomy, in the case of women; or a rejection of your sexuality, in the case of gay people; and all of these issues are directly related to the influence of Islam in our lives. It might include some crisis of faith, a lengthier process, a fear of rejection of family and community, and probably far less drama and far more introspection.

Does that make me a suitable spokesperson of ex-Muslims? No. I can't be the spokesperson for anything. Ultimately, I have been too personal and too self-centered from the earliest days of my childhood to represent any respectable human community. That includes reformists and ex-Muslims, communities that I'm proud to belong to.

However, I try to think of being an ex-Muslim. What kind of a minority am I a part of in being one? Is it a kind of identity?

Of course it is an identity. It defines who you are in the society; it defines how the society perceives you. It shapes your life maybe more than any other thing about you. If you are not a 12-Imam Shiite where I am from, you lose most of the opportunities in life. And if you are not a practicing member of one of the four "official" religions, Islam, Christianity, Judaism, and Zoroastrianism, you officially don't exist. In the forms you have to fill out to get jobs or register for anything, these options are the only four options. According to the Islamic Republic, you have no right to have jobs, study at universities, open a bank account, or, well...live. That is, unless you belong to one of these four religions.

Atheists are not only absent from official forms, they're also absent from public discourse. It's not just that you are demonized constantly and discriminated against, but your existence is also completely ignored. Deliberately ignored. "We are all Muslims". You hear that sentence more than any other in Iran. In every discussion that touches on religion—and being in a theocracy, that's almost every discussion—people take great care to remind everyone else that yes, almost everyone here is a Muslim. There are no atheists here. Even the most progressive or moderate Muslims go through the trouble of adding official religious minorities to the mix but they don't mention atheists. If they happen to be very liberal, they will throw in the Baha'i. Never atheists.

Being an atheist means that you don't exist. But that doesn't stop the media and the school and university textbooks from tirelessly arguing against atheists, without mentioning their names. One has to wonder in this society, where we are "all Muslims" why Islam needs to be defended on every channel and in every book.

Someone who has not lived in Iran has no way of imagining how omnipresent religion is. There's no street without some religious symbolism. No ritual. No event. No book without "In the Name of Allah, the Merciful, the Compassionate." No greetings or goodbyes. No bill. No official form. Think of the most secular thing and it's still religious in Iran. The only secular space I can think of is the privacy of my own room.

Being an atheist in Iran means that everything, from the walls and the floors and the streets and the houses, *everything* tells you "you're not one of us." Ultimately, being an atheist means excluding yourself from your society, completely. I *really am* not one of them.

Being an ex-Muslim is like giving up your privileges. You were the majority until a day ago, now suddenly you are the most hated minority. This, of course, doesn't mean that privilege stops from working—it's better to be a male atheist than a female atheist, a straight atheist than a gay one. But it's much better to be a gay Muslim than a gay atheist.

I think this is the most important aspect of this minority. It's not simply belonging to a marginalized group, it's leaving the non-marginalized group for one, or it's moving deeper into the margins. You were part of the dominant class. Ultimately, it's an act of betrayal, since atheism is treason. To me the word apostate ultimately means traitor. That's why it hurts the emotion of Muslims to see believers leaving their umma, the religious Brotherhood. And that's true of the dominant group and the marginalized groups. My Armenian friend tells me that coming out as atheist hurt her pious family, and they believed she was weakening the marginalized Christians and she had to stand up for the community. Atheism is an act of treason, and an individual one. You turn your back to your community, and the community turns its back to you.

There is no atheist community in Iran. Becoming an atheist means losing your community. Even if the family and friends accept you. Even if the family and friends are atheists themselves. Ultimately the world outside is so powerful that you feel excluded altogether. I was a child from a secular family who was indoctrinated at school. I made atheist friends but I have always consistently felt the pressure of marginalization.

So what is your choice? Do you announce the fact that you are an atheist? Of course, you can't—you could be hanged. But how far do you go? Do you tell your family? Friends? No one? Do you come out everywhere except where it's absolutely dangerous? Should you be a proud traitor, or should you act like the criminal you're supposed to be, hiding your opinion like a dirty secret? How much do you lie? You have to lie anyway, but it's a matter of degrees. Do you make your whole life a lie?

I believe the ex-Muslims in theocracies have these issues in common. The sense of absolute rejection, the sense of committing betrayal, loss of community, having to live a lie. It's like being exiled to a stranger land but you are still at home. It's a Diaspora in your hometown.

Ultimately, most people find the ex-Muslim experience too traumatizing and painful. For many the pain is too great. Maybe that's why there are so many de facto atheists who are Muslim in name only. But me, of course, I like it. I think it's liberating. I might be shunned and ignored, but I know I am my own man. Islam means "surrender." To me, atheism means not giving up.

Personally, I choose to come out to anyone who is not a direct threat to me. This excludes government officials who can arrest me, employers who can fire me, overly religious people who can attack me with impunity. But other than that, I'm an open atheist, proud, and I aim to normalize atheism in the eyes of other people.

I'm sure you can see why being an ex-Muslim is inherently political. Firstly, you are leaving a religion that, because of its scripture, its traditions, its major movements, and its history, is deeply political. And you do so in a society that treats religious identity as the most important identity one has, and, therefore, you become a marginalized minority.

For all of these reasons, the struggle between Islam and its apostates are inherently political. In my blog I focus on both religion and politics, because to me they are inseparable.

Not Seeing Atheists in Congress

Hemant Mehta, The Friendly Atheist

As I write this, there's not a single open atheist in elected office in Washington, D.C. We're 0 for 535.

Every member of the current Congress—everyone in the House and Senate—claims either a specific religious affiliation or refuses to answer the "religion question." There's one exception: Rep. Kyrsten Sinema of Arizona is "unaffiliated," yet even her staff has said she feels the label of "atheist" is "not befitting of her life's work." Americans without organized religion make up about 23% of the country, according to the Pew Research Center, but we have only 0.2% representation on Capitol Hill. That's more than a hundred-fold difference. Christians, on the other hand, are 71% of the country but 90.7% of Congress.

This isn't merely underrepresentation or the result of a relatively small sample size. There are bigger forces at play here, and it's worth looking into why atheists have such a hard time winning these seats.

Before I get stuck in, it's worth recognizing that while I lean politically to the left (and this chapter wears that badge on its sleeve), I recognize that not all atheists do. However, according to research, most do. In 2012, about 70% of unaffiliated voters voted for Obama.[1] Again, according to Pew Research Center, only 15% of atheists affiliate themselves with or lean towards the Republican Party.[2] I don't profess to be speaking for them, here.

---

[1] Lipka, Michael (2016), "U.S. religious groups and their political leanings," *Pew Research Center*, http://www.pewresearch.org/fact-tank/2016/02/23/u-s-religious-groups-and-their-political-leanings/ (Accessed 06/20/2017)
[2] Religious Landscape Study: Atheists, *Pew Research Center*, http://www.pewforum.org/religious-landscape-study/religious-family/atheist/ (Accessed 06/20/2017)

1) We don't vote

According to The Atlantic,[1] while the "Nones" were approximately a quarter of the population over the past several years, we made up only 12% of the electorate in both 2012 and 2014.

We're not electing people like us because we're not electing anyone, period. And if we can't be bothered to vote for people with our shared secular values, why should anyone else do it?

(It's worth noting that we don't have numbers specifically on atheists. We only have data on the Nones, which is a much larger group that includes anyone and everyone who doesn't belong to an organized religion.)

Despite our percentage gains as a group over the past decade, our voter turnout has remained frustratingly steady. And while the Religious Right is growing smaller, they remain as engaged as ever. It's that sort of apathy on our side that gives them so much power.

2) We don't vote as a bloc

In July of 2016, 78% of white evangelical Protestants said they planned to support Donald Trump. Only 67% of non-religious Americans said they would be voting for Hillary Clinton. (And that was before Trump's tax return problems escalated and the tape of him bragging about sexual assault came to light.) That's a major enthusiasm gap.

When Republicans have a candidate, the Christian Right tends to get in line and do the strategically smart thing, no matter how much they might dislike their candidate. And make no mistake, they're not bragging about Trump. This past election put that theory to the ultimate test. Trump was about as far from being a model religious candidate as a Republican could be, and yet they supported him in overwhelming fashion.

When Democrats have a candidate, Secular Americans debate how progressive that person truly is. We vote for third party candidates who have no chance of winning a national election because they're further to the left on our

---

[1] Green, Emma (2017). "Why Christians Are Disproportionately Powerful in Congress", *The Atlantic*,
https://www.theatlantic.com/politics/archive/2017/01/religion-congress/512108/
(Accessed 06/20/2017)

pet issues. We stay at home because the Democrat isn't perfect. We're too damn stupid to see the bigger picture.

Even if a Bernie Sanders-like candidate were the Democratic nominee in the future, there's reason to think a lot of Democrats would still be critical of him to the point of not voting for him at all, letting conservatives gain the upper hand.

I should note, though, that there's an obvious reason we don't vote as a bloc: There's no "We."

While different denominations of Christianity are still bound together in their beliefs about Jesus, the "Nones" are a weird mixture of atheists, agnostics, and religious people who don't belong to an organized group. While the "Nones" are a quarter of the population, the percentage of atheists is in the single digits. That means, as a group, the "Nones" include a lot of people who believe in God, Heaven, Hell, miracles, ghosts, and other forms of nonsense. I suspect if you separated the atheists from everyone else, you'd see very different results.

3) We would never listen to someone telling us how to vote

If Richard Dawkins told atheists to vote for Hillary Clinton—and he undoubtedly supported her in 2016, even though he's British—we know what the reaction from atheists would be: "You don't tell me what to do. What are you, the atheist Pope? Go to non-existent Hell."

We don't like authority. We don't do something just because a "leader" tells us to, even if we might be inclined to agree. Many of us left religion because we were sick and tired of being told to respect people who didn't always deserve it. We're not about to start now.

This idea that atheists should vote a certain way also reeks of the dogmatic thinking we abhor. We'll think for ourselves, thank you very much. If that means voting for a third party candidate who has no chance of winning a national election, too bad for the Democratic Party for not accommodating my desires. Even if that sort of "independent" thinking means the Religious Right will get what it wants.

4) We don't have atheist candidates to choose from

I could count on one hand the number of openly atheist candidates who ran for national office in 2016. They all lost. Hell, they probably only came out as atheists *because* they knew they had virtually no chance of winning. Even at the state level, the number of openly atheist candidates was relatively small (though a handful were victorious). We can't elect atheist candidates who aren't there.

And why aren't they there? Because being an open atheist is still political poison. Gallup notes that only 58% of Americans would vote for an otherwise preferable candidate from their party if that person didn't believe in a god—and that's an improvement from the past!

Given how hard it is to win an election, it's no wonder candidates might choose to keep their atheism under wraps. It's the same reason they wouldn't want to talk about their more unpopular opinions. Why give people a reason not to vote for you?

So even if we could be motivated to support one of "our own," the cost of a candidate coming out as an atheist (before getting elected) continues to be high.

5) Atheist candidates wouldn't necessarily have a "pro-atheism" platform

What would an open atheist do in Congress? Demand that we put "In God We *Don't* Trust" on the money? Remove "Under God" from the Pledge of Allegiance? Change the law to give atheist groups special tax breaks? Of course not.

The battles most atheist groups have fought over the past several years have been about maintaining neutrality, not calling for unique privilege. We're not asking for any special treatment from the government. For the most part, we just want to maintain a separation between church and state.

That means that an atheist candidate would likely be running on a typical progressive platform... which a lot of religious Democrats and Independents do already. We don't necessarily have a need for an atheist in office when others can fight our battles for us.

Meanwhile, there are countless politicians who act like their devout religious faith is *precisely* why you should elect them. They campaign on a platform of promoting Christianity and Christian principles through the government—turning our nation into as close to a theocracy as it can be within the bounds of our laws.

As I write this, we've already seen the Trump administration move in the direction of letting pastors endorse candidates from the pulpit without losing their churches' tax breaks, letting parents use taxpayer money to send their kids to private religious schools, letting faith-based business owners discriminate against LGBT customers, and letting government agencies ignore the science of climate change. And that's before we get into the conservative Christian who is now on the Supreme Court because Republicans blocked President Obama's nominee from even getting a hearing.

These are all issues that Christian Right leaders would say are direct extensions of their religious beliefs.

***

When it comes down to it, we don't necessarily *need* atheists in Congress. But we're not doing ourselves any favors by not voting for candidates who support our issues in general.

In 2016, atheists had all sorts of reasons to vote—and vote for Hillary Clinton specifically, even if she did some things that upset progressives. Given the small margins in a few swing states, if we had been more politically active and smart about it, we could have swayed the election. So could a lot of groups whose members, I hope, are currently kicking themselves.

The one thing to be optimistic about is that the demographic trends in America continue to be in our favor. But having a higher percentage of non-religious Americans means nothing if it doesn't translate into more non-religious voters supporting church/state separation. It's something we have to get better at if we want more political clout.

Patheos Nonreligious

Not Seeing God in the Military

Kathleen Johnson, NoGodBlog

It was midafternoon on a day that was much like any of the other three hundred or so days I had already spent in Iraq, except for one big difference; today, we were making plans to redeploy home. In honor of our impending redeployment, we were required to attend endless rounds of redeployment briefings, mainly rote slideshows, that at least had the benefit of being conducted in places with air conditioning and sometimes even with a working and full coffee pot. This day's briefings did come with air conditioning and a coffee pot which made me a lot less annoyed than I otherwise would have been because the setting for the meeting was in the temporary hut that qualified as the base chapel.

Forward deployed chapels are supposed to be religiously neutral in that any religious accents must be temporary and removable so that the facility can be used by troops of any faith group. This one, however, was somewhat permanently affixed with crosses and other Christian implements and it was clear this particular facility was in no way intended to be spiritually used by those of any other faith. But, it was the only air conditioned space large enough to hold the units receiving briefings on this particular day and the availability of coffee went a long way towards fostering an unusually tolerant attitude in me, and so I elected to forgo the usual round of complaints I typically engaged in when forced into a religious setting against my will.

We had settled into our chairs and had probably been there for an hour or so when we heard the familiar sound of inbound rockets. I know it was only a few seconds from the time we heard the rocket until it detonated outside the chapel but it seemed to take minutes to reach us before the explosion noise and shockwave hit us. Once it hit and exploded, we all were knocked to the floor and we huddled there while the building shook and debris fell down around us. Luckily for us, the rocket had impacted one of the many cement blast barriers that were erected around facilities throughout the camp.

Up until this point, my job in Iraq had me working in a shop that was comprised of several people of various ranks and backgrounds. Three of us were atheists, one was a Catholic, several were apathetic Christians of one type or another, but one, our shop boss, was a true fundamentalist Christian who believed our mission in Iraq was a biblically sanctioned war against Muslims, that Christians like him were a persecuted minority, and that it was his God-given duty and right to use his rank as an anvil to influence and intimidate others if they didn't subscribe to his particular flavor of whack-job Christianity, attempting to hammer and shape those around him. Much to his surprise, myself and the other atheists in the shop refused to be intimidated, which had the perverse effect of reinforcing his persecution delusion because, as he saw it, our failure to put up with him trying to bend us to his will was evidence of his persecuted minority status. Yes, it was possible to choke on the irony in that shop.

But anyway, after the blast, as we dusted ourselves off, our boss looked at me and said: "So, Master Sergeant Johnson, do you believe in God now?" I said: "No sir, I believe in blast walls and I'm never setting foot in a church again; these places are too dangerous". And I haven't.

I am pretty certain I was always an atheist. I went through the motions of pretending to believe as I was growing up and spent several of my early years thinking I was doing something "wrong" because I didn't seem to have the religious connection that those around me had (or pretended to have). After I joined the Army, I did attend church in basic training but that was only so I could get out of work details and have someplace I could nap in the air conditioning. Early in my career, I explored various Christian denominations, Deism, Unitarianism, and even flirted a bit with Wicca and nature spirituality, but ultimately veered firmly into the agnostic and humanist camps. When I was 24, I sat down to finally read the Bible for myself from cover to cover and was horrified at the content. This was a book about a mass murdering sky devil who killed children, demanded all manner of abuse, rape, slavery, and animal sacrifice in his name. And the New Testament, with its misogyny, zombies, and magical thinking, wasn't much better. After that experience, although I still considered myself a humanist, I decided the whole faith business was nonsense and happily joined the atheist camp.

Joining the atheist camp, however, left me with a problem. The military, then as it is now, heavily promotes and accommodates religious faith, particularly that of the dominant American faith group—Christianity. And those who profess to be something other than Christian risked their careers to do so.

For example, around the time I was using a base library in Korea to read up on atheist thought and get familiar with atheist organizations during the internet's infancy, I also worked directly for a unit commander who believed and stated that his fundamentalist view of Christianity was the only possible valid faith, that he expected his soldiers and leaders to be the standard bearers of that faith, and that any leader under his command who could not (or would not) be that standard bearer risked being punished on their evaluations for not having ethics or upholding "Army values." This attitude was prevalent in the 1980s and 1990s as I was coming up through the ranks as a young leader, but became much more pronounced in the years after the attacks on September 11th, 2001, when the military embraced a "God and country" philosophy in a big way. Our nation might have claimed we were not at war with the religion of Islam but those of us who served in the Muslim combat zones had no doubt that our military saw itself at war with Islam.

Interestingly, it was that military library in Korea that stocked several books from an organization called American Atheists, published by American Atheists Press, which made me realize that atheists were actually organized and had banded together to work for atheist civil rights and anti-discrimination. I immediately got on a computer, went out on the rudimentary but growing internet, found the website for American Atheists, and joined. After spending some time getting familiar with American Atheists and the other atheist, secular, and humanist organizations out there, I soon realized there was no organization specifically geared towards military atheists who are a unique population with unique challenges. Using the various free resources available at the time, like email list servers, basic websites, and early social media, I founded the Military Association of Atheists and Freethinkers (MAAF) and served as the first president for the next several years until I stepped up my role in American Atheists and handed the reigns to a former Army officer and combat veteran, Jason Torpy, who still runs the organization to this day.

By the time I served in Iraq, I was the military director for American Atheists but still a member of the MAAF, as I am today, and I became involved in a correspondence with a young Army soldier and MAAF member. This MAAF member was attempting to do what I had already done on my base, which was to hold meetings for MAAF members on his specific base in Iraq. He obtained permission to have meetings in the recreation center and posted some fliers only to have those fliers torn down, which in retrospect, was a clue that the situation was not acceptable. Once he had a meeting, he and his fellows soon became the target of an officer who started a harassment campaign intended to disrupt the meetings and prevent them from happening. The harassment had the intended effect of shutting down the meetings and the soldier eventually became the target of such extensive harassment and death threats that he had to be relocated out of the combat zone for his own safety. After filing an unsuccessful lawsuit against the Army to address the discrimination and harassment, he ultimately ended up having to leave the Army for his own safety and that of his family.[1]

Around the same time, I was quoted in a very mild *Beliefnet* article that ran in *Newsweek* magazine[2] in which I had simply pointed out that atheists in the military do face some forms of discrimination. After publication, I too became a harassment target. Indeed, after the article was published, several persons used the military email system to seek me out and email me a series of threats to have me raped, have me killed, have my family killed, and so forth. These threats were sent from new, dummy accounts that were apparently set up for the purpose of anonymously harassing me so there was no possibility of me identifying the perpetrators or even replying.

These situations were not unusual and atheists were far from the only victims of the religiously deluded as other faith groups were systematically targeted for harassment even by those charged with the duty to protect them. I only had two meaningful interactions with military chaplains over my entire career and both were awful. In the first, I had a long conversation with a chaplain who was bragging (bragging!!) about how he was able to keep a Wiccan congregation from meeting anywhere on the installation because he had convinced the base commander that they could only exercise their religious practices while skyclad (naked), which wasn't true, and that this practice combined with the ritual use of a knife made them an element too radical and too dangerous to meet on post. Then, several years later, I needed counseling to deal with a divorce and, at that time, only counseling received through a chaplain could be obtained in private. Secular counseling from real health professionals had to be reported on security clearance applications and any mental health treatment was grounds to refuse or remove a security clearance. Since I needed my clearance, I sucked it up and tried the chaplain, who ultimately refused to

---

[1] I chose not to disclose the soldier's name out of respect for his privacy but his story is verifiable via several reputable news sources that are still available for viewing today.
[2] "Atheists in Foxholes", *Beliefnet*, http://www.beliefnet.com/faiths/secular-philosophies/atheists-in-foxholes.aspx (Accessed 08/01/2017)

help me deal with my failed marriage because he was too distracted by his need to "save" me from my atheism.

I have already mentioned the shift in climate even further towards fundamentalist Christianity in the months and years following the attacks of September 11th, 2001. These are years in which the fundamentalist church machine has worked extremely hard to increase the number of chaplains in uniform, making fundamentalist Christians the fasting growing and most dominant religious group represented among the chaplain's corps.[1] These chaplains then systematically set out to change the military's culture to one that is even more religiously hard to the right than it was before. The chaplain who sabotaged the Wiccan service served before September 11th, 2001 but the one I encountered for marital counseling was several years later. From discussing this with other military atheists, I'm certain my experience was not unique, that subsequent encounters with chaplains by me and others became noticeably more pro-Christian and anti-everything else after September 11th.

The years we fought (and are still fighting) wars in Afghanistan and Iraq have been long ones for those who serve in uniform, although the fight has been largely invisible to the majority of the population who don't serve or who don't love someone who serves. One of the difficulties has been trying to convince ourselves and the world that we are and have been waging war against terrorists and those who produce terrorists, not Muslims or the Islamic religion. However, from the beginning of these recent wars, it has not been uncommon to find fighting tanks decked out in crusader or biblical imagery as they patrolled the streets of these Islamic places. Even our own equipment proclaimed this idea. For example, a company that manufactured rifle sights for the wars stamped each sight with Bible verses.[2] And it was a common practice, as it is now, to form chaplain led prayer circles prior to combat missions in which non-Christians risked isolating and alienating themselves from the people they would be fighting with if they did not pretend to participate.

---

[1] Sharlet, Jeff (2011). "Christianity in the Military: Are Chaplains Becoming Increasingly Fundamentalist?" *Huffington Post*.
http://www.huffingtonpost.com/jeff-sharlet/christianity-in-the-milit_b_747585.html (Accessed 08/01/2017)

[2] Gaskell, Stephanie (2010). *NY Daily News*. "Michigan weapons company Trijicon takes flak over soldiers' rifle scopes branded with Bible verses"
http://www.nydailynews.com/news/national/michigan-weapons-company-trijicon-takes-flak-soldiers-rifle-scopes-branded-bible-verses-article-1.458908 (Accessed 08/01/2017)

A few years ago, *Fox News* leapt upon a "story" that indicated a military chapel in Afghanistan was being forced to remove its Christian steeple, which they represented as there being some sort of anti-Christian discrimination taking place. However, the true story is that military chapels overseas, as I have already mentioned, are supposed to be neutral so that they can be affixed with temporary religious implements specific to the service being held. This chapel was simply being returned to its regulatory required state of neutrality. I ultimately ended up defending the action on *Fox News* in a segment in which I was fitted with an earpiece. However, the audio was garbled and when my segment started, I initially couldn't hear.[1] I was defending the practice from the ridiculous allegation that because most service members were Christian, than the chapel should remain Christian. This is an idea both reprehensible and unconstitutional as our constitution protects the liberties of minorities from majority tyranny.

I retired from active duty in 2008 but I am still employed by the Army as a civilian and, as such, I remain astutely aware of the issues affecting the military today. What's more, some of those things that affect Army personnel still also affect me.

For example, until recently, Army soldiers and civilians were required to submit to an online assessment to measure mental and physical health with one of the components of mental health being something called Spiritual Fitness. The intent of the measure was based on the now-discredited idea that spiritual service members and civilians were healthier, more grounded, and less likely to suffer from mental health issues and suicidal ideations.[2] Failure of any component of these assessments required commanders to be notified so that they could track and repair the alleged deficiency. To no one's surprise, when I took my assessment, I quickly discovered there was no way to pass the module without professing religious and spiritual beliefs and I was quickly determined to "lack a sense of meaning and purpose to my life" among other issues. Complaints were widespread and swift but while this version of the assessment is no longer a requirement, the effects still linger. For example, installations such

---

[1] Rodda, Chris (2012). "The Camp Pendleton Cross: The Facts vs. What the "Persecuted" Christians Are Saying", *Huffington Post*. http://www.huffingtonpost.com/chris-rodda/the-camp-pendleton-cross-_b_1124251.html (Accessed 08/01/2017)

[2] Hagerty, Barbara Bradley (2011). "Army's 'Spiritual Fitness' Test Angers Some Soldiers", *NPR*. http://www.npr.org/2011/01/13/132904866/armys-spiritual-fitness-test-angers-some-soldiers (Accessed 08/01/2017)

as Fort Hood, Texas have constructed multi-million dollar "resiliency" campuses, on which Christianity and Christian teachings are considered the primary source of "resiliency" among the troops, and these campuses and the chaplaincy fund Christian-only marital retreats in plush locations at taxpayer expense.

Much of my account to this point are stories about the past but the pernicious influence of Christian fundamentalism persists in the modern military today. The military is grappling with an epidemic of sexual assaults and sexual harassment with the primary victims being women in uniform. When I was serving in Iraq, the most dangerous threat to a female soldier was that posed by her fellow soldiers on her side, not an enemy combatant. This is still true today as the instances of reported and substantiated cases of sexual assault has never been higher. Christianity teaches that women are inferior to men and when women are inferior to men, it makes it much easier to justify victimizing them. As a recent example, the Military Religious Freedom Foundation successfully tackled a case in which an Air Force unit displayed a series of posters that explicitly favored religious belief over non-religious belief, and they were shockingly sexist as well.[1] A few minutes further exploration of this website quickly shows that Christian favoritism among the military services is a poisonous pattern that is experienced by service members who are serving now, not only those who have served in the past.

The Military Religious Freedom Foundation has documented instance after instance of covert and overt harassment and discrimination directed at the non-religious and those who don't live lifestyles acceptable to fundamentalist Christians. One major issue for the evangelical right has been the repeal of "Don't Ask Don't Tell" which has allowed openly gay service members to serve and even have their marriages treated like cis-gendered marriages with full benefits. Since then, elements within the chaplaincy have not only opposed the "normalization" of gay unions falling back on faith-based objections, but they

---

[1] Rodda, Chris (2017). "Victory for Women in the Military: Sexist Religious Posters Removed from Air Force Base", *Huffington Post*. http://www.huffingtonpost.com/entry/58b49e61e4b0e5fdf61975e3 (Accessed 08/01/2017)

have worked to effectively sabotage service members with the goal of stripping them of the civil rights they have rightly earned and deserve.[1]

Recently, a member of my own military unit committed suicide, which was a tragedy for his family and devastating to those who worked with him and called him a friend. His untimely and tragic death triggered rounds of mandatory counseling and mental health assessments that on the surface, appeared to be a laudable goal but, in practice, was afflicted with the usual pro-Christian bias and favoritism I have become accustomed to. Everyone in the unit was offered the chance to speak to the unit chaplain, but not the chance to seek and receive free secular grief counseling from a real mental health professional. Everyone in the unit was mandated to attend a peer-to-peer group counseling session with a specially trained peer. Our peer made it clear to all of us that, as a Christian with strong Christian beliefs, it was his personal belief that our dead friend was now burning in hell. At the same session, our most senior commander praised his own Christian faith and described how his faith influenced his ability to cope and lead.

Shortly before I retired, I had the occasion to attend a memorial service for all the service members in my career field who had died fighting the long and grinding wars in the post September 11th, 2001 era. This service was entirely a Christian service at which everyone present at the base in our career field was required to attend. From the opening prayer to the songs to the Bible readings to the choir to the closing benediction, every moment of the memorial service was Christian. This was a service by Christians for Christians to honor whom they perceived as dead Christians with absolutely no attempt to acknowledge those in our career field who were killed while holding other faiths or none. It was the same story for the more modest and personal memorial service for our troubled friend who was well known as not being a Christian.

The more things change, the more the bigoted right fights to keep them the same, the harder we and the organizations we represent will dutifully campaign for the rights of those who are really discriminated against. Organizations such as American Atheists, the Military Association of Atheists and Freethinkers, the Military Religious Freedom Foundation, and the Freedom from Religion Foundation will continue to advocate for those who serve.

---

[1] Rodda, Chris (2016). "Gay-Bashing Chaplain Endorsers Admit That The Military Chaplaincy Is Disproportionately Anti-LGBT", *Huffington Post*. http://www.huffingtonpost.com/chris-rodda/gay-bashing-chaplain-endo_b_13867166.html (Accessed 08/01/2017)

Seeing God in Education as Child Abuse

Michael Stone, Progressive Secular Humanist

Teaching children that the earth is only 6,000-years-old, that human beings and dinosaurs lived on the earth at the same time, and that the story of Noah's Ark is true, constitutes intellectual child abuse.

Every child deserves an education. However, many children in the U.S. and around the world are denied an education in the name of religious superstition. In the U.S. some children are denied a science education because they are being home-schooled or attend Christian schools that fail to teach the facts of basic biology, like evolution.

Instead of learning about evolution, children in extreme Christian environments are taught creationism. This is wrong, and immoral. Children have a right to a science education. Denying children a science education by teaching creationism presents a significant challenge to the educational establishment, particularly in the U.S.

Evolution is the single, unifying scientific explanation for the diversity of life on earth, and the foundation upon which the biological sciences are built.

Indeed, the scientific theory of evolution is accepted by an overwhelming majority of mainstream scientists around the world as the cornerstone of biology. To deny the reality of evolution is to deny the foundation upon which modern medicine and related biological sciences are built.

Thus, if there is a controversy about evolution, it is not scientific. The controversy is not about science, but religion. The fact is that once the theory of evolution is accepted, a literal, fundamentalist reading of Biblical creation is rendered untenable. Many Christian and other religious fundamentalists are simply unable to accept evolution as a scientific truth for this reason.

And because adults refuse to accept the scientific truth of evolution, children suffer.

Recently, a voice of reason, everybody's favorite "Science Guy," Bill Nye, spoke out against creationism in an essay published in Skeptical Inquirer.[1] Noting that creationism is "bad for science education, bad for the U.S., and thereby bad for humankind," Nye went on to note:

> "...if you, as an adult, want to hold on to a completely unreasonable explanation of the Earth's natural history that is useless from a practical standpoint, that's your business. But we don't want our kids, our science students, to be indoctrinated into that weird worldview, because our kids are the scientists and engineers of the future. They need to be the innovators that drive the U.S. economy in the coming decades."

And speaking to Popular Mechanics about the problems of teaching children creationism, and why evolution is key to a science education, Nye declared:[2]

> "Science is the key to our future, and if you don't believe in science, then you're holding everybody back. And it's fine if you as an adult want to run around pretending or claiming that you don't believe in evolution, but if we educate a generation of people who don't believe in science, that's a recipe for disaster. We talk about the Internet. That comes from science. Weather forecasting. That comes from science. The main idea in all of biology is evolution. To not teach it to our young people is wrong."

Nye is not alone. Top scientists Richard Dawkins and Lawrence Krauss also advocate for children, arguing children should be allowed to develop as critical thinkers and be protected from religious indoctrination.

---

[1] Nye, Bill (2014). "Special Report: Bill Nye's Take on the Nye-Ham Debate," *Skeptical Inquirer*, Volume 38.3
http://www.csicop.org/si/show/bill_nyes_take_on_the_nye-ham_debate (Accessed 06/30/2017)

[2] Fecht, Sarah (2011). "Science Guy Bill Nye Explains Why Evolution Belongs in Science Education," *Popular Mechanics*,
http://www.popularmechanics.com/science/animals/a6455/evolution-classroom-bill-nye-science-education/ (Accessed 06/21/2017)

Speaking with The Irish Times, Dawkins, a leading biologist, and Krauss, a leading theoretical physicist, defended a child's right to a proper education.[1]

Dawkins also said:[2]

> "There is a balancing act and you have to balance the rights of parents and the rights of children and I think the balance has swung too far towards parents. Children do need to be protected so that they can have a proper education and not be indoctrinated in whatever religion their parents happen to have been brought up in."

Krauss added:[3]

> "That means parents have a limited — it seems to be — limited rights in determining what the curriculum is. The state is providing the education, it's trying to make sure all children have equal opportunity.
>
> "And parents of course have concerns and a say, but they don't have the right to shield their children from knowledge. That's not a right any more than they have the right to shield their children from health care or medicine.
>
> "And those parents that do that are often tried and imprisoned when they refuse to allow their children to get blood transfusions or whatever is necessary for their health. And this is necessary for their mental health."

Dawkins, Krauss, Nye, and others make an interesting and compelling claim: Forcing children to accept the religious superstitions of their parents can be a form of child abuse.

For example, teaching children Biblical creationism as a legitimate scientific alternative to the theory of evolution is considered by many to qualify as a form of said child abuse.

---

[1] Humphreys, Joe (2015). "Richard Dawkins: Children need to be 'protected' from religion," *The Irish Times*, http://www.irishtimes.com/news/education/richard-dawkins-children-need-to-be-protected-from-religion-1.2116281 (Accessed 06/30/2017)

[2] Rothkopf, Joanna (2015). "Richard Dawkins on attack: "Children need to be protected" from religious parents," *Salon*, http://www.salon.com/2015/02/25/richard_dawkins_children_do_need_to_be_protected_from_religious_parents/ (Accessed 06/30/2017)

[3] ibid.

In fact, Krauss has explicitly claimed this, of teaching children creationism. Appearing on the "The Weekly," an Australian satirical TV news show, he stressed the importance of teaching children critical thinking skills. When host Charlie Pickering brought up the fact that Krauss had previously stated that teaching children creationism is a form of child abuse. Krauss doubled down on his claim, noting:[1]

> But it's true. I mean, there are different levels of child abuse. It's like not allowing your children to have medicine, not allowing your children to be vaccinated, for example, is child abuse, because you are doing them harm.

Krauss went on:

> In some sense, if you withhold information from your children because you would rather them not know what reality is really like, for fear that it is going to affect their beliefs, then you are doing them harm.

And speaking for Big Think, Krauss said:[2]

> "It amazes me that people have pre-existing notions that defy the evidence of reality. But that they hold onto them so dearly. And one of them is the notion of creationism...
> "If you think about that, somehow saying that, well, anything goes, we shouldn't offend religious beliefs by requiring kids to know - to understand reality; that's child abuse. And if you think about it, teaching kids - or allowing the notion that the earth is 6,000 years old to be promulgated in schools is like teaching kids that the distance across the United States is 17 feet. That's how big an error it is.
> "Now you might say, look, a lot of people believe that, so don't we owe it to them to allow their views to be present in school? Well, as

---

[1] Dolan, Eric W. (2015). "Lawrence Krauss: Parents who teach creationism are child abusers — just like anti-vaxxers," *Raw Story*, http://www.rawstory.com/2015/07/lawrence-krauss-parents-who-teach-creationism-are-child-abusers-just-like-anti-vaxxers/ (Accessed 06/30/2017)

[2] Krauss, Lawrence (2013). "Lawrence Krauss: Teaching Creationism is Child Abuse," *Big Think (You Tube)*, https://www.youtube.com/watch?v=UTedvV6oZjo (Accessed 06/30/2017)

I've often said, the purpose of education is not to validate ignorance but to overcome it."

Krauss is correct. Preventing children from learning the truth about the world, like teaching children that creationism is an acceptable scientific explanation for the diversity of life on Earth, is failing to provide basic educational needs. The Centers for Disease Control and Prevention (CDC) uses the term *child maltreatment* to refer to both acts of commission (abuse) and acts of omission (neglect). This can include "words or overt actions that cause harm, potential harm, or threat of harm to a child." Furthermore, they state that it comprises:[1]

> "...the failure to provide for a child's basic physical, emotional, or educational needs or to protect a child from harm or potential harm."

The leading proponent of creationism is Ken Ham, founder of *Answers in Genesis*, an organization devoted to teaching and promoting the false notion that Biblical creationism is a legitimate scientific theory. Ham and his organization produce and supply much of the literature and curriculum used by Christian schools and others to teach children creationism.

Ham and his organization are also behind the Ark Encounter and the Creation Museum. Aimed at children and located in Kentucky, the multi-million dollar facilities are part of Ham's Christian fundamentalist project to spread his flawed and misleading message based on discredited science and a literal interpretation of Genesis.

The Creation Museum and life-size version of Noah's Ark are designed to be an exercise in Christian propaganda: a deplorable attempt to deceive children and others by denying the scientific reality of biological evolution and promoting Christian mythology as scientific fact.

The 500-foot-long, $100 million ark opened in 2016, and is dedicated to indoctrinating children with ridiculous and discredited claims from the dubious field of "creation science," claims such as the earth is only 6,000-years-old, that

---

[1] Leeb, R.T.; Paulozzi, L.J.; Melanson, C.; Simon, T.R.; Arias, I. (January 2008). *Child Maltreatment Surveillance: Uniform Definitions for Public Health and Recommended Data Elements, Version 1.0*. Atlanta, Georgia: Centers for Disease Control and Prevention, National Center for Injury Prevention and Control.

human beings and dinosaurs lived on the earth at the same time, and that the story of Noah's Ark is true.

After visiting Ham's Ark Park, Bill Nye told NBC News:[1]

> "It's all very troubling. You have hundreds of school kids there who have already been indoctrinated and who have been brainwashed."

Nye lamented:

> "On the third deck (of the ark), every single science exhibit is absolutely wrong. Not just misleading, but wrong."

Nye is right to be disturbed. Children are indeed being brainwashed and indoctrinated. By teaching children creationism as a legitimate scientific theory that disproves the theory of evolution, Ken Ham's Ark Encounter is engaging in a form of the aforementioned intellectual child abuse.

The truth is that there is no scientific controversy concerning evolution. The assumption that creationism, or intelligent design, constitutes a legitimate scientific alternative to the theory of evolution, is simply false.

Simply put, creationism is not a legitimate scientific alternative to the theory of evolution. And preventing children from learning the truth about the world, like teaching children that creationism is an acceptable scientific explanation for the diversity of life on Earth, is a "failure to provide for a child's basic physical, emotional, or educational needs or to protect a child from harm or potential harm."

One example of the absurdity entailed by creationism is as follows: Answers in Genesis founding board member and self-described "Creation Scientist" Carl Kerby insists[2] dinosaurs were on Noah's Ark, explaining that Noah selected only young and small dinosaurs, and that is how they could all fit on Noah's big boat.

---

[1] Ortiz, Erik (2016). "'Absolutely Wrong': Bill Nye the Science Guy Takes on Noah's Ark Exhibit," *NBC News*, http://www.nbcnews.com/science/science-news/absolutely-wrong-bill-nye-science-guy-takes-noah-s-ark-n608721 (Accessed 06/30/2017)

[2] Dolan, Eric W. (2014). "Creationist Carl Kerby insists dinosaurs were on Noah's Ark: They took the younger ones," *Raw Story*, http://www.rawstory.com/2014/04/creationist-carl-kerby-insists-dinosaurs-were-on-noahs-ark-they-took-the-younger-ones/ (Accessed 06/30/2017)

Speaking to Bryan Fischer of the American Family Association, "Creation Scientist" Kerby said:

> "I see some people that like to mock and ridicule, especially about the dinosaurs, how did they put the big old dinosaurs on there?
> "Well, I would suggest to you they didn't take the big old dinosaur — they would have taken the younger ones. You think of a guy like me, if you're going to go repopulate a planet, you're not taking me with you. I'm old. My repopulating days are done. You take my son or my grandson. My grandson is a whole lot smaller than I am."

The stupid, it burns.

However, Ham is not alone in his desire to force creationism into the science classroom. American politicians routinely try to smuggle it into the public school classroom via various nefarious legislative efforts. From state legislatures to the highest reaches of government, creationism has powerful proponents that would happily sacrifice the intellectual health of children on the altar of religious superstition.

In fact, even Vice President Mike Pence believes that creationism should be taught in public schools.[1] When serving as a congressman, Pence made it clear that he opposes evolution, while claiming that creationism (intelligent design) provides the only "rational explanation for the known universe."

In 2002, Pence delivered a passionate speech on the floor of the House of Representatives arguing that evolution is "only a theory" and that public schools should teach the theory of intelligent design as well as the theory of evolution.

Pence told his colleagues:[2]

> "I believe that God created the known universe, the earth and everything in it, including man. And I also believe that someday scientists will come to see that only the theory of intelligent design

---

[1] Stone, Michael (2016). "Mike Pence Wants Creationism Taught In Public Schools," *Progressive Secular Humanist*, http://www.patheos.com/blogs/progressivesecularhumanist/2016/08/mike-pence-wants-creationism-taught-in-public-schools/ (Accessed 06/30/2017)

[2] Pence, Mike (2002). "Theory of the Origin of Man," *Congressional Record*, July 11, 2002, 107th Congress, 2nd Session, Issue: Vol. 148, No. 93 — Daily Edition, https://www.congress.gov/congressional-record/2002/7/11/house-section/article/h4527-1 (Accessed 06/30/2017)

provides even a remotely rational explanation for the known universe."

In other words, for Pence, the only rational explanation is "God did it."

In his speech to congress, Pence also made the false and misleading claim[1] that creationism is a valid scientific alternative to the theory of evolution, arguing that creationism should be taught alongside evolution in the public school science classroom.

The question is begged: Why is creationism so important to so many Christians? Well, it may be that evolution exposes the flimsy house of cards that is the foundation of Christianity, and by extension, all Abrahamic religions. For if one embraces science, and accepts the scientific account of evolution, one must dismiss biblical creationism as myth, metaphor, or some other euphemism for factually untrue.

Speaking for many Christian fundamentalists, Answers in Genesis President Ken Ham argues that any coherent understanding of Christianity depends upon a literal interpretation of the Bible, including a belief that the story of Noah and the account of creation offered in the Book of Genesis is historically accurate.

The fact is, for many, once biblical creationism is rejected, Christianity unravels: there is no Adam and Eve, no original sin, and no need for redemption through the blood of Christ.

In addition, once one biblical account of supernatural absurdity is rejected, all other biblical accounts of supernatural absurdities become suspect, including the very absurdity that is God. Indeed, implicit in evolution is a powerful argument for atheism. And this drives some Christians to ridiculous positions, like clinging to the untenable claim that the earth is only 6,000 years old, that human beings and dinosaurs lived on the earth at the same time, and that the story of Noah's Ark is true.

To conclude: Forcing children to accept the religious superstitions of their parents is a form of child abuse. And it follows that teaching children Biblical creationism as a legitimate scientific alternative to the theory of evolution is an example of such child abuse.

---

[1] Rabin-Havt, Ari (2016). "FLASHBACK: Mike Pence Delivers Entire Speech Denying Evolution," *Right Wing Watch*, http://www.rightwingwatch.org/post/flashback-mike-pence-delivers-entire-speech-denying-evolution/ (Accessed 06/30/2017)

Yet if we are to accept the claim that teaching children creationism is child abuse, we are left with some hard questions:

What are the implications for social policy? Should the government step in and protect children from the religious superstitions of their parents? Should parents retain the right to force their religious beliefs upon their children, even when those beliefs are demonstrably harmful to the education of the child, as is the case with the teaching of creationism?

And what about religious schools, as well as homeschoolers, engaged in the explicit task of indoctrinating children, often with devastating emotional and intellectual consequences?

How does society protect children from the damaging excesses of religion?

How does society defend a child's right to a proper education, even if that education violates the sincerely held religious beliefs of their parents?

Bottom line: The belief that Biblical creationism constitutes a legitimate alternative to the theory of evolution harms American children, and constitutes powerful evidence in support of the claim that religion breeds ignorance, and religious indoctrination is sometimes child abuse.

Patheos Nonreligious

Not Wanting to See God in Education, but Damn, He's Still there

Jonny Scaramanga, Leaving Fundamentalism

I grew up as a Christian fundamentalist in the UK—a country that supposedly has no Christian fundamentalists. Now I've made my escape, I mostly blog to show people how extreme Britain's evangelicals are, and what damage those beliefs can do. This is a story about all that. But it's mostly an anyone story of how I spent four years banging my head against a brick wall trying to get to care about children in fundamentalist schools.

Christianity—especially its evangelical flavor—has a persecution complex. US readers will be familiar with the line that the liberal media is out to get Christianity. At the slightest whiff of a chance to bash Christianity, apparently, every newspaper and TV station in the land will explode.

Here in the UK, that narrative is a bit more muted, but we still hear *Daily Mail*-esque sentiments that in today's politically correct culture there is tolerance for everything except white heterosexual Christians. The Christian Institute (an organization sometimes over-generously described as a think tank) claims that there is "widespread discrimination"[1] against Christians in the UK. In a pamphlet called "Marginalising Christians"[2] they make out that media coverage is uniformly biased against Christians.

Anyone who thinks this is anything like reality should try getting the media to cover a campaign against a Christian organization.

---

[1] The Christian Institute (2015). "Extremism Against Christians," November 2015, http://www.christian.org.uk/wp-content/uploads/extremism-against-christians.pdf (Accessed 11/30/2016)

[2] The Christian Institute (2009). "Marginalising Christians Instances of Christians being sidelined in modern Britain" http://www.christian.org.uk/wp-content/uploads/marginchristians.pdf (Accessed 11/30/2016)

I set up my blog, *Leaving Fundamentalism*, in 2012. I've mostly used it to document my efforts to expose Accelerated Christian Education (ACE), an abusive and fundamentalist system of education used in about 6,000 schools worldwide, including 30 in the UK. I've spent a lot of the last four years trying to get a national newspaper to report on ACE, and it has never happened.

I care a lot about ACE because I went to one of their schools for three years, and it really messed me up. In fact, I'm just beginning to work out how badly it messed me up, having started therapy late in 2016. Like a lot of the other survivors I've met, some of the ideas they forced on me live on as voices in my head, affecting my decisions today. I'm still learning how to be assertive and how to interact healthily with other people.

The NARIC saga

In 2008, before I ever thought of blogging, a UK government agency (NARIC— national agency for the recognition and comparison of international qualifications and skills) produced a report stating that ACE graduation certificates are as good as A Levels, the national exams taken by 18-year-old students at mainstream schools in England. This was interesting (a word that here means "fucking horrendous") because:

- The NARIC report went against every independent review of ACE ever conducted. Every academic look at the curriculum before then had concluded that it was inadequate and unacceptable.
- By what is undoubtedly a TOTAL COINCIDENCE, NARIC's report was funded by a Christian school.
- ACE teaches young-Earth creationism as a scientific fact. At the time, its high school science materials included a paragraph claiming that the Loch Ness monster is real, and this shows evolution is false.
- ACE's high school geography course included a section defending Apartheid in South Africa.

In 2009, I wrote to NARIC pointing these things out. I copied my letter to the *Times Educational Supplement* (*TES*), a newspaper for teachers. The *TES* ran it as their front-page story the following week.[1] *The Guardian* buried a small article several pages inside the newspaper;[2] but no one else was interested. That was the last time a national print newspaper reported on ACE.

NARIC evidently got a lot of mail about this and decided they didn't like me very much. Thereafter, they declined to answer my questions on the phone. They did, however, issue a public statement, part of which said:

> Any enquiries relating to the NARIC's assessment of ICCE certificates and subject matters should be addressed to NARIC directly for response.
> A copy of UK NARIC's report can be made available upon request.

I, and Paul Pettinger of the British Humanist Association, both wrote to NARIC requesting a copy of their report. They refused to make it available, saying that they were going to review their decision and the report would be available after that. Paul Pettinger left his post and was replaced by Andrew Copson, who emailed NARIC to request the report every month without fail. After something like a year of refusals from NARIC, he gave up.

In 2012, NARIC produced a second report on ACE in which they repeated their assessment that ACE students were on a par with A Levels. Again, I wrote to NARIC requesting their report, and this time they changed their story: They said that the report (which had again been funded by ACE schools) was a "commercial in-confidence document" and so would not be made public. I asked them if they could at least tell me how they had evaluated the curriculum so that I could figure out why their conclusions contradicted everyone else who had critiqued it. They replied that NARIC's methodology is proprietary and therefore a commercial secret.

You see, although NARIC provides services to the UK government, it's actually run by a private company (ECCTIS Ltd), which means it isn't subject to Freedom of Information laws and has minimal transparency. These are the

---

[1] Shaw, Michael (2009). "Fundamentalist exams on a par with A-levels," *The Times Educational Supplement*, 14th August 2009, https://www.tes.com/news/tes-archive/tes-publication/fundamentalist-exams-a-par-a-levels-0 (Accessed 11/30/2016)

[2] Shepherd, Jessica (2009). "Creationist exams comparable to international A-levels, says Naric", *The Guardian*, 31st July 2009, https://www.theguardian.com/education/2009/jul/31/creationist-exams-comparable-to-a-levels (Accessed 11/30/2016)

joys of government outsourcing. I reminded NARIC of their 2009 promise that a copy of the report would be made available upon request. They did not reply.

So this is a pretty big story, right? It had everything: religious fundamentalism, bad education, a government agency acting without transparency, and the Loch Ness monster. I couldn't get a single newspaper to cover it. The *TES* ran a small article again ("Evolution? I don't believe it. Haven't you heard of Nessie?"), and there was otherwise universal indifference. It's almost as though this media conspiracy against Christians is only in the Christian Institute's imagination.

The Nessie explosion

Then Bruce Wilson, founder of the US left-wing site *Talk2Action*, picked up my story. He'd discovered that a voucher program in the state of Louisiana was giving government funding to ACE schools, and the Nessie headline was just the right hook to make it go viral. Then some Scottish newspapers picked it up, knowing their readers would love a novelty story about a) Nessie and b) Americans with ridiculous religious beliefs. Only *The Scottish Herald* mentioned that ACE schools also exist in the UK, and they buried this near the end of the article. The rest made out that this was only happening in America.

Still, the story exploded, thanks mainly to shares on liberal sites like *Salon*, *AlterNet*, and *RawStory*. By the end of summer 2012, if you entered "Accelerated Christian Education" into *Google*, autofill suggested "loch ness monster".

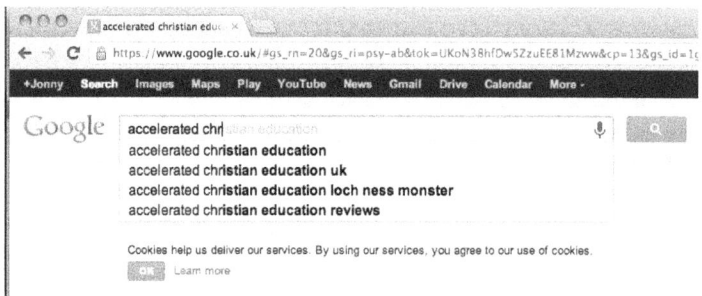

Even following this, I couldn't get an English newspaper to touch my story. And it wasn't like there wasn't more to cover. In England, a man called Stephen Dennett had been employed to carry out government-mandated inspections of ACE schools. Only one problem: Dennett was also employed at the time writing curriculum for... ACE. After I blogged about this conflict of interests, an independent journalism agency pitched this story to newspapers, and none of them would take it.

The Guardian let me write a couple of posts for their blog, and *New Statesman* did the same, but nothing ever made the news section or the print edition. The most depressing thing was that both articles received no shortage of scoffers claiming that my articles were exaggerated, misleading, or just plain false. Newspapers have run so many inaccurate stories that when I finally got a chance to expose the (admittedly unlikely-sounding) truth, people dismissed it. What's funniest about this is that *The Guardian*'s and *New Statesman*'s lawyers were *jumpy as hell*. They made me provide proof for every claim I made. I sent them scans of ACE's books to show that the stuff about Nessie, homosexuality, and apartheid really were there. They came back and said "How do you know this hasn't changed since you bought the books?" So I bought new copies of ACE's books and sent *those* scans, and they still shuffled their feet and delayed my articles for weeks. One article I wrote about racism in ACE's books got ditched altogether even after I went through that process. I couldn't figure it out. Tabloids churn out total bullshit on a daily basis with seemingly minimal repercussions, but when I wanted to tell the truth on a newspaper website, I was expected to prove every word. And people still doubted it.

In 2013, ACE removed the stuff about the Loch Ness monster from the editions it sells in Europe and Australia. I had finally embarrassed them enough that they'd been forced to take it out—my only real campaigning win in four years. This resulted in another round of Nessie headlines online and more silence from "serious" news organizations outside Scotland. ACE considered that their new Nessie-free PACE (which still said that cave paintings exist of dinosaurs, which they say is evidence that humans and dinosaurs coexisted) was a bastion of scientific credibility. Actually, it became an internet laughingstock when Richard Dawkins retweeted a picture of its last page.

I was sorry to see Nessie go. The new textbook, sans Nessie, was still full of pseudoscience and bullshit and was no better educationally, but now I'd been deprived of the guaranteed headline-grabber in my arsenal.

The BBC steps in

In 2014, finally I had what looked like a breakthrough. Anjana Ahuja contacted me about making a film on ACE for *Newsnight*, the BBC's flagship current affairs program. At the same time, I was asked onto the Jeremy Vine Show, a talk show with about a million listeners, to talk ACE, and two BBC journalists produced an article for the BBC website. This, surely, would provide the momentum to get the UK's newspapers to take notice, and ultimately force politicians to react.

My contact on the Jeremy Vine show told me that the BBC still has a reputation for the best fact-checking in the business. He thought local newspapers would carry the story now, because journalists know that if the BBC has reported something like this, it will be accurate. So I contacted the local newspapers in every city where I knew there was an ACE school, telling them what *Newsnight* had reported: ACE teaches students that homosexuality is a choice, that wives should submit to their husbands, and evolution is a lie.

There was so much more to say. ACE actually teaches students that homosexuality is an "immoral perversion", elsewhere comparing it to "murder or stealing". ACE claims it is against God's will for governments to provide healthcare or benefits of any kind. This appears to violate equality legislation and the requirement (compulsory in all English schools since 2012) for political education to contain a balanced presentation of opposing views.

Most of the local newspapers weren't interested. Think about that. Local newspapers, those organs that resort to headlines like "Footpath proves popular" and "Woman finds hat in tree" for lack of actual news, didn't want to know. And some people maintain the delusion that the media will look for any excuse to bash Christians.

Newspapers in Bristol and Windsor ran small stories, and the Manchester Evening News ran a big one. *The Independent* and *Daily Mail* ran copy-and-paste versions of the latter on their websites. *The (London) Times* managed a slightly more original web story, but again the print editions were silent. And even though websites now get more views than hard copy newspapers, it's still the print versions that set the news agenda. The Christian schools story wasn't important enough to make the "serious" section.

Finding a hook

Journalists are all convinced they can't report on something if it hasn't happened within the last ten minutes. If something really awful has been going on unreported for forty years, journalists think this is not news. Since ACE schools have been operating with impunity in England since 1979, journalists don't want to talk about it. They need a "hook." If successive governments had been burying citizens alive since 1960 to keep the unemployment figures down, this would not be news. If somebody famous stood up and said "The government burying people alive is a disgrace!" *that* would be news. Something has to happen *now* for journalists to report on. It's absolutely ridiculous, but that's part of why ACE is not in your newspaper.

For example, *The Times* reported in 1984 that ACE schools were beating their students. One school in London was routinely administering such beatings to its students, one of whom had cerebral palsy. This made the news at the time, and the nation as a whole shrugged and carried on its business. This carried on happening until 1999, when school corporal punishment was banned by law (though at my school it carried on after that, with parents now doing the hitting). But this was not news. It had been news in 1984, but the fact that the same shit was going on in 1998 was *old* and therefore not worth reporting.

Recently, it became law for schools to promote tolerance and respect for those with different religious beliefs. This is not exactly in line with ACE's repeated messages that children should not be friends with non-Christians. But "Christian schools carry on doing what they've always done despite new law" is apparently also not news. When no UK outlet would give me a platform to comment on this, I ended up writing about it for Hemant Mehta's blog, *The Friendly Atheist*.

Still, any number of things were happening with ACE which could have let journalists with an ounce of imagination expose them. The Advertising Standards Authority ruled (in three separate judgements) that ACE schools had falsely claimed that universities accept their graduation certificates. ACE schools had routinely misled parents and students about their chances of going to university, and the ASA had slapped them down. The ASA also informally resolved numerous similar complaints (from me and others) about other ACE schools. I couldn't get a newspaper to touch it; eventually the investigative magazine *Private Eye* ran a couple of small pieces.

There were more minor developments which could have provided a hook for any journalist who cared: The Trades Union Council's LGBT conference passed a resolution condemning ACE's teaching on homosexuality. Pink News got a statement from the shadow education secretary Tristram Hunt describing ACE's position as "dangerous" and "backwards". A new ACE school opened in Dover, and then closed almost immediately when it received a damning inspection report (unusual: ACE schools usually get whitewashed in inspections, because religious school inspectors are *selected for their sympathy to the religious ethos*).

The secret phone calls

In December 2014, an investigative journalist, Martin Williams, contacted me. He had secretly recorded phone calls to ACE schools in which he had posed as the parent of a gay child. He told them he was worried about his son being gay and asked if they could do anything to 'help'. More than one ACE school suggested that God could indeed cure his child of homosexuality. The most incriminating exchange happened when Martin asked if they could perform a 'deliverance'—casting out the demon of homosexuality. The teacher replied:

> "We do, but we don't do it here in school [...] We have to be sensitive because obviously we wouldn't want a deliverance going on in a room and then have Ofsted [school inspectors] walk in. That would be a bit awkward to explain …
> "Sometimes we'll have spiritual retreats for youth, for teens. These will be done over a period of three days on the weekend. We do it in a hotel in Bournemouth and all these things are going on there—deliverance and all these kinds of things."

Martin sent me some of the recordings to listen to, and they were indeed damning. Before pitching it to newspapers, he put on a live show with the comedian Josie Long. This was part of a planned series of events that aimed to bring investigative journalism to a new audience by combining it with stand-up comedy. I attended the launch in London, and the two skewered ACE brilliantly. The centerpiece was the recordings of phone calls in which ACE staff endorsed prayer and 'deliverances' as cures for homosexuality. I was giddy with excitement. Surely this was going to be the breakthrough the campaign needed.

Then we hit a roadblock. The newspapers Martin had previously written for rejected it. Then the next newspapers passed on it too. Eventually Martin gave up. No one would report on it.

Earlier in 2014, a fake memo about an Islamic plot to take over schools in Birmingham had sent the UK media into overdrive, but a genuine recording of a Christian teacher talking about exorcising a gay student couldn't find a column inch. Tell me again how British newspapers will take any excuse to bash Christianity.

I more or less gave up on the Martin's story, and swore off campaigning while I finished my PhD. Then, Siobhan Fenton at *The Independent* (once a UK print newspaper, now web-only) contacted me about doing a story on ACE. I put her in touch with several former students who talked about the sexism and homophobia they remembered from their school days, and supplied her with ACE workbooks as supporting evidence. Siobhan's initial story prompted several more former students to come out of the woodwork with more serious allegations, saying their schools performed exorcisms on them, beat them, and in some cases groomed girls for young marriages to older men.

None of this particularly surprised me, apart from the grooming. I remembered casting out demons and corporal punishment as such regular features of my upbringing that they seemed utterly mundane. I'd also spent much of 2015 and 2016 interviewing ex-students for my PhD who described similar events at their schools. Still, it was useful to have independent corroboration.

Inevitably, some people scoffed at ex-students' claims about exorcisms, so it would have been just perfect for Martin's tape to be released around then. If people were skeptical about students claiming to have demons cast out of them, a staff member offering the service ought to silence them.

Eventually, Martin got the webzine *Vice* to take the story. It looked like ACE would be exposed at last. Vice promised to do a two-part exposé, including both an article and a podcast. They were as good as their word, and both parts were released on the same day: November 8, 2016.

The day of the US Presidential election.

Fucking genius. ACE themselves couldn't have picked a better day to bury it. When I shared it on Facebook, even my friends (who know my campaigning against ACE well and knew how important this was) gave it hardly any likes. With the specter of a Trump presidency, no one could find a minute to give a damn about gay kids being abused in Christian schools.

So now what?

After four years of campaigning against ACE (during which time I also completed a PhD about former ACE students in England), I'm burned out. I've learned that I can give a talk to a Skeptics in the Pub group about ACE, and when I ask them if they'll write to their MPs about it, dozens of hands will go up. But I've also learned that once they leave the meeting, these people will remember that there are a million other demands on their time, a thousand other campaigns deserving of their support, and I'm lucky if one of those letters gets sent.

I've learned that I can have a meeting with civil servants in the Department for Education, but they are wholly at liberty not to follow up on anything from the meeting. And those civil servants may well not be in the same job this time next year, so any future meeting will start from scratch.

I recently saw a civil rights campaigner saying the only way to bring about social change is to make your demands impossible to ignore. The demands of ex-ACE students are, as British newspapers have so ably demonstrated, easily ignored. I am not capable of amplifying their voices enough to make them impossible to ignore, so I have to move on for a while, for my own health.

I guess ACE wins this round.

I have no idea what this means for Leaving Fundamentalism, my blog and campaign. I had always hoped that I would get this campaign to a point where it would have some kind of self-sustaining momentum, but I haven't built the network of people you'd need to make that happen. I helped the BHA set up Faith Schoolers Anonymous, a website for students and ex-students who have been harmed by religious schools to share their stories. I hope that in the long term this will change the way we think about religious schooling, shifting the emphasis from parents' rights to what is best for the students.

I'm sorry to subject you to such bathos at the end of this chapter, but I have no happy ending. I think that future efforts in this area should focus on helping the survivors, not on getting media exposure. What *The Daily Telegraph* will print is beyond my control, but helping an ex-ACE student rebuild their life and plug the gaps in their education is something we can do. And if I ever get the energy back to talk about ACE, that's what I'll be doing.

And then...

The above paragraph is how this chapter ended when I first submitted it for inclusion in December 2016. Then something remarkable happened: *The Sunday Times* and *The Daily Telegraph* printed stories about ACE within two days of each other.

In October, Ofsted, the school inspection service, had performed inspections of nine ACE schools on the same day and rated them all as "inadequate" or "needs improvement."[1] The schools, naturally, interpreted this as a sign of an anti-Christian agenda. Britain's right-wing press ran happily with the persecution narrative. Watchdog is picking on us, say Christian schools read *The Sunday Times* headline, while *The Telegraph* plumped for Christian schools are 'being picked on by Ofsted after Trojan Horse scandal', headteacher claims. The Christian schools' argument was barely coherent, claiming both that Christian schools were being singled out for discrimination and that Ofsted was just trying to show that it treated them the same as Islamic schools. Nevertheless, these august tomes reported their complaints sympathetically.

The Telegraph and *Times* coverage did not contain a single critical voice about the schools. Readers were not told about the homophobic, sexist, and anti-science content in ACE's materials, or the experiences of former students. The articles did not say that several of the schools were found to have either inadequate or non-existent criminal record checks for staff, missing or incomplete fire and safety procedures, and inadequate safeguarding procedures. Also unreported: two of the schools did not have an adequate supply of hot and cold water, and one had a live boa constrictor on the premises for which no health and safety evaluation had been performed.

In January 2017, numerous British newspapers, including *The Telegraph*, did report that a Christian school had kept a live boa constrictor on the premises. None of these articles mentioned Accelerated Christian Education or creationism, though, and none of them mentioned that Ofsted had also criticized the school for "an approach that is too far removed from the active promotion of respect for gay and lesbian men and women."

Fortunately, Siobhan Fenton at *The Independent* produced a third ACE article which did a somewhat better job of demonstrating why Ofsted might have found these schools inadequate. According to *The Sunday Times*, two of the schools closed shortly after their Ofsted reports were published. Off the back of this coverage, I was again invited to appear on the Jeremy Vine Show as well as BBC local radio. Although most people are still unaware of the issue, it's fair to say ACE is under more scrutiny in the UK now than at any point in its history.

It's impossible to say what difference my campaigning has made to all this. Maybe Ofsted just knew that after eighteen months of cracking down hard

---

[1] *The Telegraph* and *Sunday Times* reported that ten schools were inspected, and nine were rated inadequate or needs improvement. My fellow campaigner David Waldock requested a list of schools from Ofsted, and they only gave nine. We have been unable to find a tenth.

on homophobia in Jewish and Muslim schools, it could not continue to ignore it in Christian ones. I don't know why Ofsted conducted these inspections when it did, and it's clear that there is still confusion within the organization about what to with ACE. While some of the reports found the curriculum itself inadequate, criticizing its science content and lack of writing opportunities, one actually described the curriculum as "good." This is far from the end of the campaign, and ACE is just one of several groups of extremist religious schools in the UK.

What is very unlikely is that the ACE schools themselves have changed much. I have compared ACE materials sold today with ones from the 1980s. Some are completely unchanged, and those that have been updated have had little more than a new coat of paint. In my interviews with dozens of ex-ACE students from around the world, their descriptions of their schooling are remarkably similar, whether they last attended school in 1976 or 2009. So by rating these schools inadequate now, Ofsted has in fact admitted that they failed me and my peers. If these schools are unacceptable today, they were always unacceptable. Ofsted turned a blind eye while we were neglected and abused.

Still, whatever the reason, the future now looks more promising for British school children. It appears that bigotry and low standards are going to be addressed in private religious schools. We may even be able to look forward to a day when it is considered unacceptable to teach children that humans and dinosaurs lived together on Noah's Ark 4,000 years ago.

Part Three

LOOKING TOWARD A FUTURE IN A GODLESS WORLD

It has got to that point in the book now where we must consider both where we are going, and how we might get there. *Atheism* doesn't tell you very much about atheists. This is the common attack thrown against us nonbelievers.

Indeed, only today I was arguing with a theist about something I call the Argument from Divine Miscommunication. This is the idea that the plethora of religious revelations (experiences and holy texts) across and within religions, and all the denominations of those religions that evolve out of the varied interpretations, show us that either God does not exist, or that he is a very bad communicator.

Just take Christianity, with its purported 42,000 different denominations: if you hate gays, there is a Christianity for you; if you love gays, there is a Christianity for you; if you want socio-economic fairness, there is a Christianity for you; if you love money and prosperity, there is a Christianity for you; if you love black people, hate black people, love the environment, couldn't care less about it, right-wing, left-wing... heck, no matter who you are and what you believe, there's a theological Christian home for you somewhere.

It's almost as if we adapt our Christianity to our own core psychological dispositions or something...

The fact that there *is* so much muddled theology and varied denominational worldview construction, should tell us something.

The Ten Commandments are an interesting thing, too. Here was God's chance to properly nail his colors to the mast, to really have a go at defining the moral backbone of society. Here was God's chance to rule out slavery explicitly. To stake a claim on any number of superior moral positions.

But no. 'Twas not to be.

We could look at the Thirty Years War, Northern Ireland, or any other Christian-on-Christian conflicts over time (some 8 million perished in the former). These are the direct result of a failure to adequately communicate. But we could also extend this across religions. If God really wanted us to come to love him, to enter into that holy relationship, then he could appear to us now, universally, and say, "I'm here! And while I'm at it, you know that Islam thing, well, it's a load of old codswallop."

We then get into the whole cross on the moon idea. Indeed, we can look to extremes to clarify: either God tells us nothing, in which case we make up a load of things (for varying reasons and in varying ways) as a result of a complete lack of supernatural guidance, or God tells us everything and we are left in no doubt whatsoever that God exists, and what he wants from us.

If God put a cross on the moon now, and wrote some commands in the air in front of everyone's eyes, and so on, humanity would be left in little doubt.

On the one hand, we have no guidance and we are left to freely divine from the universe around us something about God; on the other hand, we are left with little to the imagination, being dictated everything about God and his expectations.

But at least in the latter case, we would get it right. At least humanity, as a whole, and all at once with equal access, would be given the same complete information.

Yes, there is joy in finding something when you spend a long time looking for it, but I would prefer not having to look, rather than spend a long time looking and having a larger chance of not finding it and going to hell for eternity for messing up the quest.

It's the classic issue of looking for an arbitrary, optimal level—a problem that often comes up in these scenarios. The problem is, with all our muddled confusions and doctrinal arguments and resulting death (or at the very least, getting it wrong), we must have had have a perfect amount of revelation.

Whatever amount of revelation that God decides to give us, since God is perfect and every choice he commits to is perfect (by extension), is itself perfect. This amount of revelation we have right now, this "imperfect", incomplete, confused revelation that has led to countless different and mutually exclusive religions, and 42,000 different denominations of Christianity—this level is perfect.

Since mysterianism (it's a mystery how it works, but it must be true!) is presently the preferred position du jour for understanding even the crucially important Holy Trinity, then the whole situation just looks incompetent and bizarre.

I've taken a long tie laying this out. So what did the theist say back to me?

> Seems a rather silly argument. How many different interpretations of atheism are there? Can we infer by logical extension that atheism is also false?... Are you an absurdist, an absolutist, a nihilist, humanist, utopian idealist, sadist? An angry atheist, a left-wing political atheist, a right-wing free market atheist? A positive atheist or a negative atheist? An agnostic? Narrow / broad atheist? Friendly or unfriendly? A philosophical vegan? All have access to the same "evidence" yet have many diverse opinions as to where that evidence should take them.
> So what is the argument? That we should expect to find different interpretations of physical evidence when it leads to an overall worldview of atheism, but we should expect to find exactly the same mono-culture of religion when it comes to interpretation of the theological evidence?

And there we have it, those misconceived words "worldview of atheism." *Atheism* is not a worldview. It is a single proposition to which a number of people hold, but it does not bind them together in any other way by necessity. In order to be a humanist or a left-wing political atheist, you have to do an awful lot more philosophy and politics. Yes, atheists might tend towards the left-hand side of the political spectrum, but it is not doctrinally necessitated. When we argue about politics, we are doing politics, and not atheism.

When Christians (for example) argue over the revelations and holy texts of their religion, they are doing theology. They are arguing *about their religion* and how it should be. Arguing for left-wing politics, for me as an (agnostic) atheist, is arguing about politics, irrespective of my atheism and atheology.

But if we *are* going to build up a worldview, way of living, a politics, that does take into account our atheism (but is not defined by it), then we need to think carefully about it. That is not to say the conclusions or action plans will flow necessarily out of that single proposition, that lack of belief. Not at all. Instead, we have to do all of those other things (philosophy, politics, science and so on). We often like to see ourselves as paragons of evidence-based policy making and decisions. But I know some atheistic conspiracy theorist nutjobs who play fast and loose with evidence. Atheism does not necessarily entail these add-ons.

That said, given an account of atheism, where *could* we go? What might society look like?

Let's find out.

How to Prepare for Not Seeing God

Martin Hughes, barrierbreaker

There's no one-size-fits-all answer to what happens after you stop believing in God. If there's one thing being an ex-Christian atheist has taught me, it's that no two atheists have the same history with religion, left religion for the exact same reasons, or think about what it means to have life without God in the same way. So I hesitate to give you a strict prescription, because whatever I prescribe will likely be different for you. The most I can give, really, is a description of some overall trends I have seen in my own life and the lives of others that may or may not apply to you. Because my background is in Christianity here in the United States, I'm going to focus on that context.

I'll say this: I no longer tell theists I don't know that life will be better for them if they leave Christianity. Sure, for most people, leaving Christianity is like leaving a straitjacket of rules and guidelines, and there is freedom to explore reality when you don't have to blindly agree with "because God said so" logic. But there's much more to leaving Christianity than the simple joy of not having to obey God, in most cases. Like someone weaned off a highly addictive drug, there will be benefits and, likely, some side effects.

When you are a Christian, you condition yourself to feel pleasure in certain situations, and not in others. You're given ways to deal with anxiety, worry, depression, loneliness, uncertainty, existential angst, and so on that might be more deeply ingrained in your psyche than you realize. And then there's the most intrusive thing about Christianity and other religions—the policing of relationships. Many deconversions end in divorce, due to the number of marriages held together by the concept that God is more important than the husband or wife. Many children's relationships with parents (and vice-versa) are centered on a strong sense of family faith, of the "in this house we will serve the Lord" variety, and in leaving the faith you might be disowned or estranged. Your friends might be people you go to church with, and they may not know exactly how to relate to you outside of religion. The essence of your sexuality might be tightly controlled by God, the music that you love might be colored by references to God, and the reason you get up in the morning and go to work may have something to do with God.

And then there is the afterlife. Many atheists take pride or comfort in the fact that they have the guts to give up the idea of heaven, but if the hope of heaven was a big part of your Christianity, that pride might be tinged with a bit of regret (at least at first). All those dreams you may have had of one day seeing your grandfather, or the friend who was killed while deployed in Afghanistan, or the relative who committed suicide—all those dreams have to die. Of course, so will your concern that they will go to hell, which is a positive. But giving up the idea of heaven can be a difficult adjustment. Perhaps, before, you were living for an afterlife in paradise, and now you have to live for the here-and-now.

The cold, hard truth, as far as I can see it, is that the deeper your connection to Christianity was, the harder it will be to leave it. No, I'm not talking about the lack of belief in God or gods—saying and thinking that God doesn't exist is often pretty easy. What might be more surprising is that your belief in God may have created habits or ways of thinking that might not be all that easy to shake off. That belief has also sustained relationships that might have grown to be very important to you, it may sustain hopes and dreams that are deeper parts of your motivation than you anticipated, and it may contain assumptions that you may gradually have to either unlearn, or relearn in a completely different framework.

And you will probably hurt people. That was the most surprising thing for me. I left religion fully expecting to get hurt by every Christian I knew; I was ready for the abuse. What I wasn't prepared for, though, was the genuine concern and worry people close to me had concerning my decision to leave religion. I wasn't prepared for close family members to cry, for hours, what I knew were genuine tears of concern because they were afraid I was going to go to hell. I was prepared to be disowned; I wasn't prepared for family members to go out of their way, through deep personal anguish of their own, to figure out how to adjust to me and learn to relate to me as I became beet-red angry at the core of everything they thought was valuable in the world. I had no idea that simply not believing that the God of the Bible didn't exist—just that simple fact—would cause so much turmoil in THEIR lives as they struggled to learn how to transition from loving the passionate servant of God to the outspoken atheist.

I also wasn't prepared to keep struggling with things like fear of death. Five years after I've left Christianity, my fear of death is finally starting to diminish, but it wasn't easy. Then, in addition, I had to find new motivation to get up in the morning, and nowadays that's starting to develop as well. I've lost friends, and gained friends. Most of the friendships I've kept have had to be rebuilt from the ground up.

I don't want to lie to you and say that you're going to enter a cute rose garden full of nothing but happiness, because leaving religion is usually not like that, especially if you do it in your late twenties and afterwards. When the dust settles, your life will be different, and likely not all for the better – though some parts may be.

You'll likely need another support group outside your religious circle, and places to vent your frustrations as you change, but remember that the rules of who people are don't automatically change when you become an atheist. One common thing I've seen is atheists who think that atheist groups can be more easily trusted than most churches, and thus let their guard down, making themselves ripe for people to take advantage of them. So don't set yourself up for disappointment. Group dynamics happen in most groups—any problems you saw due to politics in church may happen, to an extent, in any atheist groups you join. Joining a community of atheists is helpful when you've had enough of the religious drama, but if you rely on it too much, and expect from it too much, you may eventually be disappointed when you find out that the people in it are human, not paragons of virtue. If you have a hero, be prepared for that hero to be exposed, in some ways, as a villain; if you are against a villain, be prepared for them to turn out to be, in some ways, like a hero. The truth is that there are very few, if any, villains or heroes. We're all just people.

If you're a Christian considering leaving your church, I don't want you to go in expecting utopia. It's a bit like coming out of a cult or a gang. Someone coming out of a cult might initially get a sense of euphoria from the freedom, but it's important to remind them that eventually there will still be bills to pay, work to go to, relationships to create or end, and anger that some people you love remain in the cult and there's nothing you can really do about it. There's the practical reality of the day-to-day. Enjoy the freedom, but don't have a false expectation of utopia.

Let me give you some strategies to access positivity, though.

First, don't forget to embrace the reason God's nonexistence was important to you in the first place. Yes, we all arguably left God for rational reasons—the logic and the evidence didn't match up. But *why* did the question of God's existence or nonexistence become important enough to you to take it seriously? Was it because the concept of God didn't allow you to explore the beauty of existence as deeply as you wanted? Then explore. Was it because God made rules about who you could love and when? Then love freely. Was it because leaving God would give you independence? Then embrace a life independent of God. Sometimes it's tempting to focus so much on starting with a "fresh" slate after leaving God, or to get caught up in the post-deconversion turmoil, that the reason we left God in the first place becomes forgotten, and we miss out on the appeal of godlessness that made us intrigued in the first place.

One thing that's awesome about being an atheist is that you don't have to respect religious barriers to your actions or who you decide to associate with, and when. I think it's a good idea to find ways to connect with people, and in your newfound freedom they don't have to all do with religion. Because there is no God, and we're all just people, right? I found some meaning in joining marches and protests, and also in taking up social justice causes through writing. Yours may be different—it might be playing volleyball, or watching football, or having a Netflix night where you watch your favorite shows. You can even visit other religious traditions out of curiosity—there's no Atheist God who is going to be pissed at you for exploring the way other people think and conduct their lives.

Because you will be going through so many changes upon leaving God, you might go through an existential crisis every once in a while as you rebuild your way of thinking. One thing that will help in coping with that is exploring what other atheists or agnostics you relate to have said or thought before you. As an atheist, you have access to a wide range of secular philosophy. If it's bewildering, at first, to be faced with all the different ways proposed to you concerning how to cope with the world, a good idea might be to find a philosopher or philosophy that resonates with you now, and feel free to disagree with some aspects of it and embrace other ideas.

I'm not going to tell you to fight against religion, if you get meaning from it. I did for the first couple of years after I left Christianity, nearly constantly, and I still do, albeit a bit less frequently. But don't feel like that's an obligation. I made the mistake of feeling, sometimes, like fighting Christianity was a responsibility or something I had to do to make up for all the time I was a Christian. Other times, I thought that getting rid of religion was a desperate project that had to be completed in order to make a better world. I don't think that now, so I don't have a constant sense of evangelistic urgency anymore. I do get into the occasional debates and instances of outrage, but the longer I have lived without God, the less other people's religion has been a part of my life. It's certainly not this way for everybody; some people are in terrible circumstances that make atheism extremely difficult. If you're one of those people, fight away. But I encourage you to do it naturally—don't feel obligated to do it, and don't feel like you have to shut up about it. Just do what you feel you need to do.

If you're a religious person reading this who is thinking about what life after God is going to be like for you, remember: the longer you wait, the more difficult things are going to be. If you want to leave, it's better to do so sooner than later. If this life is truly the only one you get, then you should live it on your own terms as much as possible instead of spending more of it being entangled deeper and deeper into dogma that, deep inside, you know is not true. It hurts a bit at first, and then you'll likely have euphoria as you leave, and then you'll have to sort your life out…but after that, it's just life. The world is open to you.

I'd like to say one more thing, in closing.

All that love you once had for God—maybe try putting it into people. That's something I found—when I stopped loving God, I had a lot of love in my heart that I had to put somewhere—and I've saved some of it for myself, but I have had a lot to give to people. There's something about reaching out to others that can make your life deeply meaningful. I'm not saying that you have to follow or trust others blindly, or be naïve and think that they're perfect. I'm just saying that this is a place to put your love that can enrich your life.

No, this isn't a one-way street. You can also feel free to be loved by other people, in return—people who will love the parts of you that perhaps a mythical God thought was wrong. You'll be told by other people that you don't have that right, that you should keep your feelings to yourself, that you have to conform to religiously-based ideals of what those "sinful" parts of you are supposed to mean to be you. Those voices don't know what they're talking about. You're as much a part of the world as anything else, and you should feel free to express that. Feel free to talk to close friends about it, celebrate it in videos and blog posts, and communicate it to people who disagree with you, if you dare. This can be a valuable exercise for many people; I've found that communicating my journey honestly often seems like a way to carve out a place in this world where I fit. And when I do that, I oftentimes hear other people in my position who say I'm helping them, too—sometimes from very surprising places. If you're honest, you never know who will come out of the woodwork and say, "me too."

The best thing about living without God is that you're one step closer to being right. This is not to say that you're right about everything. There is more freedom to be right on issues, but there is also a lot of freedom to be wrong. But if you want to embrace a more nuanced, more open and more realistic view of people, becoming an atheist is a good first step. At least, it was for me. One major reason to become an atheist is for other people. Although you may make a lot of people sad by leaving a religion, becoming an atheist is often a prerequisite to having a more thorough, nuanced view of people that can allow you to treat them better, especially if your former religion had strict, not-to-be-questioned definitions of and protocols for what is right and what is wrong. For many people—myself included—becoming an atheist was a small price to pay for having a more accurate view of people. Christians often like to think we leave for solely selfish reasons, but in many ways I left so that I could better help people and see solutions that would make this world a better one for more individuals.

No, I didn't promise you utopia. But do you really want me to? All the empty promises in church, the demand that I always rejoiced in commands I didn't necessarily think were true, the overwrought encouragement to believe in a larger-than-life God...frankly, I got tired of all the overpromising and underdelivering. I'm not going to do that here. You have the freedom to have a realistic view of life. And in spite of Christian apologists saying it's a nightmare, it's not, in most cases. It just feels more like reality. Like in a previous life you were in a bubble separated from the world or distanced from it, and now, although there are still questions, you have the freedom to embrace the "real" world more directly, without God in the way. So no, atheism isn't necessarily offering you utopia.

It's offering you something that's arguably better: the freedom to embrace reality, instead.

Not Seeing God in Life's Meaning and Purpose

Gleb Tsipursky, Intentional Insights

According to traditional and unfortunately still mainstream perspectives, the meaning and purpose of life is to be found only in God. An example is *The Purpose Driven Life* (2002), a popular book written by Rick Warren, a Christian mega church leader.[1] Yet is this true? This article will explore the scientific research on meaning and purpose, and illustrate how we can find a secularly-informed approach to meaning and purpose in life.

Meaning and Purpose: Health Benefits

Before proceeding, let's clarify some terms. Scholars on meaning and purpose define "purpose" to refer to a broad aspiration in life that motivates one's everyday activities. They use "meaning" as a more overarching term to refer both to one's life purpose, but also one's broad comprehension of one's life, self, and the world. However, since life meaning and purpose are used interchangeably in everyday speech, I will use them interchangeably in this chapter to refer to the broader concept encompassed by "meaning" in the scholarship.[2]

Now, why should we care about this broad overarching drive and the comprehension of one's life, self, and the world? I have heard comments from many secular folks who dismiss the value of gaining a sense of meaning and

---

[1] Warren, Rick (2002). *The Purpose Driven Life* (Nashville: Zondervan)
[2] Steger, M.F., Sheline, K., Merriman, L., & Kashdan, T. B; Eds. T. B. Kashdan and Ciarrochi, J., (2012). "Acceptance, Commitment, and Meaning: Using the Synergy between ACT and Meaning in Life Research to Help." *Cultivating Wellbeing: Treatment Innovations in Positive Psychology, Acceptance and Commitment Therapy, and Beyond.*

purpose. I generally respond to them by pointing to the research on the vital role of having a deep meaning and purpose for mental and physical wellbeing. Research shows that people who have a clear answer have better lives.[1] They can deal much better with both everyday life and the most challenging situations. The classic research on meaning and purpose comes from Victor Frankl, an Austrian psychiatrist who lived through the concentration camps of the Holocaust. He described how those who had a sense of meaning and purpose in their lives were most likely to survive and thrive in the camps. He conducted research demonstrating this both during and after his concentration camp experience.[2]

Recent studies illustrate that people who feel that their life has meaning and purpose experience a substantially higher degree of mental wellbeing. For example, Michael F. Steger, a psychologist and Director of the Laboratory for the Study of Meaning and Quality of Life at Colorado State University, found that many people gain a great deal of psychological benefit from understanding what their lives are about and how they fit within the world around them. His research demonstrates that people who have a strong sense of meaning and purpose have greater mental wellbeing in general. They are more satisfied on a day-to-day basis, as well as at work.[3] Adolescents, in another study, are shown to feel less depressed, anxious, and are less likely to engage in risky behaviors the greater their search for, and sense of, meaning.[4]

A deeper sense of life meaning and purpose also predicts better physical health. Greater meaning and purpose has been associated with a reduced risk of Alzheimer's disease.[5] An increased sense of life meaning and purpose correlates with reduced risk of heart attack, the leading cause of death in the United States,

---

[1] Seligman, M., (2002). *Authentic Happiness* (NY: The Free Press), pg. 30-44.
[2] Frankl, V.E. (1964) *Man's Search for Meaning* (London: Hodder & Stoughton), pg. 101-36.
[3] Steger, M. F., Dik, B. J., & Duffy, R. D. (2012). "Measuring Meaningful Work: The Work and Meaning Inventory (WAMI)." *Journal of Career Assessment* 20.3: 322-337.
[4] Brassai, L., Piko, B. F., and Steger, M. F. (2011). "Meaning in Life: Is it a Protective Factor for Adolescents' Psychological Health?" *International Journal of Behavioral Medicine* 18.1: 44-51.
[5] Boyle, P.A. et al. (2010) "Effect of a Purpose in Life on Risk of Incident Alzheimer Disease and Mild Cognitive Impairment in Community-Dwelling Older Persons." *Archives of General Psychiatry*. 67.3: 304-310.

and stroke, another of the top five leading causes of death.[1] With such benefits for mental and physical wellbeing, it is no wonder that a strong sense of life meaning and purpose predicts longevity, whether in the United States or around the world.[2]

Thinkers on Meaning and Purpose

Faith-based, mainstream perspectives perceive the meaning and purpose of life to be found only in the divine. An example of a prominent recent religious thinker is Karl Barth, one of the most important Protestant thinkers of modern times. In his *The Epistle to the Romans* (1933), he calls modern people's attention to God in Christ, where the true meaning and purpose of life must be found.[3]

Rick Warren represents a more recent and very prominent religious thinker, whose book powerfully shaped the public dialogue on life meaning and purpose. Warren's book epitomizes the traditional, conservative, faith-based perspective on meaning and purpose in life. In his book, he argues that the most basic question everyone faces in life is "Why am I here" and "What is my purpose?" The answer that Warren provides is that "real meaning and significance comes from understanding and fulfilling God's purposes for putting us on earth." The book describes five specific purposes that Warren claims God has for all of us: 1) We were planned for God's pleasure, and thus the first purpose is to offer real worship; 2) We were formed for God's family, and thus the second purpose is to engage in real Christian fellowship; 3) We were created to become like Christ, so the third purpose is to learn real discipleship; 4) We were shaped for serving God, so the fourth purpose is to practice real ministry; 5) We were made for a mission, so the fifth purpose is to live out real evangelism.[4]

While Warren represents the mainstream faith-based view, some thinkers disagree with the notion that religion is the only way to find meaning and

---

[1] Kim, E. et al. (2013) "Purpose in Life and Reduced Risk of Myocardial Infarction Among Older U.S. Adults with Coronary Heart Disease: A Two-Year Follow-Up. *Journal of Behavioral Medicine* 36.2: 124-133; Kim, E., et al. (2013). "Purpose in Life and Reduced Incidence of Stroke in Older Adults: The Health and Retirement Study." *Journal of Psychosomatic Research* 74.5: 427-432.
[2] P. A. Boyle, "Purpose in Life is Associated with Mortality Among Community-Dwelling Older Persons. *Psychosomatic Medicine* 71.5 (2009): 574-579.
[3] Barth, K. (1933) *The Epistle to the Romans* (London: Oxford University Press).
[4] Warren, Rick (2002). *The Purpose Driven Life* (Nashville: Zondervan)

purpose in life. The prominent philosopher John Dewey argued for a pragmatic and naturalistic approach to evaluating life's big questions, such as finding meaning and purpose. He called for empirical testing and validation of any abstract claims, grounding out such claims in how they would guide behavior, and then evaluating whether such conduct would be beneficial. In other words, Dewey's approach to meaning and purpose would involve seeing how any framework of thinking about meaning and purpose actually guided human action, and then evaluating whether that action actually led to a richer and deeper sense of meaning and purpose.[1]

Jean-Paul Sartre, in his 1957 *Existentialism and Human Emotions*, advances the notions of "existentialism," the philosophical perspective that all meaning and purpose originates from the individual. The challenge for modern individuals, according to Sartre, is to face all the consequences of the discovery of the absence of God. He argues that people must learn to create for themselves meaning and purpose.[2]

The well-known philosopher Paul Kurtz argued for a new approach that he calls *eupraxsophy*. He uses the term, which literally means "good practice and wisdom," to describe a specifically secular and non-religious approach to life. In the tradition of Dewey, he argued for a pragmatic, naturalistic, and empirically validated approach to human values and big life questions, including meaning and purpose in life. Kurtz specifically emphasized the important role of placing humanity within its context of the natural world while also orienting toward hope and optimism about the future.[3] These sentiments echo Kurtz's earlier writings, such as in his *Forbidden Fruit: The Ethics of Secularism*, where he calls for developing a rationally-based sense of ethics and morals, which includes a sense of meaning and purpose derived from a realistic appraisal of nature.[4] A more recent prominent thinker is Greg Epstein. In his *Good Without God: What a Billion Nonreligious People Do Believe*, he advocates striving for dignity as a means of finding "meaning to life beyond God." According to Epstein:

---

[1] Dewey, J. (1976). "The Logic of Judgments of Practice," in *The Middle Works, 1899–1924*, vol. 8, J. A. Boydston (ed.).
[2] Sartre, J.-P. (1957) *Existentialism and Human Emotions* (New York : Philosophical Library).
[3] Kurtz, P. (2012). *Meaning and Value in a Secular Age: Why Eupraxsophy Matters: The Writings of Paul Kurtz*, N. Bupp ed., (New York: Prometheus).
[4] Kurtz, P. (2008). *Forbidden Fruit: The Ethics of Secularism* (New York: Prometheus)

"we are not wicked, debased, helpless creatures waiting for a heavenly king or queen to bless us with strength, wisdom, and love. We have the potential for strength, wisdom, and love inside ourselves. But by ourselves we are not enough. We need to reach out beyond ourselves—to the world that surrounds us and sustains us, and most especially to other people. This is dignity". (93)[1]

Michael Martin, a notable secular philosopher, is particularly vocal in claiming not only that one can lead a meaningful life without belief in a deity, but that the Christian approach to morality and meaning has deep flaws. In his 2003 *Atheism, Morality, and Meaning*, Martin outlines the deep impact of the Judeo-Christian legacy on American society and culture, especially its sense of morals and ethics. He highlights the dangers of basing one's sense of morals and life meaning on the idea of imitating the life of Jesus and the Divine Command Theory. He then demonstrates convincingly how one can derive a sense of meaning in life without religious belief, instead focusing on a reason-oriented, empirical perspective.[2] Another notable recent thinker is Michael Shermer, who states in his *How We Believe: The Search for God in an Age of Science* (2000):

> I am often asked by believers why I abandoned Christianity and how I found meaning and purpose in the apparently meaning- and purposeless universe presented by science. The implication is that the scientific worldview is an existentially depressing one. Without God, I am bluntly told, what's the point? If this is all there is, there is no use. To the contrary. For me, quite the opposite is true. The conjuncture of losing my religion, finding science, and discovering glorious contingency was remarkably empowering and liberating. It gave me a sense of joy and freedom. Freedom to think for myself. Freedom to take responsibility for my own actions. Freedom to construct my own meaning and purposes and my own destinies. With the knowledge that this may be all there is, and that I can trigger my own cascading changes, I was free to live life to its fullest.[3]

---

[1] Epstein, G. (2009). *Good Without God: What a Billion Nonreligious People Do Believe* (New York: Harper).
[2] Martin, M. (2003). *Atheism, Morality, and Meaning* (New York: Prometheus)
[3] Shermer, M., (2000). *How We Believe: The Search for God in an Age of Science* (New York: W.H. Freeman), pg. 236.

Likewise, Sam Harris, in his *Waking Up: A Guide to Spirituality without Religion* (2014), states that

> Separating spirituality from religion is a perfectly reasonable thing to do. It is to assert two important truths simultaneously: Our world is riven by dangerous religious doctrines that all educated people should condemn, and yet there is more to understanding the human condition than science and secular culture generally admit. (6)[1]

Along the same lines, in *Atheist Meditation Atheist Spirituality* (2015) and *Exploring Your Life: Mindfulness Meditation and Secular Spirituality* (2015), Mark W. Gura agrees with Harris that atheists and humanists can use meditation as a means to access secular forms of spirituality, to attain stress-release and self-actualization without beliefs, or faith in God(s), pseudoscience or the supernatural, but he goes a step further. Gura argues that secular meditation can also produce a psychological state of mind that is, in-and-of-itself, a source of meaning and purpose, if meditation is used as the source of contentment in one's life. Gura's point is that sources of meaning and purpose that are external to ourselves change, expire, and are likely to disappoint us, while secular forms of meditation can provide an internal equilibrium that is under our own control.[2]

Other naturalistic-oriented thinkers have approached the conceptual space of meaning and purpose through different lenses. For example, Andy Norman uses the conceptual lens of "mattering" as a way to get at meaning and purpose. In a December 2014 piece for *The Humanist*, he wrote:

> "Stable mattering maps offer the promise of sustainable meaning—a sense of purpose...Religious ideologies are best understood as crude, fanciful mattering maps—well intentioned but clumsy attempts to afford a stable sense of meaning and shared sense of purpose."[3]

---

[1] Harris, S. (2014). *Waking Up: A Guide to Spirituality Without Religion* (New York: Simon & Schuster)
[2] Gura, M. W. (2015). *Exploring Your Life: Mindfulness Meditation and Secular Spirituality*; *Atheist Meditation Atheist Spirituality*, (Inneraction Press).
[3] Norman, A., (2014). "Getting Humanism Right-Side Up A Reality-Based "Mattering Map" and Alternative Humanist Manifesto," *The Humanist*, December 22, 2014.

At the core, Norman's concept of mattering is using a different semantic lens to describe the same empirically-oriented approach to purpose and meaning.

The approach taken by these more recent thinkers is in line with the perspective taken by Dewey, Sartre, and Kurtz. Are these naturalistically-oriented thinkers correct? Can we have the mental and physical wellbeing benefits of a rich sense of meaning and purpose without belonging to a faith-based community?

Research on Meaning and Purpose

What does the research show? First, it is vital to recognize that studies do indicate that a strong religious belief correlates with a rich sense of meaning and purpose. Research on the psychology of religion illustrates that "for many, the most salient core psychological function of religion is to provide a sense of meaning and purpose in life" (149).[1] Survey-based studies affirm such individually-oriented psychological research. For example, a study of the population of Memphis found that the extent to which religion has salience in a person's life correlates with a heightened sense of meaning and purpose.[2] Another study used the General Social Survey, which tracks demographic, behavioral, and attitudinal questions across the United States. The researcher investigated how the degree of belief in God relates to a personal sense of life purpose. The data showed that people who indicated they are confident in the existence of God self-report a higher sense of life purpose compared to those who believe but occasionally doubt, and to nonbelievers.[3]

Parallels exist in global comparative research on religion and life purpose. One study encompassed 79 countries, using the World Values Survey. It found that more religious people in more religious countries experience a greater sense

---

[1] Batson, C. D. and Stocks, E. L. (2004). "Religion: Its Core Psychological Functions," In J. Greenberg, S. L. Koole, & T. Pyszczynski (Eds.), *Handbook of Experimental Existential Psychology*, (New York: Guilford Publications). pp. 141–55.

[2] Petersen, L. R. and Roy, A. (1985). "Religiosity, Anxiety, and Meaning and Purpose: Religion's Consequences for Psychological Wellbeing," *Review of Religious Research*, Vol. 27, No. 1 (1985), pp. 49-62.

[3] Cranney, S. (2013). "Do People Who Believe in God Report More Meaning in Their Lives? The Existential Effects of Belief," *Journal for the Scientific Study of Religion*, Vol 52, No. 3, pp. 638-46.

of life satisfaction across a variety of dimensions, including life meaning and purpose.[1] A 2007 survey by Gallup of 84 countries used the following question: "Do you feel your life has an important meaning or purpose?" The report on this survey highlighted the following as the brief summary: "Takeaway: Regardless of whether they affiliate themselves with a religion, more than 8 in 10 respondents across 84 countries say their lives have an important meaning or purpose. However, religion does make a difference: Those who claim no religious affiliation are more than twice as likely as those who do claim one to say they do not feel their lives have an important purpose."[2]

Such generalized takeaways provide support for mainstream opinions and religion-oriented thinkers who use such findings to support their claims that religion is the way to gain meaning and purpose. Yet digging deeper into the data raises questions about the evidence for such claims. For example, the study cited above on 79 countries also found that more religious people have less life satisfaction, including a sense of meaning and purpose, in less religious countries. Moreover, forms of worship that do not promote social connectedness do not correlate with a heightened sense of life satisfaction.[3] Other studies illustrate similar findings. For instance, religious affiliation with community belonging leads to a higher degree of life satisfaction than religious devotion in private settings.[4] Another investigation underscored that extrinsic religious devotion, meaning a focus on religion for means such as in-group participation and social status, correlates with higher happiness and life meaning. However, intrinsic religious orientation, defined as religion that is deeply personal and defining one's lifestyle, does not correlate with a greater sense of happiness and life meaning.[5]

---

[1] Okulicz-Kozaryna, A. (2010). "Religiosity and Life Satisfaction Across Nations," *Mental Health, Religion & Culture*, Vol. 13, No. 2, pp. 155-169.
[2] S. Crabtree and B. Pelham, "The Complex Relationship Between Religion and Purpose: Worldwide Data Show Religious Conviction Isn't necessary, But It Helps," December 24, 2008
http://www.gallup.com/poll/113575/complex-relationship-between-religion-purpose.aspx. (Accessed 2/24/15)
[3] Okulicz-Kozaryna, A. (2010)"Religiosity and Life Satisfaction Across Nations," *Mental Health, Religion & Culture*, Vol. 13, No. 2, pp. 155-69.
[4] Bergan, A. and McConatha, J. T. (2001). "Religiosity and Life Satisfaction," *Activities, Adaptation & Aging*, Vol. 24, No. 3, pp. 23-34.
[5] Sillick, W. J. and Cathcarta, S. (2014). "The Relationship Between Religious Orientation and Happiness: The Mediating Role of Purpose in Life," *Mental Health, Religion & Culture*, Vol. 17, No. 5, pp 494-507.

These results should give pause to any intellectually honest people examining the ties between religion, meaning, and purpose. After all, the data seems to show that socially-oriented religious practice in religious communities leads to a stronger sense of life meaning and purpose, while private and inner-oriented religious practice does not. In that case, is it religion or social and community bonds that lead to a deep sense of life meaning?

Research conclusively demonstrates that social affiliation is key to a deep sense of life purpose, regardless of religious affiliation. As an example, 4 studies showed significant correlation between whether people experience a sense of belonging and their perception of life meaning and purpose. Study 1 highlighted a correlation between questions asking for a sense of belonging and life purpose at the same time. Study 2 strove to remove the possible biasing that may occur by asking these questions at the same time. It first asked people about their sense of belonging, and 3 weeks later inquired into their sense of life meaning. The data was similarly indicative of a clear correlation between belonging and life meaning. Studies 3 and 4 primed participants to experience a sense of belonging and a variety of other experiences, and found that priming people to experience belonging resulted in the highest perception of life meaning for study participants.[1] A meta-review of many studies on life meaning and purpose similarly indicates social belonging as vital to a sense of life purpose.[2]

These findings fit well with my own research on secular societies, specifically on the Soviet Union. My research illustrated how Soviet community and cultural centers offered citizens many opportunities to find meaning and purpose in life, as well as fun and pleasure—although they also certainly wanted to spread communism throughout the world, and put a lot of efforts into this goal as well.[3] Present-day societies with a more secular orientation than the

---

[1] Lambert, N. M. et. al. (2013). To Belong Is to Matter: Sense of Belonging Enhances Meaning in Life," *Personality and Social Psychology Bulletin*, Vol. 39, No. 11: 1418-427.
[2] Steger, M. F. (2012). "Making Meaning in Life." *Psychological Inquiry* Vol. 23, No. 4, pp. 381-385.
[3] Tsipursky, G. (2014). "'Active and Conscious Builders of Communism': State-Sponsored Tourism for Soviet Adolescents in the Early Cold War, 1945-53," *Journal of Social History* Vol. 48, No. 1 (Fall 2014): 20-46; Tsipursky, G. (2012). "Having Fun in the Thaw." *The Carl Beck Papers in Russian and East European Studies* 2201, pg. 1-67; G. Tsipursky, "Integration, Celebration, and Challenge: Youth and Soviet Elections, 1953-68," in Ralph Jessen and Hedwig Richter eds. (2011), *Voting for Hitler and Stalin: Elections under 20th Century Dictatorships*, 81-102.

United States have similar stories to tell, as illustrated by research on contemporary Denmark and Sweden.[1]

In fact, research shows that the important thing is simply to *have* a sense of meaning and purpose in life, regardless of the source of the purpose.[2] Going back to Frankl, his research suggests the crucial thing for individuals surviving and thriving is to develop a personal sense of individual purpose and confidence in a collective purpose for society itself, what he terms the "will-to-meaning and purpose." Frankl himself worked to help people find meaning and purpose in their lives. He did so by helping prisoners in concentration camps, and later patients in his private practice as a psychiatrist, to remember their joys, sorrows, sacrifices, and blessings, thereby bringing to mind the meaning and purposefulness of their lives as already lived. According to Frankl, meaning and purpose can be found in any situation within which people find themselves. He emphasizes the existential meaning and purposefulness of suffering and tragedy in life as testimonies to human courage and dignity, as exemplified both in the concentration camps and beyond. Frankl argues that not only is life charged with meaning and purpose, but this meaning and purpose implies responsibility, namely the responsibility upon oneself to discover meaning and purpose, both as an individual and as a member of a larger social collective.[3]

Frankl's approach to psychotherapy came to be called *logotherapy*, and forms part of a broader therapeutic practice known as existential psychotherapy. This philosophically-informed therapy stems from the notion that internal tensions and conflicts stem from one's confrontation with the challenges of the nature of life itself, and relate back to the notions brought up by Sartre and other existentialist philosophers. These challenges, according to Irvin Yalom in his *Existential Psychotherapy*, include: facing the reality and the responsibility of our freedom; dealing with the inevitability of death; the stress of individual isolation; finally, the difficulty of finding meaning in life.[4] These four issues correlate to what existential therapy holds as the four key dimensions of human existence,

---

[1] Zuckerman, P. (2008). *Society Without God: What the Least Religious Nations Can Tell Us About Contentment.* (New York: New York University Press), pg. 57-75.
[2] Steger, M. F. (2012). "Making Meaning in Life," *Psychological Inquiry* Vol. 23, No. 4: 381-85.
[3] Frankl, V.E. (1964) *Man's Search for Meaning* (London: Hodder & Stoughton), pg. 101-36
[4] Yalom, I. D. (1980). *Existential Psychotherapy*, (New York: Basic Books), pg. 6-10.

the physical, social, personal and spiritual realms, based on extensive psychological research and therapy practice.[1]

Meaning and Purpose: Secular Communities

So believing in God and going to church is not the only way to attain a strong sense of life purpose and meaning. You can gain it in venues that are secular and provide an opportunity for community ties and a chance to reflect on life purpose and meaning just as religious communities have traditionally offered.

In the United States, such venues are few and far between, but their numbers are growing. I belong to the Humanist Community of Central Ohio, an affiliate of the American Humanist Association. Other national secular groups have many local affiliates as well. Those in college and high school can go to Secular Student Alliance chapters, while children and teenagers enjoy lively discussions and fun activities at Camp Quest. Moreover, interfaith venues exist that welcome both secular and non-secular people, for example Unitarian Universalist (UU) congregations. Many have distinct groups for secular people, such as the UU Humanist group at the congregation I attend, the First UU Church of Columbus, united by a national UU Humanist Association.

So if you want to gain a rich sense of life meaning and purpose, without an externally imposed and God-oriented framework, check out local secular affiliates of national organizations. You will likely find a place to reflect on deep life questions from reason-based perspectives, and gain an opportunity to enter communities where you can form strong social bonds and great friendships. Such activities, according to the scientific literature, are very likely to increase our sense of life meaning and purpose.

The material from this article is adapted from my 2015 book, *Find Your Purpose Using Science*. The workbook aims to help reason-oriented people avoid the physical and mental health ailments associated with an insufficiently strong sense of meaning and purpose. It combines academic research, an engaging narrative, and stories from people's everyday lives, and provides a set of exercises readers can do to help them figure out their own sense of meaning and purpose. Since I wrote the workbook, a free app has been developed using the approaches described therein to help people evaluate their own sense of

---

[1] Cooper, M., (2003). *Existential Therapies,* (London: SAGE); Mathers, D. (2001). *An Introduction to Meaning and Purpose in Analytical Psychology* (Philadelphia, PA: Brunner-Routledge).

meaning and purpose, at www.intentionalinsights.org/findyourpurpose. These offerings are informed by my own scholarship on meaning and purpose, my experience as a teacher, and my role as President of Intentional Insights (www.intentionalinsights.org), a nonprofit devoted to empowering reason-oriented people to improve their own thinking, feeling, and behavior patterns, and thus reach their goals. Please reach out to me to learn more about how to adapt recent scientific findings on how our brain works to improve our lives at gleb@intentionalinsights.org, and my workbook is available at Amazon and elsewhere.

Not Seeing God when Raising your Kids

Stephanie Savage, Miracle Girl

Look, I understand how you feel. Really, I do. Now that you've finally broken free of the stranglehold of faith, you just want to breathe the fresh air of reason and filter out the stultifying miasma of ignorance. Out with the bad air, in with the good.

But your children can't so easily avoid the malodorous cloud of religion that surrounds them whenever they leave your faith-free home. Religion is like the air next to a smoking section. No matter how far into the nonsmoking section you sit, the wind will carry the smoke wherever you go.

You can't put a gas mask on your children to protect them from secondhand religion. Yet, with proper guidance, they will be able to avoid the pitfalls I fell into in my nonreligious childhood. Blindly navigating through a society still smothered by the fog of pre-scientific myths, I bumped into countless obstacles along the way.

As you will see, I'm not exactly a poster child for the coming generation of secular-raised kids. No one would put my childhood forth as a model to emulate, nor could my mother write a how-to book on godless parenting. Instead, my childhood would be more in the line of a cautionary tale, a how-not-to book on growing up in a world still mired in just-so story mythologies and messiah cults.

Yet, in my often absurd experiences, there are many lessons on the potholes in the road to raising secular children. You may not want to have anything to do with the religion you were brought up in, but your children will be living in a culture dominated by the superstitions you left behind. It's a lesson I learned over and over again during my childhood. Listen to my stories and beware. And maybe have a laugh or two in the process.

A key to understanding my crazy, mixed-up, secular childhood is that my mom was an agnostic, not an atheist. For her, Judaism brought nothing but ambivalence. The Jewish deli was her tabernacle. To religion, she said…meh.

Like many Jews of her generation, she was raised with a weak-tea version of Judaism. Hers was the Judaism of Passover Seders and Hanukkah gelt. Her dad would buy pork chops, then burn them to a crisp to kill the trichinosis he imagined lurked in every bite.

Being a third-generation American, Jewish culture meant little to her. And it didn't help that she grew up in the era of *Gentleman's Agreement*, when anti-Semitism was still expressed openly. When she wore a small Star of David, kids threw rocks at her. Can you blame her for not caring to identify with a world with which she felt no religious connection?

My mom divorced my father when I was two. And my tenuous connection to Jewish culture was extinguished when I was eight, after we moved away from our family in Miami. But my earliest adventures in godforsakeness were to occur before those ties were broken.

Being an agnostic and a Jew besides, my mom had resolved not to raise me with the Santa Claus myth. This was the late 60s and early 70s—an era that valued "letting it all hang out" and held profound distrust of those in authority. My hippieish mom felt uncomfortable teaching me a lie.

She was working and attending college at the same time, so I was in preschool before it was de rigueur. Preschoolers wind up catching many communicable diseases; I picked up a belief in Santa. My mom decided, reluctantly, that the Kris Kringle myth was harmless enough and played along.

She dutifully took me to the mall to see Santa Claus like all the other kids. But that came to a crashing halt when I was four. I was sitting on Santa's lap, happily telling him what I wanted for Christmas (we "celebrated" Christmas because neither Hanukkah nor Christmas meant anything to her). As I spoke, I naturally looked up at Jolly Saint Nick. Huh, what's that gap between his beard and his face? It took a moment to process, but then I realized with a jolt that Santa was a fraud.

After I rejoined my mom, I said in high dudgeon, "Santa is a fake!" I thought about it for a bit, then continued, "And all those Santas, in all those malls, they're all fake too!" I can remember my rising indignation.

My mom was impressed at the level of deductive reasoning for one so young. And since my belief in Santa wasn't her doing in the first place, she had no incentive to continue the charade. She fessed up, but told me that I shouldn't spoil it for my friends.

Dale McGowan has used the revelation that Santa is a myth as a self-teachable moment for his kids. But as I said, my mom was an agnostic...and an invariably direct one, at that. When I was old enough to understand, she explained the arguments for and against God's existence and left it up to me to decide for myself. I think Dale's method is a wonderful example of subtly guided secular parenting. Yet, you can see how well my mom's method worked out with me, as well.

Lesson One: Myths are a communicable disease.

My next stumble on my nonreligious path also occurred when I was four. I was walking with my mom when a group of Orthodox Jews strolled past us.

With the tactlessness of early childhood, I pointed to them and exclaimed, "What are those funny beanies they're wearing, Mommy?"

I don't personally remember this incident, but my mom loves to tell the story. I think that's because it illustrates how ignorant I was about Judaism as a child. And of course because it's funny. But I think this is more of a practical lesson in what happens when you raise a secular child without any knowledge of religion whatsoever.

Lesson Two: Ignorance isn't bliss. If you don't teach your children about religion, society will school them for you.

I had never stepped foot inside a synagogue, so I had never seen a yarmulke before. That ignorance made the next incident all the more shocking to me.

I was about six, and I had a best friend I'll call Peter, though time has stolen his actual name. One day, Peter turned to me and asked me out of the blue, "Are you a Jew?"

I looked at him for a long moment, puzzled at why he was asking the question. I didn't really know what Jew meant, but I did know that I was one. I had memorized a rote, sing-song refrain from my mom that I recited whenever I was asked about our religion, "We're non-practicing Jews." But what that really meant I had no idea.

"Yes," I replied

"My dad says you killed Christ," Peter told me matter-of-factly.

Not *the Jews*, but *you*. All three feet of me somehow managed to nail Jesus up on the cross 2000 years before I was born.

I shot back, "That's not true!" But I didn't really understand what I was denying.

Still, I think I had a better idea of what Christianity was from pop culture than I did about Judaism. While I knew that there were people who hated Jews,

I wasn't aware that some Christians blamed the Jews for Jesus' crucifixion. Peter's dad was apparently determined to inform me of that fact.

Peter later told me that he wasn't supposed to play with me anymore, but we still secretly played together sometimes, though less frequently than before. I have no way to know how he really felt about the matter, although the way Peter phrased it suggests that he didn't truly comprehend what his dad was saying, either. But Peter couldn't have been more confused than I was. I barely had a conception of what religion even meant.

Lesson Three: Teach tolerance, but also about society's intolerances (especially if they concern your heritage or religious beliefs).

By the time we moved to the buckle of the Bible belt, Birmingham, Alabama, I was a middle schooler who was at least familiar with the concept of religion. Yet, I was still a gefilte fish out of water in the intolerant and evangelical Deep South.

The casual racism I saw was a major culture shock for me, as a budding little liberal who idolized Martin Luther King enough to tell bullies, "I'm a pacifist. I don't believe in violence." And then they would beat me up. I must have missed that bit from the old news footage.

This was our second move after my mom remarried. Richard was raised a Southern Baptist, but he was a committed Unitarian—yes, they do exist—by the time of their marriage. He's now a Unitarian minister.

My favorite Unitarian church was the one in Springfield, Illinois because it was little more than daycare. We did fun projects like carving balsa wood sailboats and my all-time favorite, as an aspiring paleontologist, fossil hunting. I still have the tiny clamshells embedded in slate I collected on our "expedition."

The Unitarian church in Birmingham, however, was a nonreligious version of a Christian Sunday school. Instead of Noah's Ark stories, we learned nice, liberal moral lessons. In other words, it was b-o-r-i-n-g.

But being a Unitarian had its advantages in the hotbed of Christian fundamentalism that is the Deep South. Whenever people would ask about my religion—and in the South they frequently do—I could truthfully answer that we were Unitarians. I'm convinced that most of them had no idea that the Unitarian Universalist church had evolved from Christian beginnings into what I term "organized agnosticism." There are so many Christian sects out there that for all they knew we could've belonged to one of those crazy Pentecostal churches who think the Bible commands them to go around bobbing for apples in piranha tanks, or something.

At any rate, this was my closest brush with anything approaching religion when I was growing up. Unless you count the few months in my mid-childhood when I began silently praying…

Now I lay me down to sleep,
I pray the Lord my soul to keep,
If I should die before I wake,
I pray the Lord my soul to take.

I suppose I must have heard it on TV or in a movie. Why did I do this, pray tell? My fearful, neurotic little mind interpreted this child's prayer as a threat, not an exhortation to God to accept me into Heaven. Pray to me or I'll kill you in your sleep.

God had become the monster under my bed, or perhaps a mobster demanding protection money.

I eventually decided that praying to a god I didn't really believe in, just in case he actually existed, was silly. I stopped cold turkey and—spoiler alert—God didn't snuff me out in my sleep.

Lesson Four: Religion is contagious, too. Inoculate your children when they're young by explaining religious practices to them. You wouldn't want them to pick it up like chicken pox.

Just as I was old enough to have a glancing idea of what religion was, I was also beginning to gain an understanding of what it meant to be agnostic. Thus, I was filled with anxiety when I entered 6th grade and one of my teachers would lead the class in prayer before we could head to the cafeteria for lunch.

Did you say *prayer*? you may be saying to yourself, aghast. In *school*? But that's unconstitutional! Yup. Remember, this was the Deep South. I thought that this was just that one teacher, but when I entered 7th grade, my home room teacher began every day with a different child reading from the Bible. I ducked down my head and "prayed" I wouldn't be called.

Don't tell me school prayer is harmless. (Okay, so maybe *you* wouldn't.) For those two years, I lived in fear that I would be found out. And it only ended when we moved.

Each noon, as the rote lunchtime prayer commenced, I was so afraid of anyone catching me not praying that I would mouth the words.

By his hands we all are fed.
Thank you, Lord, for our daily bread.
God is great and God is good,
And we thank him for our food. Amen.

In my mind, I wasn't really praying if I didn't say it out loud. Oh, I suppose I could've objected. Then, those bullies would've again had a chance to test my pledge of nonviolence.

While the monotone of that pointless prayer droned on, I couldn't help wondering why we should be thankful for the puck-like biscuits they served in the cafeteria. And how good could God be if all he could provide us was that gelatinous Salisbury steak? Thanks but no thanks.

But of course I said none of this. I was already being picked on daily, so you can forgive me if I deliberately used my Unitarianism as a dodge. Saying I was an agnostic was out of the question in that deeply fundamentalist environment. And mentioning that I was Jewish was hardly better.

In our recently desegregated school, I witnessed racial fights on an almost daily basis. Considering everything I had seen, tolerance was not a reasonable expectation. And with my Yankee accent, I didn't have a prayer of a chance of fitting in.

Lesson Five: Hopefully, this will never happen to your kids. If it does, who ya gonna call? Breach busters! In other words, contact the Freedom from Religion Foundation or the ACLU.

During the Pledge of Allegiance and the recitation of the Girl Scout pledge, I always mouthed the word God as well. Even so, when auditions for the Girl Scout Christmas play were held, I felt no hesitation about trying out.

I was so excited when I snagged the lead role with the most lines: Joseph. That's right, for the second time in history, a Jew went searching for room at the inn. Actually, it was the first, since the manger story is as fake as the animals in a lawn crèche.

I remember beaming with pride when our Girl Scout leader told me that my performance was the best. They even used my doll as the baby Jesus. It never occurred to me that I had portrayed the father of the man Peter's dad accused me of killing. But my profound ignorance would lead me to far worse.

By this time, I was well familiar with the existence of anti-Semitism, even if I continued to feel no real connection with my heritage. I had yet to see the inside of a temple, so why would I want to risk being beaten up for a culture that seemed to have no relevance to my life?

Still, I was curious about the Holocaust. These were the days before *Schindler's List* and the TV miniseries that gave the genocide its name. All I knew was that six million of my people had been slaughtered for that thing about my heritage I knew hardly anything about.

When writing a biographical book report, I always picked someone I was curious about. So, when we were given an assignment to profile a famous historical person, I chose a man I wanted to learn more about: Adolf Hitler.

That was not the worst part.

Due to my ADHD, my mind often blanks out and I miss important details. In this case, it was the fact that we were supposed to read the report out loud in class...as the person we were profiling. I caught the second part and had dutifully written my paper in first person.

Even in my ignorance, I knew pretending to be Hitler was a no-no. On the day of the assignment, when in horror I discovered my mistake, I went to the teacher and tried to back out of reading my paper aloud. When she refused, I told her who I was profiling. But she still wouldn't let me off the hook.

So, I stood in front of that class filled with Christian children and said, "I'm Adolf Hitler and I killed six million Jews."

It's a good thing I don't believe in Hell because that episode might have been my ticket to perdition.

Lesson Six: If you still haven't taught your children about their ethnic and religious heritage by the time they're adolescents, it might bite them in the ass.

We left my stepfather behind and moved to Los Angeles when I was 12. One day, when I was about 14, I was having an imaginary conversation with myself, as I am wont to do. In the course of the dialog, I said *if there is a God* to the invisible conversationalist in my mind. Then I stopped and thought about it. Suddenly, I realized that I went from day to day assuming there was no God. Did I really have any doubt? That's when it hit me that I had become an atheist; I just hadn't realized it until that moment.

That was it. No exhaustive searches for the truth or heart-rending decisions. Instead of **BOOM**, it was more like…pff.

Over the course of a few years, I engaged in a series of discussions with my mom over why she still clung to that last shred of belief in the possibility of God's existence. Her stance boiled down to, if there's no God, who sparked the Big Bang?

I would always counter, so who made God? And is it really easier to believe that an all-powerful god—who has always existed—set the universe in motion? She would reply something along the lines of, true, but still... She was mostly there. Not quite an atheist, but not really a believer, either.

Then, one day when we had that God disputation, she said, "Yeah, I suppose I'm an atheist too." For a while, my mom would waver a bit. From talking with other people raised in faith, however tenuous, I understand how hard it is to break free of religious dogma inculcated since childhood. But now my mom is more zealously atheistic than I am. She's all out, as it were.

Lesson Seven: Even if you fail to heed the other six lessons, your kids might still turn out okay. When they're old enough, they might even teach you a thing or two.

The religion my mother wanted nothing to do with was intimately tied with my ethnicity, which complicated my journey tremendously. As I like to say, the religion I don't practice is Judaism. My experiences were therefore not completely universal. Still, I believe my rocky passage through the shoals of secular childhood holds many lessons for parents who left other faith traditions.

So far, I've only talked about the possible traps on the way to raising secular children. But what positive things might you expect? Well, for one thing, I've observed that many adults raised without faith harbor less bitterness against religion. And why not, we weren't force-fed belief along with our Cheerios™. Personally, I tend to react to religion's myriad absurdities not with anger, but with incredulity. I have trouble understanding how anyone could believe in what I term the Great Big Genie in the Sky.

Yet, religion remains far more prevalent in society than apostasy. Your children's friends will therefore mostly be believers. Just as Santa Claus was catching for the preschool me, you'll need to vaccinate your kids so they'll carry the antibodies of critical thinking. You wouldn't want them to catch a case of faith.

The good news is that your children may well find their paths easier than yours or mine. The 2014 Pew Religious Landscape Study showed that each new cohort of Millennials has been progressively more secular than the preceding one. Nonetheless, the US remains one of the most religious of all Western nations. Though you may wish to forget the religion you left behind, your children will need your guidance to navigate through a society where Bronze Age beliefs continue to hold sway.

If you don't, you and your children will live to regret it. I'm lucky I never stood in front of a class and proclaimed, "I'm Judas and I killed your savior and Lord."

Patheos Nonreligious

Not Seeing God in Religion

Alan Duval, A Tippling Philosopher

I've had the pleasure of being a writer on 'The Tippling Philosopher' for over a year, now. My personal research is primarily on the psychology of morality and values—and tippling—so I'm fairly comfortable straddling religion and politics, especially in pubs. As such, I wanted to approach the question of whether we can look forward to a godless world from the point of view of the intersection between the psychology of theistic belief, and the influence of religion (aka society and politics).

To be able to look forward to a godless world, one has to understand the mechanisms that underpin the god concept. I will discuss two key mechanisms that perpetuate belief in gods, namely: how the human mind generates gods, and the influence of religion on the maintenance of belief in gods.

To do so, it's necessary to discuss some definitions: *what is a god*, and *what is religion?*

What is a god?

Broadly speaking, there are two ways to answer the question of what gods are. The first is to ask a number of believers how they describe the gods in which they believe, and to then look for commonalities in the answers. The second is to look at the psychology that underpins those beliefs. That being said, the latter obviously relies upon the former, to at least some degree.

The vast majority of gods in human history were in pantheons, often with a hierarchy, and always with distinct powers and personalities (the fact of hierarchy in pantheons is our first brush with the idea that politics is embedded in religion). Indeed, the only thing differentiating pantheons from human society is the supernatural element (and the question of whether or not they exist). These gods seem like abstractions based on human experience, in the same way that a centaur is based on the experiences of a human and a horse, but not on the experience of a centaur.

While a believer might assign a primary attribute to a given god, I would say that the god in question is actually a placeholder, a vivified definition of that attribute. In pantheons there is often a king of the gods, and whilst this is often the most powerful god, as befits a ruler, it is not powerful in the same way that the gods of the various monotheisms are. Indeed, a striking thing about monotheistic gods is that they are powerful in an even more abstracted sense. A goddess of wisdom might manifest her power through lending insight to the follower that it is wise to favor, but a monotheistic god is omniscient. A king of the gods might have power over all of the gods, but a monotheistic god is omnipotent. And so on.

What you end up with, in the case of a monotheistic god, is a peg upon which almost anything can be hung. Any claim about a monotheistic god's attributes might make some sense in isolation—as was the case with each pantheon god, each with a primary attribute—but as soon as these abstracted attributes are applied to a single entity they becomes logically untenable. Much has been made of the difficulties inherent in omniscience and omnipotence. Additionally, what does it mean to be both infinitely merciful and infinitely just?

The gods of pantheons are reified concepts, humanized metaphors; the monotheistic god is an omnishambles.

What is Religion?

Let's dispense with the usual first hurdle. No, religions don't require gods. The go-to example is of course Buddhism. That having been said, I think there is at least one god-like aspect in Buddhism (and many other non-theistic Eastern religions): karma. The anthropomorphic element has either been completely abstracted out, or was never recognized as anthropomorphic to begin with. Isn't karma a combination of justice and mercy? Aren't both justice and mercy concepts in the moral space? They are certainly not physical constants, and thus not universally applicable. How are the good and bad actions and intentions that are central to karma measured, and by whom?

The apparent lack of a god in Buddhism sounds an awful lot like Daniel Dennett's (2013[1]) *homuncular functionalism* as it relates to consciousness.

---

[1] Dennett, D. C. (2013). "A Cascade of Homunculi." *Intuition Pumps and Other Tools for Thinking* (pp. 91-95). London: Allen Lane.

Homuncular Functionalism is the idea that while explaining the mind by recourse to lots of little men is fallacious (these little men have minds that also need to be explained), if one can eventually abstract these little men down to the point where they are engaged in sub-routines of sub-routines that could be taken over by a mechanistic process, such as a logic gate/brain cell, then we can build consciousness back up in mechanistic terms. Karma is an almost-mechanistic process applied to moral cause and effect. It will never be abstracted down to a purely physical law because it is ultimately social or even judicial in nature.

I am the LAW

What defines religion, in a judicial or practical sense, if an actual god is not necessary, let alone sufficient? It should come as no surprise that this is an ongoing debate, not least of which is in legal circles, where the limitations on the right to practice one's religion is a regular question. In 'Constitutional "Religion"—A Survey of First Amendment Definitions of Religion', Jeffrey Oldham (2001[1]) concluded that:

> ...the Court has implied a range of definitions but never explicitly defined religion. Lower courts, more adventurous in this realm, have given the impression that defining religion is difficult and risky. Scholars have attempted to bring clarity to the issue by proposing definitions with various approaches, including functional, content-based, and analogical methods. From the analysis of each of these types, one may conclude that the functional definitions are more common but often lead to strange results, while the content-based conception results in a narrower classification.

That's a fairly non-committal outcome from fifty-or-so years of jurisprudence and centuries of both philosophy and theology. Though it does show that focusing on the god/no-god aspect will result in a "narrower classification."

To illustrate the difficulty in coming up with a clear distinction between religion and not-religion I will turn to a psychological definition from the work

---

[1] Oldham, J. L. (2001). "Constitutional Religion: A Survey of First Amendment Definitions of Religion." *Texas Forum on Civil Liberties & Civil Rights, 6;* 117.

of Vasillis Saroglou (2011[1]). He proposes the 'Four B's' of religion: Believing, Bonding, Behaving, and Belonging. In extremely paraphrased form:

1. Belief (generally in something transcendent) is the condition of entry to the community
2. Bonding ensues (generally through self-transcendence in response to the thing believed in)
3. Behaving in accordance with expectation maintains membership
4. Belonging is the benefit obtained from maintaining belief, bonding with fellow believers, and behaving in accordance with expectation

Key to Saroglou's analysis is the dynamics of variation:

1. Believing – Literal to Symbolic
2. Bonding – Negative to Positive
3. Behaving – Self-focused to Other-focused
4. Belonging – Exclusive to Inclusive

If we replace the symbolic god(s) with the literal universe, we get (more or less):

1. I believe in the scientific method
2. I bond with others around this belief
3. I behave in accordance with my understanding of the world based on this belief
4. I belong to the scientific community (or all mankind viewed as scientific entities, if you prefer)

It is the literal-to-symbolic and self-focused/other-focused continua that define the difference between the "true believer" and the more casual believer who gains comfort from the rituals and sense of community.

It seems as though the nature of the object of belief is pivotal in defining religion, but we've ascertained that a god need not be central. I suggested above that there is a supernatural element in the process of karma. It really is just

---

[1] Saroglou, V. (2011). "Believing, bonding, behaving, and belonging: The big four religious dimensions and cultural variation." *Journal of Cross-Cultural Psychology*, 42(8), 1320-1340.
https://cdn.uclouvain.be/public/Exports%20reddot/psyreli/documents/2011.JCCP.4BRD.pdf

another way of saying that 'God/the universe has a plan for you' but, meanwhile 'God/the universe moves in mysterious ways.' Then again, as with the gradual abstraction that takes place in homuncular functionalism, the abstraction to a mechanism with human-shaped elements precedes abstraction to an explanation that doesn't have those human elements. That last step is not always possible. I would suggest that this is the case with karma. Where we can reduce down to a non-human-mediated mechanism, we have a scientific theory, in all of its reductionist glory. Where we can't, where we have human-shaped mechanisms, be they tiny homunculi, or universe-spanning gods, or the ghosts and goblins in between, we have the supernatural, and thus religion.

I just feel that I'm right

Other entries in this volume have mentioned Kahneman's (2003[1]) Emotional (System 1) path, which is quick, intuitive, associative and in most cases good enough; and Reasoning (System 2) path, which is slower, sometimes counter-intuitive, rule-based, but more likely to land on a better answer. Religion is the reliance on intuitively satisfying, non-specialist consensus (System 1). Science is the reliance on engaging with the facts of the matter in a deliberate and concentrated way (System 2). A complication of this admitted over-generalization is that theology and apologetics are the application of System 2 reasoning to justifying System 1 conclusions. Meanwhile, a specialist in a complicated topic (requiring the use of System 2) may well have flashes of creative intuition (System 1).

The object of belief in religion seems to be the incompletely abstracted, still somewhat anthropomorphic (and thus supernatural) explanation. It is easier to accept these human-shaped explanations because we are human-shaped, so they slot more easily into our cognitive make-up. Kahneman calls the feeling of rightness due to the ease with which the features of an explanation can be accepted, cognitive ease. This feeling can be caused by features of an idea that have nothing to do with being right, and everything to do with how often one is exposed to the relevant features of the idea (and we're exposed to being human daily).

As you might imagine, in light of all of this, I see the idea of a post-religious society as unlikely, in part because, with no firm definition of what

---

[1] Kahneman, D. (2003). "A perspective on judgment and choice: mapping bounded rationality." *American Psychologist*, 58(9), 697-720.

"religion" in fact is, the concept of post-religiousness is meaningless; and in part because Believing, Bonding, Behaving, and Belonging, whilst eminently descriptive of religion, is also descriptive of virtually all social undertakings.

Believing, Bonding, Behaving, and Belonging

In his original paper, Saroglou seeks to illustrate that religion is unique by noting other social phenomena that involve some combination of believing, bonding, behaving, and belonging, but not all four. I suggest that whilst his examples might seem to be accurate, any missing element in each may merely be less explicit, rather than missing (much like the "god" of karma). He gives philosophical systems as an example—like religion, there is an interest in existential claims, possibly impacting morality, but unlike religion there is no emotional/ritual dimension, no bonding. I would suggest that spirited intellectual debate is a form of bonding. It is quite ritualized, or formalized, if you prefer, and it is a means of not only affirming one's beliefs/values as it relates to the given philosophical system, but also seeks to remove a point of disagreement about the system itself between two adherents (or an adherent and an a opponent).

But who is it that does the Believing, Bonding, Behaving, and Belonging, regardless of whether it is religions or philosophical systems?

The Other Holy Trinity – Me, Myself, and I

A very important, and I think under-discussed, aspect of the psychology of theism is how the understanding of the self impacts upon the fact and quality of belief (and not just because of cognitive ease). One obvious trinity of selves that we all have is what we believe about ourselves, what we aspire to be, and the reality of our "selves." It is ironic that the third image is the one we don't (and probably can't) know. For a number of Christians, the idealized self is expressed as the desire to be "Christ-like." If you happen to believe in the "fallen" nature of human existence, then you probably have a far more negative view of your present self than other (non-believing) people do. If you aspire to being "Christ-like" and believe in your fallen nature, you must necessarily see the difference between your present self and your ideal self as insurmountable (so it's just as well that you probably also believe in miracles).

It is interesting to note that many people view their future self in idealized terms (whether as "Christ-like" or not) and, importantly, as someone who is not them. This is why we offload the need for better behavior to our idealized selves (in some future time, when we are more Christ-like). If, six months ago, I "planned" to write one chapter of my own book, each month for the following twelve months, and to date I've written none (this is true), the normal response to this failure would be to literally double down on the original "plan" and assign my idealized self the task of now writing two chapters a month in the remaining six months. In other words, I remain committed to the decision of my past self—a self who did not have access to the knowledge that I would fail to write any chapters in the intervening months (of course, it also wasn't privy to the knowledge that I would write this chapter in less than twelve hours of concentrated effort).

To assume that a person who has not so far engaged in a desired behavior will suddenly do so, and at double the intensity, is irrational. Acceptance of my failure and a revised plan to write an outline and make some notes in the next month is more achievable, and less daunting. To do this, however, would be to update my beliefs about myself, and particularly my idealized self, in accordance with the demonstrated, if somewhat confusing, facts of the matter. This is a process that Carl Rogers spoke of as self-actualization—improving yourself in accordance with your beliefs about yourself—and it is antithetical to a desire to be "Christ-like." Christ is an externality imposed upon you, and as such does not reflect the internal reality of you as an individual, and it is unable to be updated in response to new data. If you also view yourself as fallen, then what you believe about yourself will not change much, regardless of the success in approaching the stated goal of being Christ-like (whatever that means).

The Great I AM

My position on the impact of the self on belief in God is most powerfully shaped by a study from Nicholas Epley and colleagues (2009[1]). Individuals were placed in an fMRI scanner and asked to think about themselves, and agents external to themselves—George Bush, the average American, Bill Gates, or God—they

---

[1] Epley, N., Converse, B. A., Delbosc, A., Monteleone, G. A., & Cacioppo, J. T. (2009). "Believers' estimates of God's beliefs are more egocentric than estimates of other people's beliefs." *Proceedings of the National Academy of Sciences*, 106(51), 21533-21538. http://www.pnas.org/content/106/51/21533.long

were then asked to think about their own opinions, and those of the external agents, on such salient topics as abortion, the death penalty, marijuana legislation, and same sex marriage. The participants had a marked difference between thoughts about themselves and thoughts about others, except in the case of God. Thoughts about God were almost indistinguishable from thoughts about the self. It seems that if we subtract the self from God, there is almost nothing left. God is the empty peg on which to hang the definition of self (a collection of omni-words that we define our own benevolence, potency, and knowledge in relation to).

The one external agent that showed some commonality with the self (and therefore God) was Bill Gates. Presumably, because being highly successful and wealthy is something that we all "plan" for our "future selves." (Along these lines, John Steinbeck has been paraphrased as saying that the American poor see themselves as "temporarily embarrassed millionaires.") I would predict that, had the participants also been asked to think about Jesus' opinion, the result would have been between self and other, and the location, in relation to Bill Gates, would depend upon the individual's opinion of Jesus.

A God of the people

God, then, is a mind-first phenomenon in the same way that the centaur was. Reliant upon exposure to things outside the self, but created within the mind, definitional of the self, and projected outwards. Where the centaur is a cut and paste job, God is the ultimate abstraction. You will notice that this abstraction leads to some problems beyond the omnishambles mentioned previously. If God is an abstraction from exposure to people, then the most obvious hurdle to a clean abstraction is gender. Either the abstraction is genderless (and no longer quite so human-seeming), or it is gendered, and (at least) one gender loses out. It's worth noting here, that some classical depictions of the devil are hermaphroditic.

This abstraction process relates to one particular approach to God, probably the approach that gave rise to the god-concept in the first instance, and almost certainly the process that gave rise to the God of monotheism. People who fervently believe in this God have socio-political tendencies that reinforce this notion of God, predicated as it is on an abstraction process that relies on the self, and terminates in a singular definition, and as such doesn't cope with binaries, let alone spectrums. Such individuals tend to be both politically and religiously conservative, and often authoritarian (as we'll soon see). Individuals whose God concept is predicated on this abstraction (and a belief that this internal phenomenon is external) have a preference for highly homogenous communities. This homogeneity allows them to maintain the abstraction. Women are dehumanized, people of differing races, religions, orientations, and opinions, are shunned for their negative impact on "God."

The other approach to God is the belief in the value of belief (e.g. Dennett, 2009[1]). Here, I would suggest, the cognitive underpinning just outlined, the over-simplified and externalized abstraction, is not engaged with in quite the same way. The desire to represent more facets of society than can be achieved by a single abstraction, is manifested in the Catholic saints. The Catholic Church is Roman in its conception, and the Romans were notorious for their pantheon, and syncretism. Syncretism is the inclusion of other religious practice and thought alongside that of the main religion. Maybe there are vestiges of the Roman pantheon in modern Catholicism. That being said, just as there are left-leaning conservatives, and right-leaning liberals, it doesn't seem terribly far-fetched to suggest that there are Protestant-leaning Catholics (not interested in the saints) and Catholic-leaning Protestants. One need only look at the spread of Evangelicalism from Protestantism to Catholicism to see this in action.

Believing

It seems that there is belief, predicated on the experience of the abstracted self, misunderstood as an external phenomenon, and there is belief in the value of that belief, but without the cognitive machinery required to get to "true" belief. It seems likely that this "belief in belief" is in fact quite similar, cognitively, to belief in lots of gods, with a stated preference for one. Then again, having a preference for the self, but recognizing there are other, perfectly valid selves out there, is a more accurate description of reality. The next step then is the recognition that there are an awful lot of things out there that have nothing to do with human society, so if we are using a human-shaped pattern to understand it, we are probably wrong (as with karma). This is, in effect, a description of the means by which we arrived at the scientific process—exploring the world as

---

[1] Dennett, D. (2009, July). "The folly of pretence." *The Guardian.* https://www.theguardian.com/commentisfree/belief/2009/jul/16/daniel-dennett-belief-atheism (Accessed 06/23/2017)

selves, initially embedded in an intensely social environment, and gradually learning how to explore the general (non-social) environment in a more scientific, less supernatural way.

The base from which we believe whatever we believe is the self that we inhabit. So, of course our understanding of the world is impacted by what we believe about ourselves. It's often said that we all yearn to be part of something larger than ourselves. If you believe in an extrapolation from self to God that is based on a highly homogenous society, then your horizons for this are incredibly narrow (the attempt to make that God the creator of everything is so narrow that it comes with a preference for a timeline that broadly matches the span of written human history). If you believe yourself to be one of many selves, existing under a god, your horizons are broader. If you believe in the existence of as many gods as there are people (more or less), your horizons are broader still. If, however, you see yourself, and a society of other unique selves, bound by our joint existence in a particular time and place, your horizons are the broadest they can reasonably be. There are steps beyond this, of course, but I think these are the extrapolations based on lack of awareness of the boundary conditions that children often adopt as they mature, and that some adults maintain.

Speaking of children, some are raised in environments in which they are encouraged to explore, and for whom appropriate social behavior is modeled. They are allowed to discover themselves in the context in which they find themselves, both physical and social. Others are not, as these paragraphs from a 2014[1] Pew article on the values parents seek to instill in their children make abundantly clear:

People who express consistently conservative political attitudes across a range of issues are more likely than other ideological groups to rate teaching religious faith as especially important—and the least likely to say the same about teaching tolerance.

By contrast, people with consistent liberal opinions stand out for the high priority they give to teaching tolerance—and the low priority they attach to teaching religious faith and obedience.

In addition, the consistent liberal valued empathy for others, and curiosity, among the top five most important values, and no other segment did.

---

[1] "Teaching the Children: Sharp Ideological Differences, Some Common Ground." (2004, September 18). *Pew Research Centre - U.S. Politics & Policy.* http://www.people-press.org/2014/09/18/teaching-the-children-sharp-ideological-differences-some-common-ground/ (Accessed June 23, 2017)

By contrast the consistent conservative valued obedience in the top five most important values, unlike any other segment. It is curious that those respondents tagged as mostly conservative have only one difference from the consistently conservative; they value independence ahead of obedience.

The upshot of these preferences is that the children of consistently liberal parents are encouraged to understand themselves and other people through interest, curiosity, and tolerance for difference. They come to believe what they have experienced, and what they have understood from other people who have had experiences they have not had. The children of consistently conservative parents believe what they are told to believe, with little-to-no self-expression or self-understanding, often in a social context filled with people ostensibly similar to them.

Pew used political types in their study, but other Pew studies (2016[1,2]) make it clear that the consistently liberal are most likely to be atheist, agnostic, or unaffiliated, with quite a few liberal Christians thrown in. Conversely, with 81% of the consistently conservative parents noting that religion was important, 59% saying it was one of the most import values to instill in their children, there are relatively few atheists and agnostics in their ranks.

Bonding

There is less effort involved in "keeping up appearances" if you hang out with people whose views are relatively close to your own. My primary point in the 'Believing' section is that children raised in a consistently conservative environment do not have the room to develop their own beliefs, given the emphasis on religion and obedience. Children are naturally curious. Consistently liberal parents encourage this, within reason. Consistently conservative parents do not, without reason (or at least none that the child is party to).

Curiosity is a child's natural inclination, and in some more so than others. Often, the only way to curb this is through distraction or violence. Corporal punishment, sometimes culminating in outright abuse, is far more common in

---

[1] Lipka, M. (2016, June 1). "10 facts about atheists." *Pew Research Centre - Fact Tank - News in the Numbers.* http://www.pewresearch.org/fact-tank/2016/06/01/10-facts-about-atheists/ (Accessed June 23, 2017)

[2] Lipka, M. (2016, February 23). "10 facts about atheists." *Pew Research Centre - Fact Tank - News in the Numbers.* http://www.pewresearch.org/fact-tank/2016/02/23/u-s-religious-groups-and-their-political-leanings/ (Accessed June 23, 2017)

highly religious households (see my extended treatment of this topic[1]). The relationship is strong, but indirect, in the same way that counties with historical ties to the Ku Klux Klan are more likely to vote Republican than those without that history, even decades after the local chapter is closed (McVeigh, Cunningham & Farrell, 2014[2], see also Matthews, 2014[3]).

Behaving

Children have a natural inclination towards curiosity and exploration. A child raised in an environment where this is seen as misbehaving is going to have problems with another natural drive, attachment. To be clear, attachment isn't bonding (Benoit, 2004[4]), at least not as discussed above, but it is generally recognized as the template for future relationship behavior. In a child, "the attachment system is activated by natural 'clues to danger' (e.g., separation from the attachment figure, physical illness, or pain) and terminated by 'clues to safety' (most notably, physical contact with the attachment figure)" (Granqvist, 2010[5]). However, if a child's internally generated curiosity is met by a response with negative valence (cold shoulder, angry words, physical violence), then the attachment figure will often be exhibiting "clues to danger" and "clues to safety"

---

[1] Duval, A. J. K. (2016). "Duval on Moral Epistemology, pt. 3.2: Conservatives and Corporal Punishment." *A Tippling Philosopher*. Retrieved June 23, 2017, from http://www.patheos.com/blogs/tippling/2016/10/13/duval-on-moral-epistemology-pt-3-2-conservatives-and-corporal-punishment/
[2] McVeigh, R., Cunningham, D., & Farrell, J. (2014). "Political Polarization as a Social Movement Outcome 1960s Klan Activism and Its Enduring Impact on Political Realignment in Southern Counties, 1960 to 2000." *American Sociological Review*, 0003122414555885.
http://www.brandeis.edu/now/2014/december/cunningham-kkk-impact.html
[3] Matthews, D. (2014). "Study: The KKK helped Republicans win the South." *Vox*.
https://www.vox.com/2014/12/10/7372495/ku-klux-klan-republican
(Accessed June 23, 2017)
[4] Benoit, D. (2004). "Infant-parent attachment: Definition, types, antecedents, measurement and outcome." *Paediatrics & Child Health*, 9(8), 541–545.
https://www.ncbi.nlm.nih.gov/pmc/articles/PMC2724160/ (Accessed June 23, 2017)
[5] Granqvist, P. (2010). "Religion as Attachment: The Godin Award Lecture." *Archive for the Psychology of Religion* 32, 5-24.
https://www.researchgate.net/profile/Pehr_Granqvist/publication/233504585_Religion_as_Attachment_The_Godin_Award_Lecture/links/0a85e532d34ac43f3f000000.pdf (Accessed June 23, 2017)

simultaneously. As such a child will be drawn to and repelled by the attachment figure. We can see that bonding is predicated on behaving in a manner that the attachment figure considers appropriate.

Should bonding be conditional on believing? It seems as though Saroglou (2010) did mean for believing, bonding, behaving and belonging to be in this order—the '4 B's' are predicated on *beliefs* expressed through *rituals/emotions* (that foster bonding) and ultimately the *moral rules* (behaving) accepted by the *community/group* (to which one belongs) (p. 1322).

It should be obvious that children don't believe as adults do. There are three interrelated reasons for this:
1) immature faculties (in physiological terms)
2) lack of exposure to a range of data
3) the interaction between these

Punishing a child for behaving in a non-adult fashion is punishing a child for being a child. Note, also, that the conservative religious communities that have a tendency towards homogeneity are themselves deficient in reasons two and three. It seems fair to say that the maturing of faculties, the increased exposure to data, and the interaction between these, is the process of becoming mentally adult. Conservative religious communities, therefore, are self-infantilizing, by limiting exposure to data (mostly in the form of other people from other countries, and especially those of other faiths, but also people of other races and sexual orientations. This limited exposure leads to immature faculties by virtue of the (lack of) interaction between the outside world and the brain. This is the outcome of failing to allow children to explore the world with a proper attachment figure. Through several routes, it also leads to the "parenting" style that creates this outcome.

Belonging

The feeling of unconditional love, the sense of belonging that a child enjoys, is a product of liberal upbringings, whether atheist or theist. Children who are raised in detrimentally permissive liberal households are a tiny minority, contrary to what children raised in even moderately conservative households are led to believe. The children of authoritarian religious parents, however, tend to have a sense of belonging that is entirely conditional on appearing to believe the same as the congregation, regardless of what they actually believe. Children brought up in liberal religious households tend to grow up to be more liberal than their parents, whether they become members of even more liberal congregations or become non-believers (Altemeyer, 2006).

Conclusion

What we have seen is that Believing, Bonding, Behaving, and Belonging is a pretty good description of adult religious practice. What we also see, though, is that fervently religious parents fail to follow this pattern, in this order, when it comes to their children. These parents focus on behavior, making bonding conditional, and forcing belief upon their children as a ticket to belonging. Liberal parents (whether religious or not) tend to encourage children to believe what makes sense to them. Bonding is a product of parental love, not conditional on belief. Behaving flows naturally from the interaction between belief and bonding, and improves over time, through exposure to more data.

Adult religious belief conforms to Believing, Bonding, Behaving, and Belonging, and liberal-leaning parenting does, too (possibly because religious belief is a yearning for a liberal parent). Liberal-leaning parents who are believers generally raise more liberal believers—this eventually leads to non-religious children that become non-religious parents. Authoritarian religious parents lead to authoritarian religious children, not through encouraging Believing, Bonding, Behaving, and Belonging, but through demanding Behavior based on parental Belief that gives rise to contingent infant attachment (Bonding) and contingent adult attachment (Belonging). Authoritarian religious parenting also leads to the types of self-understanding that lead to so-called "true belief" in "God" which is simply an externalized sense of self (due to having most rules imposed from outside, with few beliefs predicated in a sense of self).

There will always be individuals who are psychologically predisposed to seeing gods, so there will never be a society without gods. However, because religion, as described by Saroglou (2010), is also a description of liberal parenting, and because liberals, whether moderate or otherwise, outnumber conservatives, both moderate and otherwise, the future will eventually have many more "religions" that do not have gods at their center, and some of them may even be religions that have nothing supernatural at their center at all, such as humanism.

What Comes after Not Seeing God

Hank Fox, A Citizen of Earth

The day I left home to go to Reason Rally 2016, a friend—who knew I'd be driving eight hours to get to Washington DC and another eight hours to return that same night (!)—asked me "Why are you going to this thing?" I gave him a flip answer as I stepped out the door: "Hey, it's the Atheist Woodstock!" Thirty seconds later, I poked my head back in and answered seriously: "Because when I went to the one in 2012, it was the first time in my life as an atheist I felt welcome, and free, and *home*."

If our one desire as atheists is to be a loose body of free individuals, nothing more need be done. We're there and getting more there all the time. But if we want to have our own place in the world, a permanent place, a home, we need something bigger than atheism. Something sturdier. Longer-lasting. Self-perpetuating. Because atheism alone can't get us there.

Here's why I think so, and what I think that "something" is.

Three Boats

Think of the future as an archipelago of possibilities, with all the things-to-come each on its own island. One island might contain a future of clean beautiful cities and unspoiled wildlands, of education and wealth; another might present a future of grit and poverty, overpopulation and starvation; a third might lack humans altogether; a fourth...you get the idea.

Every one of us will eventually arrive on one of those islands, to live in some sort of future. But most of those futures will be, in broad terms, of someone else's making. In that future, whichever one we reach, we'll pay whatever *they* charge us for our student loans. We'll dress in what *they* sell in the stores. We'll listen to the music and see the movies and read the books *they* provide. We'll vote for the candidates *they* offer us. We'll eat the foods—and the ingredients in those foods—*they* put on the shelves, in stores *they* own. We'll celebrate *their* holidays. We'll receive the medical care, or lack of it, offered by *their* hospitals. We'll tread lightly under the scrutiny of *their* cops. We'll obey *their* laws, or go to *their* prisons. Because the only boats going to that distant archipelago are *theirs*.

Who are the owners of those vessels? Who are *they*? Government. Corporations. Religion.

Government: Organized and powerful, government can and does direct money, labor, and planning toward large-scale projects that can span decades or longer. Supposedly created to serve its citizens, it can have goals that have nothing at all to do with long-term benefits to ordinary people. It can create laws, operate police forces, courts and prisons. It can interfere in the lives of its citizens in ways large and small. It can even engage in wars, sending young men and women off to die in some scorching hellhole, for no good reason.

Business: Large corporations plan for their own future, a future of survival and profit in an environment of competition and scarce resources. Corporations have goals to benefit themselves first, customers second. Yes, they have to keep customers happy in the short term, but that doesn't mean they actually have to benefit—or even keep from harming—those customers in the long. If there's more money in sugary carbonated soda than in fruit juice or tea, guess which product will get the advertising budget? If lottery tickets are a more profitable sell than savings accounts, what's going up on all the billboards? Which will be available in every convenience store? If a profitable product like tobacco actually harms the customer, but nobody can prove it without a protracted legal fight pursued over decades, will they sell it? You bet they will.

Religion: Not just people in random Brownian motion, but tens or hundreds of millions gathered together with common beliefs and goals—dictated, supposedly, by an actual god—operating out of one or more churches in every city, town, hamlet and neighborhood in the U.S. Religion can set and enforce social mores with real consequences that might range from public censure to shunning—in the past, even to death—and it functions across generations.

None of these "boats" travel alone. They rope together to smooth the journey. The boat of business sails in close touch with the boat of government. Considering there are something like 15,000 lobbyists in Washington DC, allegedly spending $3 billion a year to influence legislators, and most large corporations pay little or nothing in taxes, the corporate boat is not only well-fueled and -powered, it is avidly assisted by the vessel of government. Government, in turn, leans heavily on business for navigational cues.

The boat of religion gets all sorts of perks from the government, and does everything it can to reflect influence back into government. It succeeds: Government officials pay constant homage to religion, treading carefully on any issue that even remotely relates to it. Case in point: the Catholic molesting travesty was out in the open for years before law enforcement slouched into action.

So where's the boat that has room for atheists, or atheist goals? Say we want to reach the island where schools—all schools—teach evolution. Not as some also-ran topic covered in a day, not as a suggestion given no more weight than creationism, but as the rock-solid heart of every discussion of Earth biology. Who's going to make that happen? Who's going to get us there?

Government? Uh, no. They're going to waffle and test the air, veer away and carefully not get involved. Corporations? Nope. They're gonna sit this one out too, kids. Churches? Ha! Not on your life. They're the ones who got us to *this* island, the one where teachers are afraid to teach.

How are we going to get those actual science classes for every kid in America—the ones that explicitly say creation didn't happen but evolution did? Answer: We're not. It's not going to happen. There is no boat going there. *Generations* of schoolkids will come and go with inferior science education.

There's this island we want to get to, but there's some whole other island—another future entirely—we'll arrive at. We'll get the future that government, business and religion will take us to. You and I might want a cure for Alzheimer's in five years, but if government won't help fund the research, if universities, hospitals and pharma companies won't do the research, and if religion blocks the research, or owns the hospitals that might otherwise apply or test the treatment, there will be no cure for Alzheimer's in five years. Not here, anyway.

But isn't it enough just to be atheists? If we free ourselves and others from the grip of religion, won't good things automatically follow? No. Atheism alone isn't going to get us to any particular future because, beyond the bit about individual freedom (no small thing!), it has no built-in direction. Atheism by itself isn't even a thing. It's a non-thing, an opposed-to-this-other-thing thing. It can work immense changes on individuals, but as a larger social force, a force aimed at some particular future, it is dramatically rudderless.

If atheism isn't going to get us there, and the three boats aren't going to get us there, what can we do?

How about we build our own boat? To have any hope of creating a future of our choice—possibly any hope of having a future at all—we pretty much have to.

So let's talk about this imagined boat of ours. Let's talk about *culture*.

Culture

In simplest terms, culture is all the things you learn from your parents, peers and elders, and then pass on to your own children and grandchildren. Culture is just about everything you do. Your culture is the unwritten handbook on how to live life on scales both large and small.

It's what you eat, the utensils you use to eat it. What to wear and how to wear it, what language you speak and the regional accent with which you speak it. Where to live, how to relate to your fellow men and women and children, what to learn and what to do with it once you've learned it.

It's the haircut you sport, the songs you sing, the dances you do, the way you court and wed and cohabit, the way you welcome children into the world and bid farewell to departing elders. It's the games you play, the slate of acceptable careers laid out before you, the type of jokes you tell, even the words you're allowed to use. It includes your ceremonies and holidays, the things you read and don't read. It presents you with life goals—a lion skin, a sheepskin, an eagle feather, a position of respect and honor within your tribe. Ways to deal with strangers and outsiders. Entertainments, contests, rules for interpersonal conflict. Women's ways, men's ways. It offers something for every social and psychological need humans have. For some of us, it's the protective underwear we don at night, and even the shortlist of positions acceptable for (married-only, heterosexual-only) intercourse!

The substance of culture is taught to each new generation, but culture itself is probably automatic. Drop a group of ignorant kids on an island, isolate them for a hundred years or so, and their descendants would emerge possessing a complete culture, containing every possible thing they needed to live day-to-day—every ceremony, recipe, song, and article of clothing.

At its best, culture provides you a Home, a place of acceptance, support, and stability. It gives you an identity, an automatic sense of self. At its worst, it acts as something of a cage, trapping its people within it, oppressing them, offering the threat of punishment or ouster to those who don't stay in line. But to most of us throughout history, the price has apparently been worth it.

Here in the U.S., it seems to me culture comes in three general "grades"—which I label Full Culture, Fractional Culture, and U.S. Overculture.

Full Culture

Already described above, full cultures cover every aspect of life, providing both game and gameboard for living. They present an elaborate social framework with all the details worked out.

In New York state where I live, full cultures include the Amish and Hasidic Judaism. However confining or silly they might look to those of us outside them, from the inside they provide a place of warmth, safety and familiarity, which most would only reluctantly leave.

But other than these, which make a deliberate attempt at island-like isolation and purity, few of us have anything even close to a complete culture. Here in the United States, they're actually hard to come by. Instead we have the other two types.

Fractional Culture

Harley Davidson culture, gamer culture, NASCAR culture, Star Trek and Star Wars fan culture, Renaissance Festival culture, countless others. They contain certain rules and traditions, but those rules address only that one small part of life. Everything else has to be borrowed.

Fractional cultures, it seems to me, arise because they satisfy the yearning for a tribal home-place, a sense of inclusion with "My People." You and yours have a team, a band, a sport. But they fall apart on the rest of life. Science fiction fandom might provide you with the details of how to conduct yourself during late-night filking, but it's mostly silent on funeral traditions, or what to wear to work. As an avid Yankees fan, you might attend all the games, go to after-parties with fellow Yankees fanatics, wear Yankees caps, and for all I know drink Yankees beer and dance the Yankees dance. You might even be enough of a Yankees fan to have a Yankees-themed wedding—all the while feeling included and safe in the cherished Yankees traditions—but you're not going to ask for the Yankees meal on an airplane. You're not going to confine yourself to exclusive Yankees positions for sex (I'm guessing catcher's mitts and face guards would be involved), or send your kids to Yankees school every day.

U.S. Overculture

All of us outside full cultures live in a huge, blended mess of subcultures I call U.S. Overculture. Overculture provides guidance for every aspect of life, but it does so in fractured, massively oversupplied form, presenting us with many different models for weddings, scores of courtship rituals, diverse ways of bidding goodbye to the departed, a dozen traditions for observing holidays—including distinctly different holidays—and countless potential suggestions for every other aspect of life.

You can have a cowboy wedding, a Catholic funeral, a Hello Kitty birthday party, Goth hairstyles and makeup, biker clothing, Montessori schooling for your kids, Wiccan holidays, any of thousands of other traditions, ceremonies and activities…without actually belonging to any specific home culture. All of us in fractional cultures, or no culture at all, call on this overculture every day of our lives in order to fill sociocultural needs.

Overculture provides ton lots of traditions and foods and clothing, songs and dances and everything else, but the one thing Overculture fails to provide is any sense of belonging. It gives you no Home, instead leaving you adrift on a choppy cultural sea. Most of us manage only some vague identification as "American."

The Worm in Overculture

We might think living in U.S. Overculture is perfectly fine, and miss a home culture not at all. We might even interpret the lack of a home culture as the ultimate freedom. After all, we don't have to wear a beard and work a farm our entire lives. But that freedom comes with a degree of exposure and vulnerability—because a great deal of U.S. Overculture arrives as purely predatory marketing. Rather than socially-useful traditions, this culture largely supplied by corporations is an extended sales pitch aimed at nothing but profit.

On the streets of any large city, some large percentage of the faces you see will have a cigarette stuck in them. This pricey, health-destroying social practice wasn't something that got passed down by generations of wise elders, it was relentlessly advertised into existence by tobacco companies. We might imagine "A Diamond is Forever" to be cherished, ageless tradition, but it arose out of an ad campaign begun in 1947, before which sensible brides-to-be much preferred husbands to spend limited household money on washing machines or cars. Yet today, the central element of a "proper" proposal is a diamond engagement ring, the pricier the better—even to the point of crippling debt for the couple just starting out.

Do either of these customs truly benefit the people who follow them? Not in any way. People trade money for illusion.

Full cultures serve as guardians for the people within them, but those of us living in U.S. Overculture have little or nothing to perform that function. An active ad campaign can be projected at us or our children, and there is no social mechanism, no equally active protective force, to oppose it. Left to evaluate the thing as lone individuals, many of us simply adopt whatever it is because it is new, different, and briefly entertaining. For every new thing presented, lottery scratchers or vape sticks, Beanie Babies or Pokemon Go, hot yoga or K-2, car surfing or brain piercing (any day now), large numbers of us are right there, sucking it up.

Even if you as an individual detect the falsity, the uselessness, the actual physical harm of something, any public show of resistance will meet with instant unthinking opposition from those already under the spell. "Hey, vape pens are awesome, man! They're way healthier than cigarettes!" "But Beanie Babies are a great investment!"

—No, new things are not automatically bad. But they're not automatically good, either. Having a home culture with a collective of smart, trusted advisors helps you breast the daily flood of marketing, huckstering, and outright lies.

Religion and Culture

Speaking of the Amish and Hasidic Jews, note that both cultures are rooted in religion. In fact, every tribe, city-state and nation I ever heard of throughout human history had religion at or near its heart. Every culture had holy men, monuments, temples, gods, complex myths of afterlives and paradises and places of eternal punishment, plus numerous everyday rules and injunctions about how to relate to the supernatural—some of which you broke on pain of death.

Except for the part about death, that very much includes the society we live in here and now. As every atheist knows, you can't sneeze without a chorus of god-bless-yous—often from complete strangers. The U.S. is well-salted with Ten Commandments monuments, many of them still on public land, police vehicles in some jurisdictions defiantly carry goddy bumper stickers, military leaders pressure subordinates to attend religious services, goddy signs and billboards are everywhere, biology teachers are nervous about using the word "evolution" in science classes, and there is a never-let-up insistence across the nation to say prayers at public meetings. Every disaster has people giving thanks to God for their survival, no matter how many others died in the event. With "In God We Trust" on every bill and coin, even we atheists hand out religious tracts with every cash transaction.

Where has that left atheists? Out in the cold. There has never been a time or place we could truly feel welcome. If you're an atheist, probably most of the people you know—including your own family—tolerate rather than welcome you. In some countries, being an atheist can be a death sentence. Even here in the United States, there are places you'd be wise to hide it. There is no place we fit. Non-god-believers are not safe, or free, or home in much of the "civilized" world today.

We even take part in *borrowed* holidays. Those of us who enjoy Christmas do so only by resolutely telling ourselves it's a *mostly* secular occasion. You know, with the gift-giving and Santa and all. And yet, as we are frequently reminded by goddy neighbors, it remains *Christ-Mass*.

It doesn't have to be that way. We could have our own holidays. We could have our own everything.

Culture, Rebooted

Religion itself is cultural. Draw a Venn diagram of Religion and Culture, and the circle of Religion would be wholly contained within the circle of Culture. It might occupy only one small area of the Culture circle, as it does in U.S. Overculture, or it might almost completely dominate it, as it does in conservative Christian, Jewish or Islamic sects.

Culture is not religion; culture is the container religion comes in. There might be a lot of things people think are religious, but which are only cultural, things that can be teased out and considered separate from religion. A perfect example, understandable by just about any atheist, is morality, which might be presented as specifically religious, but really isn't. You no more have to be religious to care about others, to attempt to be a good person, to not lie and steal and kill, than you have to be able to ride a bicycle in order to get to work.

There's nothing that says the Venn circle of culture *must* contain a circle of religion. It's just that we've never tried it. Maybe never even been in a position to try it. Until now.

Imagine a specifically, emphatically non-religious culture, created—for the first time ever in the world—by newly freed and connected atheists. Imagine a culture founded in reason and science rather than superstition and mysticism. A culture that reveres education, excellence and careful thought, that has as its champions teachers and intellectuals rather than ridiculously costumed priests and jingoistic uniformed "heroes." Something that helps guard us from the lies and silliness projected at us daily via TV, radio, Internet, magazines, newspapers and billboards.

Give it a working title: Take all the religious cultures collectively, past and present on Planet Earth, all the tribes, city-states, kingdoms and nations, and call that Alpha Culture—Alpha because it came first. Call this new non-religious culture Beta Culture. "Beta" not because it comes second, but because it comes *next*.

(Yes, I'm aware there's already a "beta culture." Doesn't mean the term can't be repurposed. If it's a problem, think of the two as Culture 1.0 and Culture 2.0.)

So what is this Beta Culture? It is, or could be, a crowd-sourced, deliberately-constructed culture with the specific aim of providing a permanent socio-cultural home for reason-minded people—atheists, agnostics, freethinkers and secular humanists.

In the islands-of-the-future metaphor, it would be a new boat aimed at that far archipelago, a cultural tool to carry us to a future in which we have a place. It might not get us there directly, but it could influence the courses of the other three boats, a lot more than a demographic of rootless individual atheists who currently have no choice but to catch a ride with others.

Beta Culture would be a first in at least two ways: First in that it contained no religion or mysticism. Second, it would be the first culture deliberately constructed by the (hopefully) rational people who were to live within it.

Built up one piece at a time from within, it would presumably possess an important third difference: It would be a culture that deliberately sought to empower and strengthen its members, rather than to control and limit them.

Culture's Gifts

The home-feeling—which I call "Place"—is only one of the assets of a home culture. Cultures also offer Values, Ways and Goals.

Values serve as the guides and arbiters of good behavior: Honor your mother and father. Be generous to the less fortunate. Never lie to a child for any reason (which apparently is not a widespread cultural value!).

Ways are all the outward physical displays of culture: Wear a cowboy hat and a big silver belt buckle. Quit school at 14 and work the family farm. Never eat pork.

Goals are the menu of personal aims, careers and benchmarks of success: Raise a big family. Go to college. Kill a lion all by yourself.

What would Beta Culture include?

Place

A sense of Place, the homey feeling culture provides, would happen simply by Beta Culture existing. But I'd like us to also have our own meeting place. Inevitably, the idiots will call it the "atheist church." I call it the Nexus.

If my own small town can have nearly 80 churches, many of them occupying pricey downtown properties, there's no reason why there can't be one permanent meeting place for Beta Culturists. Every city and town of any size should have a Nexus—untaxed just as churches are untaxed. It might contain a freethinker library and reading room, a networking center and coffeehouse (free coffee for math and science majors!), plus rooms for meetings, discussions and classes. I picture a media center and computer lab, maybe a room for a visiting speaker to stay the night, or even safely secular child care for working Beta parents.

Values

Every culture has a set of core values—its basic concepts of who and what "we" are. What we hold dear, what we're proud of in contrast to all other, lesser cultures. In building Beta Culture, the easy part would be finding things to include. The hard part would be making it work, deciding on the various traditions and values and making them stick.

Of course its most basic value is atheism. Rationality. A reason-based lifestyle and view of the world. In attempting to create a fully non-religious, non-superstitious, non-mystic-woo-woo culture, this is something on which it could not afford to compromise. Loosen that rule and you end with just another religio-mystical culture, and damn, it's been *done*.

In Beta Culture, there would simply be no place for the faithful, the superstitious or the woo-woo mystical. Prospective members would be either firmly convinced the universe works by physics and chemistry—that there are no such thing as gods or ghosts, spirits or mystical forces—or not. Only one of those positions gets you through the door.

There are values that flow out of reason. I picture Beta as powerfully oriented toward education—not just school and college, but some degree of permanent, ongoing studiousness throughout life. This educational emphasis would be one part of a broad push toward empowerment and support for its individual members.

I see Beta as equalitarian, as post-racial and, necessarily, as futurist. It would also be basically activist—including a muscular humanism aimed at making the world a better place.

I imagine it as very much an international thing—not just in the culture itself, but in those who chose to be members. Every Beta—while legally remaining a citizen of his/her home country—would first consider himself a "Citizen of Earth" rather than of historic tribes and nations.

I picture Beta as a champion of evolution, not just the subject, but the broader implications—the interrelatedness of all life on earth. I also see it as a strong proponent of real sex education—including contraception, safety and *permission* from an early age.

I would expect it to be oriented toward health, fitness and longevity for all its members. Considering the opposition it will face, every member will be something of a warrior. Being healthy and strong helps not just us as individuals, but everyone around us.

Ways

In the U.S., we have two national holidays—Veterans Day and Memorial Day—honoring soldiers, nothing at all to recognize some of the other heroes of civilization. Allow me to float the idea of an international SALT Day, a day to honor Scientists, Artists, Librarians and Teachers.

How about Conscience Day to recognize the warriors of conscience and justice—the whistleblowers, war protestors, and fighters for social justice who have carried us forward into betterment, but who've been treated like traitors and criminals for their labors? —Hell, we could honor people who *choose* not to have children.

Superhero Day would remind us annually (quarterly?) to devote time to volunteering, cleaning up neighborhoods, assisting the elderly or handicapped. Memory Day would be an annual event to come together for remembering friends and relatives, sharing with each other the stories and pictures of the otherwise unheralded people who have shaped our lives and communities. I can even see some merit in a just-for-the-hell-of-it Aunts, Uncles and Cousins Day.

In place of Christmas, why not Krismas? Jokingly devoted to the fictional Kris Kringle, it could be a weeklong celebration at the end of each year, with gift-giving, visiting, gathering, singing, dancing, performing, formally honoring the accomplishments of friends and family over the year, with lots of eating and drinking included.

Speaking of joking, maybe humor should be a part of any deliberately-designed rational culture. The Flying Spaghetti Monster could be a permanent 'patron saint,' a gently sarcastic counterpoint to god-belief. To poke fun at the pomposity of priestly costumes and other church frippery, there might be a tradition of Big Funny Hats worn on at least one annual occasion. Rather than Easter we could observe Wester, a western-themed dig at the religious holiday, held on the same weekend.

More seriously, we would have our own ways to observe births and deaths, graduations and other milestones of life. We could have all sorts of daily and annual and special-occasion Ways that were not just secular, but that celebrated reason.

Goals

Addressing the theme of empowerment, I'd want the Nexus to offer regular classes in leadership, public speaking, bargaining and persuasion and assertiveness—not only to advance the atheist cause but to enhance and strengthen individual members in their own personal lives.

Considering what I said earlier about asking for a Yankees meal on an airplane—when it comes to Beta Culture, I *do* want a Beta meal on an airplane. For myself, I want a sandwich made in the past two hours, with whole-grain bread and a couple of slices of fresh-roasted free-range chicken breast. I want it to have a fresh salad alongside, with unwilted lettuce, crunchy croutons, tasty avocados and fresh, flavorful tomatoes—all of it made with no artificial ingredients.

That meal is an assertion that Beta Culture must have at least the same sort of determined impact on the world as Jews and Muslims, with their kosher and halal demands. Such assertions are a public statement of "We exist; we demand others honor and respect our customs and traditions."

There would be both initial and ongoing World-Café-type sessions to iron out details and values of the culture and the goals of the people within it, including gender ethics, dietary observances and the focus of activism in broader society. Beta Culture might include integral side projects such as media watchdogging or issue activism—possibly a flatly stated opposition to genital mutilation for both girls *and* boys.

I imagine a Book of Good Living collected online with non-religious guidance for daily life, for anyone who chooses to read and consider it. It might include tidbits such as "Take pictures of your parents, lots of them, something to keep you company in the long years alone." Or perhaps "Live your life in such a way that nobody has to pick up after you." Or maybe even "Never leave your dog in a hot car." But definitely, "Hey, dummy, if you're on the freeway and people are passing you on the right, get the hell out of the left lane."

I'd like there to be deliberate efforts at recruiting and youth outreach, at least as aggressive as that done by churches in every city and town in America. I go further in picturing religion-superstition detox classes for young and old, for those interested in discovering and removing from our heads the last remnants of religious unreason. I'd like to see such things as Reason Rangers (like the Girl Scouts/Boy Scouts)—possibly arising out of Camp Quest—and Reason Riders motorcycle club (it already exists) as public aspects of the culture.

Beyond local efforts, I want us to undertake a worldwide push for increasing the numbers of "out" atheists—*10^9 by 2029*—one billion atheists by the year 2029.

More than any other goal, I'd like it to be a culture of strength, empowerment and independence rather than one of weakness, fear and whining.

The Way of the World

In the era of mass communication, which has pretty much reached maximum saturation with the Internet, most of what we and our young people internalize comes from someone else—corporations, pundits, professional liars and manipulators. The persuasive pitches are everywhere. And everything in them, every word and musical note and motto, is aimed at gaining profit or power. Helping anyone live a better life is a distant second.

Which means: If you don't teach your kids your culture—your values or ideas or wisdom—someone else will come in and teach them theirs. If you don't *have* your own culture, other people will decide the way you and yours live large parts of their lives, often to the very thoughts that occupy your mind.

With no home culture, you yourself won't be immune to it. Sooner or later you'll fall for one of those seductive pitches for inclusion and coolness and victory. If you do this thing, buy this thing, wear this thing, you will win, you will succeed, you will belong. Living in a constant surround of these pitches, you may not even realize you're doing it.

I might feel fewer reservations about all of this if the world was full of good people, generous and compassionate, interested in your welfare and the welfare of your kids, but the fact is, much of the content of U.S. Overculture is exploitative rather than supportive.

Already in the Pipeline

To repeat, there's the future we *want*, and the future we'll *get*. As literally nobody but freethinkers give a damn about a specifically rational future, the future we most want...

Will.

Not.

Happen.

Churches, other cultures, broadcast media, corporations, and even governments will pursue their own self-interests, with no concern for your needs and desires, but worse, no long view of human survival on planet Earth.

For those of us in science fiction or tech fandom who happily imagine the Technological Singularity, that moment when advances take place so rapidly the rising curve of change goes completely vertical and all predictive models break down, let me present this alternate concept—The Dark Singularity: The curve of negative change accelerates until it goes vertical in the other direction—downward to chaos. Human population continues to rise; human appetite and carelessness finally outstrips the ability of our planet to recover; all the elephants and rhinos, lions and wolves, whales and dolphins and mountain gorillas vanish; shortages of energy, food and clean water spark riots; war breaks out pretty much everywhere; martial law is declared everywhere; and those few sitting pretty in an ugly, diminished world are either government officials and billionaires in fortified retreats, or survivalist fanatics dug in with guns and Bibles.

You think that can't happen? Point to one coordinated worldwide social force aimed at preventing it. Hell, the main issue causing a lot of this—still-rising human population, with something like 80 million extra people per year, *a city the size of Los Angeles arriving on Earth every 3 weeks*—is a subject about which we can't even have a useful public discussion.

If we were 200 years in the future, looking back for details of the fall of civilization, I'm convinced we'd see people of this time as very much in the midst of it. The drowning of New Orleans, the decay of Detroit, global warming, extinctions and invasive species, broken ecosystems, the rise of global terrorism, the electing of messianic figures to public office rather than competent public servants, damaging technologies used to pursue progressively scarcer petroleum, on and on. These are all data points in a collapse *already in progress*.

The Flaw in Unbelief

Compared to religion, atheism is really rather fragile. It has sprung up and died out several times in the U.S. alone. Its recent resurgence is most likely due to the existence of the Internet. Outside that, there's really not a lot to support and preserve it.

Here's the eye-opener I realized a few years back: *Under the lash of strong emotions, humans become less intelligent.*

Scary, right? But true. In conditions of fear or panic, higher parts of the human brain temporarily *shut down*.

If the Internet goes down for some reason—a solar flare or some such event—if there is an incident of nuclear terrorism anywhere in the world, if even some small version of the imagined Dark Singularity happens, a majority of our panicked fellow humans will leap toward the certainty of religion and churches and authoritarian government, unquestioningly supported by a pliant, uncritical corporate-owned media.

Churches will gleefully snatch up these new devotees, telling them to clasp their hands and close their eyes, to read their Bibles and chant its magic verses, to get down on their knees and pray, to give and give and give in order to bribe God into letting them and their loved ones live.

Anyone casting the least doubt on that mindset will be the enemy, unAmerican traitors to all things good, and a lot of scared, angry fellow citizens will jump in to intimidate them into silence.

That would be the end of the noble mind-adventure of freethought. Bye-bye, outspoken atheists, hello religious fascism.

You're sitting there right now, intelligent and educated, and you probably can't imagine a mob coming to your door and dragging you out, or a riot that smashes your windows and breaks down your doors, sets your home or business on fire. But I can imagine it, because I grew up in the Deep South among people who were not all that far advanced from the lynchings and murders of the KKK's worst days. Old men told us kids the stories, and they were stories of *pride*.

The witch burnings of yesteryear are absent today not because we humans have evolved beyond them, but because our culture disallows such acts *at this moment*.

But that culture is maintained by humans. It can be abandoned and replaced by humans, sometimes in days. You saw what happened after 9/11—suddenly we were discussing the merits of torture, arguing whether we had *too much* freedom in public places, and launching off into a war that killed and terrorized hundreds of thousands of real people *who also thought nothing bad would happen to them on any near-future day*.

The more afraid and desperate we are, the crazier it will get.

Making It Happen

Here's the rub: How do you create an entire culture?

I suspect it would take very little effort. Cultural creation already happens, and on a near-daily basis. At the least prompting, people take on actions and beliefs that become cultural traditions, perpetuating them indefinitely. Some years back the song "Tie a Yellow Ribbon Round the Old Oak Tree" made a splash on the radio, triggering a sudden leap onto the public stage of ribbon-tying as a way of welcoming returning soldiers. Now ribbons and ribbon-shaped magnets are everywhere, tasked for every social cause.

The way attendees at Reason Rally 2016 reacted with smiles and selfies to a strolling Flying Spaghetti Monster, it was obviously already a much-loved icon of the movement. Yet it arose sheerly out of a sense of fun.

We figure out the basic framework and put it out there. If it's a good idea, people will show up and be part of it, commenting, contributing, coming up with fun or useful things to include, arguing over the details and the aims, and one day there it would be. The short-term challenge might be in laying down the foundation, the basic concepts, before its growth outraced the underlying goals of reason and reality.

The larger challenge would be in creating something that was livable long-term, and paid off on the promise of enhancing the lives of people who join in it.

For years and years, evangelism was a taboo in the atheist community. Deliberately trying to get people to give up religion was seen as a self-thwarting shortcut. If people were seduced into atheism simply because it was the latest fad, without working it out for themselves, they'd be no better than religious people, right?

But in this case, that's not a problem. People coming into it would either want to be there, or they wouldn't. Besides which, we've already started selling atheism. We know we have the *right*; our problem is in believing we have the *duty*.

Moreover, considering that religion and religious observances are such an integral part of even modern cultures—Catholicism for example—and that most prospective atheists will come from such cultures, by inviting them into atheism we're basically asking them to give up not only their religion, but their home culture, and often even the loving closeness of their families. To offer them none of the same tribal inclusion in return seems both morally shabby and counterproductive. How many who might otherwise be open atheists stay where they are in order to enjoy the continued safety and warmth of their home traditions and tribe? For millions, especially the weaker and more vulnerable among us, atheism by itself might seem a poor trade.

Where and how do we get the features and attributes of our own culture? Two ways: 1) Make them up. 2) Steal them.

Make them up: If we decide every Beta middle schooler should go off every morning with Great Humanist Quotes fortune cookies to share with other kids, that's doable. If we want every partner bonding (wedding ceremony) to include a traditional bat'leth fight with designated champions to determine who cleans the bathroom for the first two years, nothing would stop us. The limits are human nature, and our own imaginations.

Steal them: The entire world, now and for all its history, is a mine of ideas for designing our own unique cultural environment. We can borrow, copy, or shamelessly expropriate customs and lifeways from any and every culture on Earth, past and present, real and fictional. So yes, we could all wear Star Trek uniforms. Or sporrans and plaid kilts (with underwear, my people, please!). Or leather jackets with flaming skull insignias and embroidered patches saying "Born to Raise Questions."

Borrow cultural goodies from the Amish. Steal from the Catholics. Copy good stuff from the Romans, the Mormons, the Japanese, the Italians, the Navajo. Borrow, copy, steal...and make it ours.

Cultural appropriation? —Eh. No. Nobody has a copyright on culture, and borrowed traditions take nothing away from the source. I wouldn't expect the group to flaunt yarmulkes, feathered headdresses or dreadlocks, but cultural appropriation is a moot issue, it seems to me. Lots of people wear cowboy hats, and—as someone who grew up with real cowboys, a group no less fiercely proud of our cultural apparel than Hasidic Jews or Sikhs—I find some of them fairly annoying. But I would never tell people they have no right to wear a cowboy hat, that I'm somehow mortally offended by it. I wouldn't join in any screaming chorus of thin-skinned offense junkies, demanding those people instantly cease all cowboy-hat-related activities and apologize to us delicate, sensitive cowpokes. If people copy your culture, it doesn't make you a *victim*, it makes you an *icon*.

Other than registered trademarks (which might be an issue with the Star Trek uniforms), nobody owns body decorations, hats, clothing or customs. What one or more groups in history have done, others can do, and the original doers lose nothing.

Hazards

We face two hazards already resident in our psyches—complacency and misplaced optimism.

Rich and safe and well-fed, we're prone to be complacent about dangers. Hey, nothing could really go wrong, right? We went to college, we know how to read and think and figure out this atheism stuff, and pretty much everybody else is just like us—same values, equivalent intelligence, same fearless approach to life. All we need do is be patient and rational, and explain things to them, and they'll come around.

Living in the modern age, we're optimistic that someone else—Brighter People Out There in the World—will work out all the problems. Scientists will solve the challenges of food and water and energy; educated, Empowered Women will spontaneously have smaller families and solve the population problem; Environmental Activists will save the whales and mountain gorillas; and the coming generation of smart, engaged Youth will burst out into the world and fix everything else that's broken.

Yeah, and all those public-spirited multi-national corporations will pitch in and help, even if it means reducing their bottom line, right? Riiiiight.

All we have to do, we happy optimists, is sit back and live our lives, go green and recycle, pick up our litter, continue to drive our SUVs to the grocery store to buy organic fruits and vegetables, and it's all going to work out.

Except it isn't. Complacency and optimism, when you have real problems, can kill you.

Forging ahead, we'll make mistakes. Not every bright idea that pops into our heads for inclusion will be viable. Not everything we add at the beginning should stay forever. Continuous discussion and self-checking has to be a part of it. But hazards and all, we shouldn't be afraid to make the experiment.

Target for Tomorrow

Sooner or later, there has to be that civilization that very deliberately embraces science and reason and rejects superstition, don't you think? I mean, really, shouldn't we have that *at some point*?

But we don't have it yet. We do not live in that civilization.

Get that? You do not live in a rational society. No, it's not a living hell. Not for *you*. But for a lot of other people, and the planet itself, it's pretty bad. Rather than casually accepting this status quo, I think you have to reject it almost violently. Every one of us has to reject it, to establish some bare minimum for being humans on Planet Earth. And until we start figuring some of this stuff out—for instance, "What is the basic intellectual and moral set every adult must be *required* to have?"—we'll continue on as we have been.

On a planet of diminished resources, radical human overpopulation, vicious inequality and mistreatment of women and minorities, all that, there's a demand for this basic human society. But we don't have it yet. Considering present-day politics and media, we may even be moving away from it.

Again, some of us might say "People have the right to believe whatever they want." And again I'd say yes, that's true—if they stay home and don't buy anything, don't drive, don't participate, don't vote, don't have kids they will subject to their idiot beliefs and behaviors.

In a real world, we can have a civilization based on reason and science and reality in which everyone participates, or we can have one based on outlandish fantasy and suffer the very real consequences. So far, we've had one based on fantasy and—in my opinion—it's been an utter disaster. And it's getting worse, *right now*.

I want a society that survives the disaster-in-progress, that picks up the pieces afterwards with this new way of thinking. What I don't want is a society that reboots using all the old software. I want something that kicks us out of the cycles of mystical thralldom, something that allows us to live on this planet into the distant future, without wrecking it or ourselves.

Who do you want at your side in the midst of a civilization-wide disaster, working to live through it and later repair it? Goddy mystics who will react with screaming panic, or fall to their knees and pray for the Rapture? Or people who will look at the falling bits with, yes, deep regret, but also with calm determination and say "Let's fix this, and then find a way to never let it happen again"?

I know whom I want. I want a community of cooperative, rational individuals. What I emphatically don't want is a bunch of faith-professing strangers telling me I need to get right with Jesus or, equally poisonous, a bevy of "Don't tell them the truth; they might panic" government officials.

We've already taken a step back from the negative religious fantasy culture. Now we need to take a step forward, with a positive reason-based culture of our own making.

Like it or not, you cannot be free of culture. You will be subject to cultural values, trends and standards all your life. As things stand, all of it will come from others. A lot of it will be based in unreason, and predatory. If you have to be immersed in culture anyway, why shouldn't it be something you helped create?

I expect the movement to have enemies. There are people—even a lot of atheists—who will instantly hate the idea of creating an atheist culture. But it's a club you don't have to join. Nobody has to be a part of it. It's also not some sort of horrifying nightmare that needs to be stomped with lug-soled boots. It is one option among many in response to an uncertain future.

But reality-based thinking and living is not just a luxury to be possessed by the few, or some flickering candle that can be allowed to go out every few years. It's important. It's a light that *must* be kept burning, a trend that *must* grow.

In the end, I believe atheists have a lot to offer the world. I think people would see that. If we did this thing, we might be surprised at the number of people who'd want to be a part of it.

And if we did, and they did, the human future just might be brighter, and better, and *there*.

Onward

So here's this airy-fairy fantasy someone had, right? This impractical utopian dream. Probably best to sneer and turn away. Get back to the real world. Except the real world—as it really is—is why we should be thinking about this. Look around you and tell me everything you see is all peachy-keen with you, and all we need is more lovey-love-love, kumbayah. That things will all work out in the end because of fate or something. Because stories always have happy endings, and because somewhere out there, the smart, rich people are working out all the problems. Hey, any day now we'll all have flying cars and robot housekeepers, immortality and world peace.

Except sometimes—too often, as every mom and dad knows—the person who has to fix things, or pick up the mess, or be the grownup, is you. Or it doesn't get done.

Someone has to be the responsible party, the person or group with an eye on the future of Planet Earth, a planet that could be unburdened by irresponsible consumption, irrational beliefs, blithe lies and destructive craziness.

It could be you.
It could be us.
It could start now.

Patheos Nonreligious

Afterword

Staring Back at the All-Seeing God

Dale McGowan

Like many adult atheists I've met, I loved mythology as a kid. The Greek and Roman stories I read Monday through Saturday were always so much more riveting and memorable to me than the Bible stories I heard in Sunday school.

One of the creatures I remember so vividly was Argus Panoptes, the giant whom Hera ordered to guard the nymph Io so Zeus wouldn't seduce her. Argus was right for the job: A hundred eyes covered his entire body. Even when some of them slept, at least one eye was always wide awake. I used to picture myself tiptoeing past his sleeping form, terrified, only to have the one open eye spot me and the other 99 snap open as one.

The image of the many-eyed gaze that you cannot escape rose in my imagination once again as I read this book by my friends and colleagues at Patheos Nonreligious. But this time, the eyes are not in the service of a god but are turned around, glaring unflinchingly back at God—and finding nothing.

In a way it's even more powerful than Argus, this collection of eyes, because each is connected to a separate mind, seeing (or in this case not seeing) God from a different perspective—philosophy, psychology, neuroscience, folklore, ethics, science, medicine, even religion itself. Not seeing God from all of those vantage points, through all of those unblinking eyes and probing minds, yields an absence more compelling and complete than any single view could achieve.

Engaging one clear and courageous thinker is among the great joys of intellectual life. But I think there's also something special about a crowd of human minds turning as one, away from the paralyzed traditions in which they were often raised, and casting the withering gaze of humanity on the empty space where the gods were said to be.

If this appeals to you as well, there's no need to stop here. Join the ongoing conversation at Patheos.com/Nonreligious.

Dale McGowan
Managing Editor, Patheos Nonreligious

Author Biographies

Galen Broaddus is a writer, web developer, and certified Secular Celebrant with the Center for Inquiry, with whom he successfully challenged Illinois' marriage statutes in order to permit secular celebrants to solemnize marriages in the state. More information about his celebrant work can be found at centralillinoiscelebrant.com. He also blogs at *Across Rivers Wide* on the Patheos network.

Jonathan Burrello is a globetrotting cartoonist, teacher, comedian, and skeptic. Originally from upstate New York, he has lived in the middle of Kansas, Los Angeles, Seoul, Madrid, and Montreal and has explored many more wondrous places in distant lands on his days off. When he is not creating deeply introspective cartoons he enjoys watching obscure movies and taking long, meandering walks. When describing what it is like to walk away from religion he says, "It was like removing a giant stick that was up my ass."

Neil Carter is a high school math teacher, a father of four, and a writer for Patheos under the name Godless in Dixie. He lives in Jackson, Mississippi, and primarily writes about living as a skeptic and former evangelical in the heart of the Bible Belt. He is a charter member of the Mississippi Humanist Association, and also a state representative for both the Secular Coalition of America and for the Openly Secular campaign.

Kevin Davis is a blogger, author, and secular activist focused mainly on fighting back against church/state separation violations and the harms that aggressive indoctrination can cause, especially in public school settings. He's the head writer and editor for *SecularVoices*, a Patheos blog, and is the co-founder and Executive Director of Young Skeptics, an elementary-level after school program for kids, focused on critical thinking and evidence-based reasoning. Kevin's first book, Understanding an Atheist: A Practical Guide to Relating to Nonbelievers is aimed at improving relationships between the religious and their atheist loved ones.

Alan Duval was born in New Zealand to English parents. His early career was in systems and database administration, though with a nearly 20-year sideline in

DJing (mostly pop and retro). He maintains a broad taste in music, from acid jazz to death metal... and is distraught at the passing of Prince O)+->. In his mid-30s, Alan took on a degree in psychology at Birkbeck College, University of London. The decision to take psychology was due, in no small part, to his son's mild (and relatively high-functioning) autism. Having secured a first class honors, and a distinction for his dissertation on moral psychology, Alan is currently looking for an appropriate PhD in moral psychology, though moral philosophy or philosophy of mind are possibilities given his interest in these fields. In the meantime Alan works for a Big Data consultancy, and ponders the ethics of Big Data. Alan contributes to *A Tippling Philosopher*.

Matthew Facciani, M.A., began his academic career in cognitive neuroscience and later switched to sociology where he is now finishing his PhD at The University of South Carolina. Facciani has published academic work in neuroscience, psychology, and sociology journals. Currently, his main research area investigates why people reject scientific evidence. Facciani is also involved with secular and gender equality activism. Once Facciani finishes his PhD, he plans to become a college professor and science communicator. Facciani's blog and podcast are both titled *According to Matthew*.

Daniel Fincke earned his PhD in Philosophy from Fordham University and taught at a variety of universities for eleven years. Since 2009 he has blogged about ethics, atheism, social issues, and philosophy more generally at *Camels With Hammers*. Since 2013, he has taught private videoconference philosophy classes with live, interactive small groups and offered philosophical advice services to help people apply philosophical tools in solving their personal problems. Learn more at http://danielfincke.com/dr-daniel-finckes-philosophy-classes-welcome-page.

Hank Fox is the author of *Red Neck, Blue Collar, Atheist: Simple Thoughts About Reason, Gods & Faith*. A former blogger on the Patheos network (*A Citizen of Earth*) and Freethought Blogs (*Blue Collar Atheist*), he now blogs independently as A Citizen of Earth. A native Texan who grew up with rodeo cowboys and has ridden bulls, he has had a wide variety of careers – truck driver, carpenter, pastry chef, photographer, freelance writer, graphic designer, sign maker, draft horse driver, wilderness guide, and magazine/newspaper editor, among others – in Texas, California, Nevada, Arizona and New York. He now lives in Upstate

New York and works with drug and alcohol abusers. He has been exploring the concept of a godless culture since 2010.

Luciano Gonzalez is a Puerto-Rican atheist, activist, and researcher. He graduated from the University of North Carolina at Greensboro in May of 2017 and is currently working as a writer for numerous sites such as *LatinoDad* and the Patheos Nonreligious channel. He is a passionate voice who can easily be identified on social media and is focused on reporting on stories that aren't making the news or deserve more press coverage and nuanced discussions than they currently get.

Andrew Hall is the author of the comedy/atheist blog *Laughing in Disbelief* on Patheos' Nonreligious Chanel. He has entertained many over the years with his comical stories, jokes, and godless memes. He co-hosts the podcast *Naked Diner* and has interviewed notable notables like comedian W. Kamau Bell, and Trae Crowder, the Liberal Redneck. Andrew is a devoted father, a curmudgeon, and an atheist. Somehow he mixes all of those things together when doing stand-up comedy. Andrew was brought up to be a good Baptist. Mom was the organist and choir director of their church. Andrew's father was a deacon. At thirteen he chose to be baptized. His interest in science slowly eroded his faith (thank you, Carl Sagan). He came to realize faith can get in the way of exercising compassion. When he isn't working on being funny, he is spending time with his two children and raising them as pious atheists.

Martin Hughes is the writer of the *barrierbreaker* blog on Patheos. His blog focuses on breaking barriers in religion, race, class, and gender. He also teaches English at the university level, and enjoys expressing himself through the written word while encouraging others to do the same

Kathleen Johnson is the Vice President and Military Director of American Atheists and the Editor of the *NoGodBlog* on Patheos. She is the founder and past President of the Military Association of Atheists and Freethinkers.

Jeana Jorgensen earned her MA and PhD in folklore from Indiana University. She has taught anthropology, folklore, and gender studies at the University of California Berkeley, Butler University, Indiana University, and Indiana University-Purdue University of Indianapolis. She publishes academic research as well as blog posts on topics ranging from gender and sexuality in fairy tales and dance to the history of sex education. She blogs at Patheos as *Foxy Folklorist*.

Hemant Mehta is the editor of *FriendlyAtheist.com*, appears on the *Atheist Voice* channel on YouTube, and co-hosts the uniquely-named *Friendly Atheist Podcast*. He is a former National Board Certified high school math teacher in the suburbs of Chicago, where he taught for seven years, and still serves as head coach for their competitive Speech/Forensics team. Hemant has served on board of directors for Foundation Beyond Belief and the Secular Student Alliance. His books include *I Sold My Soul on eBay* and *The Young Atheist's Survival Guide*. At Patheos, he blogs at *Friendly Atheist*.

Kaveh Mousavi is the pseudonym of an atheist ex-Muslim living in Iran, subject to one of the world's remaining theocracies. He is a student of English Literature, an aspiring novelist, and part-time English teacher. He is passionate about politics, video games, heavy metal music, and cinema. He was born at the tenth anniversary of the Islamic Revolution of Iran. He has ditched the Islamic part, but has kept some of the revolutionary spirit. He blogs at *On the Margin of Error*.

Jonathan MS Pearce is a philosopher, author, blogger, public speaker and teacher who lives in Fareham, Hampshire, UK with his partner and twin boys. He has spent many years philosophizing about all things religious and…well, all things, actually. He has a penchant for discussing free will, or its illusion, and how this affects society. Pearce has written a number of books (including fiction: check out his zombie apocalypse series dealing with aspects of philosophy), edited others, and contributed to more still, and public speaks to various groups around the UK concerning the topics he covers. He is surprised there is any time left in the day to breathe. You can find him on the Patheos network, blogging at *A Tippling Philosopher*.

Stephanie Savage's first published work appeared in *American Atheist Magazine*, which is not surprising for someone later called "Funny, profane and adamantly atheistic" by the *Washington Post*. But it wasn't until she emerged from a six-week coma to proclamations of an authentic Miracle of God™ that she began focusing on secularist nonfiction. Since then, Stephanie's writing has appeared in such publications as *Skeptical Inquirer*, *Free Inquiry*, and of course *Patheos*, where she blogs as *Miracle Girl*.

Jonny Scaramanga grew up as a charismatic Christian and can still pray in tongues as a party trick. He has a PhD from the UCL Institute of Education, where he researched the experiences of students in Accelerated Christian Education schools. He has talked on this subject for BBC Newsnight, BBC1's The Big Questions, The Jeremy Vine Show (BBC Radio 2), The Sunday Programme, and Out of the Ordinary (BBC Radio 4). He has written for *The Guardian*, *New Statesman*, *Salon*, *AlterNet*, and the *Times Education Supplement*. He has been quoted in The Independent and the Herald Scotland. Now he plays guitar in a touring band and tries not to think about abusive asshats who run Christian schools.

Bob Seidensticker graduated from MIT in 1980. He has designed digital hardware, programmed in a dozen computer languages, and is a co-contributor to 14 software patents. After leaving Microsoft, Bob wrote the book *Future Hype* about technology change—how we see it and how it really works. He now focuses on the atheism/Christianity debate. His novel, *Cross Examined: An Unconventional Spiritual Journey*, explores the issue in a fiction format. Bob writes a widely read atheist blog on the *Patheos* network, Cross Examined.

Andrew Spitznas is the film critic at Patheos' Secular Cinephile blog. A member of the North Carolina Film Critics Association, he also contributed a chapter to the print anthology *Faith and Spirituality in Masters of World Cinema, Volume II*. A board-certified psychiatrist, Andrew has spoken to academic audiences about psychological themes in movies. He lives in East Tennessee with his wife Jessica, his three teenagers, and their five dogs.

Michael Stone writes the *Progressive Secular Humanist* blog at Patheos Nonreligious and is the CEO and Founder of the popular Facebook page, Progressive Secular Humanist Examiner.

Dr. Gleb Tsipursky serves as the President of Intentional Insights, a nonprofit devoted to promoting rational thinking and wise decision-making in politics and other life areas. Its main current focus is the Pro-Truth Pledge, a project that aims to reverse the tide of lies and promote truth in public discourse through combining behavioral science and crowd-sourcing. A best-selling author, he has written *Find Your Purpose Using Science* and other books, and is the author of the forthcoming *The Alternative to Alternative Facts: Fighting Post-Truth Politics With*

Behavioral Science. He regularly publishes pieces on these topics in prominent venues such as *Time, New York Daily News, Psychology Today*, and reason-oriented venues such as *The Humanist, Skeptical Inquirer, Free Inquiry, American Atheist Magazine*, and *Patheos*, He has appeared as a guest on mainstream venues such as network TV, including affiliates of Fox, ABC, and others, and radio stations such as NPR, WBAI, KGO, and 700WLW, as well as reason-oriented podcasts, such as *Ra-Men Podcast, The Scathing Atheist, Danthropology, Sensibly Speaking*, and *The Humanist Hour*. He researches decision-making and emotional and social intelligence in politics and business as a professor at Ohio State. He is available to speak to reason-oriented groups through the AHA, SSA, and CFI Speakers' Bureaus.

Warren Tidwell is a lifelong resident of Alabama who has used blogs and social media to organize thousands of volunteers and secure millions in financial and material donations for disaster relief and recovery efforts. He worked as a volunteer in rural Hancock County, Mississippi in the aftermath of Hurricane Katrina and drove over 11,000 miles in 12 weeks to create a network of small non-profits in the south-eastern United States after the 2011 tornado superoutbreak. As a result of these extensive networking efforts, Warren was also able to help set up operations when subsequent tornado outbreaks affected Joplin, Missouri, and Piedmont, Oklahoma. Warren sparked a worldwide movement when he started 26 Acts of Kindness after the tragic shooting at Sandy Hook Elementary. Warren is currently on a one-year deployment with the Humanist Service Corps working in the "witch camps" of Northern Ghana. His dream is to do humanitarian work with his son when he is older.

Suzanne Titkemeyer is the admin at [No Longer Quivering](). She's been out of the Quiverfull Evangelical world for ten years now and lives in Costa Rica with her retired husband and assorted creatures. If eye rolling was an Olympic sport, she would take the Gold every time.

www.ingramcontent.com/pod-product-compliance
Lightning Source LLC
Chambersburg PA
CBHW070555100426
42744CB00006B/281